EQUAL BEFORE THE LAW

Iowa and the Midwest Experience

SERIES EDITOR
William B. Friedricks
Iowa History Center at Simpson College

*The University of Iowa Press gratefully acknowledges
Humanities Iowa for its generous support of the
Iowa and the Midwest Experience series.*

Equal Before the Law

How Iowa Led Americans
to Marriage Equality

Tom Witosky and Marc Hansen

UNIVERSITY OF IOWA PRESS
IOWA CITY

University of Iowa Press, Iowa City 52242
Copyright © 2015 by the University of Iowa Press
www.uiowapress.org
Printed in the United States of America

The University of Iowa Press is a member of Green Press Initiative
and is committed to preserving natural resources.

Printed on acid-free paper

Library of Congress Cataloging-in-Publication Data
Witosky, Tom, author.
Equal before the law : how Iowa led Americans to marriage equality /
By Tom Witosky and Marc Hansen.
p.   cm
ISBN 978-1-60938-349-7 (pbk), ISBN 978-1-60938-350-3 (ebk)
1. Same-sex marriage—Iowa—History.   2. Same-sex marriage—Iowa—Cases.
3. Same-sex marriage—United States—History.   4. Gay couples—Law and
legislation—Iowa.   5. Gay couples—Law and legislation—United States.
6. Unmarried couples—Legal status, laws, etc.—Iowa.   7. Unmarried couples—Legal
status, laws, etc.—United States.   I. Hansen, Marc, (journalist) author.   II. Title.
KFI4303.W58   2015
346.77701'68—dc23   2014034893

Contents

Acknowledgments

This book could not have been written without Mark Cady's guidance, insight, patience, and friendship. The chief justice of the Iowa Supreme Court and author of the *Varnum* decision made himself available at every turn. Sometimes he even pretended to enjoy our company.

Supreme court justices aren't the most vocal group when it comes to discussing the anatomy of their decisions. As a rule, they don't advocate for themselves, hit the campaign trail, or publicly defend their opinions. Yet Cady, Marsha Ternus, Michael Streit, David Baker, and David Wiggins recognized the historical significance of the case, understood the importance of the story, and were instrumental in helping tell it.

They gave generously of their time and answered most of our questions, but not all. When Justice Wiggins says he won't talk about something, he "WON'T TALK ABOUT IT!!!" We'd also like to thank the lawyers, the legislators, the entire Lambda Legal crew, and the countless others on both sides of the issue who tried to keep us on track.

The big heroes, of course, are the couples who put their lives on hold for several years to fight for marriage equality, those who took the time to give us the who, what, where, when, and whys. They include Kate and Trish Varnum; Larry Hoch and David Twombley; Chuck and Jason Swaggerty-Morgan; and, of course, Dawn and Jen BarbouRoske. Not only did the BarbouRoskes never make us feel like bad houseguests who keep coming back, they (Bre and McKinley in particular) always made us laugh.

As always, good friends encouraged us throughout the process: Bill Barnhart, whose wise counsel gave us direction; Melissa Ludtke, whose support was invaluable in the early and later stages; Sharon Pilmer, whose belief and insight into the book's potential bolstered our resolve; and the

Grossfeld family—Stan, Stacey, Sam, and Zoe—who graciously opened their home to us on our visit to Boston.

We also acknowledge Robert Dykstra, the author of *Bright Radical Star: Black Freedom and White Supremacy on the Hawkeye Frontier*. Professor Dykstra's book and advice assisted greatly in placing the *Varnum* decision into the proper context of the state's history.

Also deserving much praise is Diane Witosky, our chief copy formatter/motivational leader: "This book won't get written by itself, you know!" When the directions said, "Change the formatting of selected text in the document text by choosing a look for the selected text from the Quick Styles gallery on the Home Tab," Diane was all over it.

Finally, we are much indebted to Catherine Cocks and Rebecca Marsh of the University of Iowa Press for their deft editing touch and the way they break it to us gently.

MICHAEL GARTNER

||||||||||||||||||||||||||||||||||||||||||||||||||||||||||||||||||||||||||||||||

Foreword

They seemed an unlikely mix of couples in an unlikely place to be pioneers in the march toward gay marriage in America.

There were six couples. Some were older, some younger. Some had children. Some had none. There were three male couples, three female. They seemed the most ordinary of people from the most ordinary of towns in the most ordinary of states.

In fact, though, they were extraordinary people in an extraordinary state. For equality, for fairness, for dignity and, especially, for love, the twelve men and women were willing to take their private lives public. And they did so in a state whose supreme court has for 175 years routinely upheld the ideas of fairness and of liberty and of equality—usually decades before the Supreme Court of the United States found its way to similar rulings. As it turned out, the six couples were in the right place, at the right time.

But the story of how Iowa, the very heart of the heartland, became just the third state—after Massachusetts and Connecticut—to recognize that all men and women were equal and thus could marry whomever they chose is a story about far more than six gay couples and seven honorable justices.

It is a story of politicians wrestling with their consciences—and, sometimes, the consciences losing—and of lawyers wrestling with the law. It is a story of legal strategies and political showdowns. It is a story of important people who stood up, and equally important ones who ducked down.

And it is a story of little children fiercely wanting what their schoolmates had: married parents.

Reporters Tom Witosky and Marc Hansen are Iowans who—like many Iowans—watched with interest but not surprise as the case of *Varnum v. Brien* unfolded in the courts in Des Moines. Recently retired from the *Des Moines Register*, they resolved to take a long look at how the case arose, how it played out, how it was decided, and how it affected the state and some of its people.

The result is this book.

Varnum was an important decision, and this is an important book. Years from now, when gay marriage is routine across America, people will wonder how it was that Iowa was a leader, how it was that the opponents were outmaneuvered in the legislature, and how it was that three supreme court justices lost their jobs in an aftermath that was far more contentious than the case itself. Who were the people that made it happen—the lawyers, the politicians, the judges, the couples, and the partisans who battled it out in judicial elections after the fact?

The answers are all in these pages.

It would be hard to put all this in context if you weren't an Iowan thoroughly familiar with the state and its people. It's important to understand the values the future chief justice learned growing up on a farm, the role religion played in the lives of several justices, the rising role of the political Far Right at the time the *Varnum* case was working its way through the system. It's important to understand Midwest populism and what Meredith Willson meant when he wrote the song "Iowa Stubborn" ("And we're so by God stubborn / we can stand touchin' noses / for a week at a time / and never see eye-to-eye. / But we'll give you our shirt / and a back to go with it / if your crops should happen to die.") Hansen and Witosky know all this, because they have lived it, watching and writing about Iowans and Iowa issues day in and day out.

Because of their backgrounds as knowledgeable Iowans and as fair and accurate reporters, they were able to get access to virtually every person with a voice in the story. Chief Justice Marsha Ternus walked them through the process at the supreme court, and Justice Mark Cady, who wrote the *Varnum* decision, talked them through the process of writing the decision. Lawyers on both sides, politicians of every stripe, and, of course, the couples—and some of their children—told how they came to be involved and how their views evolved. No voice is missing.

Iowa became a state in 1846. The next year it adopted its motto, "Our Liberties We Prize and Our Rights We Will Maintain." The *Varnum* case is a further guarantee of those liberties, a further maintenance of those rights. And this book by Witosky and Hansen explains how it all came about.

EQUAL BEFORE THE LAW

||||||||||||||||||||||||||||||||||||||||||||||||||||||||||||||||||||||||||||||||||||||||||||

CHAPTER ONE

Injured Child

As she ate breakfast before kindergarten, five-year-old McKinley BarbouRoske learned a terrible truth about her parents.[1]

The conversation was weekday-morning matter-of-fact. McKinley, by all appearances, was off in her own little world, paying scant attention to the grown-ups at the table. Jen BarbouRoske was telling her longtime partner, Dawn BarbouRoske, about a conversation the night before with another nurse in the University of Iowa Hospitals neonatal unit. The coworker was stunned to learn that Jen and Dawn weren't married and that same-sex marriage was prohibited in Iowa. As McKinley's two moms quickly discovered, McKinley was paying close attention.

"You're not married?" she cried out, huge tears rolling down her cheeks. The very notion was absurd. How could they not be married? Jen was "Mommy" and Dawn was "Mema." They were her parents. They'd always been her parents.

But the answer was no. Not yet. Not in Iowa. The year was 2003. George W. Bush, running for a second term as president, had felt compelled to go on record. Marriage, he announced, was between one man and one woman, and it was time "to codify that one way or the other." It was time mainly because the Massachusetts Supreme Court was about to become the first state in the country to make civil marriage legal for same-sex couples, and the backlash was soon to be felt across the nation. Writing for the majority in a 4–3 ruling, Chief Justice Margaret H. Marshall would say, "The exclusive commitment of two individuals to each other nurtures love and mutual support; it brings stability to our society.

For those who choose to marry, and for their children, marriage provides an abundance of legal, financial, and social benefits. In return, it imposes weighty legal, financial, and social obligations."[2]

But the BarbouRoskes weren't living in liberal-leaning Massachusetts or Connecticut, the second state (in 2008) to sanction same-sex civil marriage. They were living in not-so-liberal Iowa—a rural midwestern state with an influential core of social and religious conservatives who specialize in steering the Republican Party to the right during its first-in-the-nation presidential caucuses.

Despite Iowa's white-bread image, the reputation doesn't always match the reality. Although the 2014 election screamed otherwise, Iowa is not a conservative stronghold. It isn't a perennial red state. Much of the time, it is a purple-clad political cross-dresser. From 1984 heading into 2014, the Hawkeye state had been represented in the United States Senate by one Republican and one Democrat. True, Republican Terry Branstad is now setting longevity records as governor. Since 1969, however, two Republicans and two Democrats have held the job. What's more, in five of the last six presidential elections, starting in 1988, Iowa voted Democratic. Before that, the voters largely favored Republican presidential candidates. But lately, what Iowa seems to do best is help elect the winner.

For a long time, Hawaii and Massachusetts were seen as the true marriage-equality pioneers: Hawaii for its high-court ruling in 1993 recognizing civil marriage for a same-sex couple (only to have the court decision overturned by a constitutional amendment five years later) and Massachusetts for being the first to make it stick. The politicians in Iowa and almost everywhere else saw what the court in Hawaii had done and dug in their heels. How can this happen? How can a small, relatively obscure deliberative body far from the mainland be allowed to redefine one of life's most sacred institutions?

In February of 1996, the week before Iowa's presidential caucuses, Republicans in the Iowa House responded to Hawaii by introducing their own Defense of Marriage Act (DOMA). To same-sex Iowa couples considering a wedding and honeymoon in Hawaii, the message was clear: Hold off on the celebration. When the law is passed, your marriage will not be legally recognized back home.

In 2003, around the time McKinley BarbouRoske learned her parents weren't married, the prospects for most same-sex couples in the United States still seemed bleak. An Associated Press poll found that most Americans favored laws banning gay marriage and that they would punish any presidential candidates supporting marital equality or even civil unions. But change was on the way. The decision that was to decisively turn the tide in favor of marriage equality would come from flyover country, and McKinley BarbouRoske's family would play a key role.

The Iowa Supreme Court decision in *Varnum v. Brien* firmly and deeply rooted the chief principles enumerated by all subsequent decisions overturning laws banning the marriage of a same-sex couple:

- Gays and lesbians could not be deprived of equal protection under the law because of their sexual orientation.
- Prohibiting them from civil marriage was not connected to any important government objective.
- The ruling wasn't about anyone's religious views as much as it was about preventing government from endorsing a religious belief and about protecting the freedom of religious organizations to define marriage as they choose.

As Justice Mark S. Cady wrote in the opinion, "Civil marriage must be judged under our constitutional standards of equal protection and not under religious doctrines or the religious views of individuals." But, he added,

> this approach does not disrespect or denigrate the religious views of many Iowans who may strongly believe in marriage as a dual-gender union, but considers, as we must, only the constitutional rights of all people, as expressed by the promise of equal protection for all. We are not permitted to do less and would damage our constitution immeasurably by trying to do more.[3]

Cady didn't say it in so many words, but the implication gradually became clear to the rest of the country. These weren't wild counterculture claims coming from the so-called coastal elite. The court, in fact, was espousing core American ideals.

By the fifth anniversary of the decision, an estimated six thousand same-sex couples had been married in Iowa. In rapid succession, sixteen states followed Iowa's lead — as did the U.S. Supreme Court. In 2013, the high court gutted a major section of the federal Defense of Marriage Act and let stand a lower court decision declaring California's Proposition 8 unconstitutional.

This book tells the story of the decades-long legal struggle for marriage equality in Iowa and the now-snowballing acceptance. Clearly, Iowa's decision wasn't a first; it followed similar court outcomes in Massachusetts, California, and Connecticut. But unlike those decisions, Iowa's court ruled unanimously, setting an unmistakable tone of necessity and inevitability reminiscent of the 1954 school desegregation decision, *Brown v. Board of Education*.

In the immediate aftermath of the *Varnum* decision, Kenji Yoshino, Chief Justice Earl Warren Professor of Constitutional Law at New York University School of Law, said,

> This is a remarkable decision not only because it occurred in the Midwest, but also because it was 7–0.
>
> The three prior courts to rule in favor of same-sex marriage were 4–3 decisions. . . . It was a more aggressive opinion in that there was absolutely no toe-hold for naysayers to find in the opinion. And so this makes the opposition to same-sex marriage much more like opposition to interracial marriage.[4]

In an article written for the *New York Times*, Yoshino even equated Cady's effort in *Varnum* with Warren's fifty-five years before:

> Chief Justice Earl Warren strove mightily to get a unanimous opinion in *Brown v. Board of Education* so that the moral principle of desegregation would be accorded its full moral force. Given that he invokes *Brown*, one wonders how hard Justice Mark S. Cady, the author of the opinion today, struggled to find the words that would allow his court to speak — from the heart and heartland — with one voice.[5]

Legal scholar Patricia Cain, a law professor at Santa Clara University, also predicted a substantial impact from the decision: "Iowa may be the last state to extend marriage equality by court decision, but it may serve as a major impetus for other states to follow legislatively." Why? Because the decision addressed the impact on religious groups. "This break in the silence about religion and its role in the same-sex marriage debate is a positive step forward," she said, inserting a useful dose of reason into an otherwise intemperate debate.[6] By supporting marriage equality in middle America, the Iowa Supreme Court caught the attention of a nation that, before *Varnum v. Brien*, typically thought of "gay marriage" as an issue for only New York, California, Massachusetts, and other coastal states.

Back in Iowa, McKinley BarbouRoske was too young to understand the stakes. She wanted only what most of the other kids had. It would not be long before the United States Supreme Court shared her concerns. In the nation's slow-simmering same-sex marriage debate, much ink was spilled and energy expelled conjecturing that children were somehow imperiled by living in the homes of same-sex couples. Official acknowledgment of their mere existence would take a long time.

It would come ten years later in the Supreme Court of the United States as the justices delicately probed the constitutionality of California's ban on same-sex marriage. In the oral argument, Justice Anthony Kennedy noted evidence that some forty thousand children lived in California with same-sex parents. Those children, Kennedy added, "want their parents to have full recognition and full status." Denying children such recognition, he said, could result in "an immediate legal injury . . . and that's the voice of these children." It was a flesh-and-blood moment in a case that hinged on technical questions. Who had the right to litigate the California ban in court? Exactly who was injured here? Addressing the lawyer seeking to uphold the ban, Kennedy said, "The voice of the children is important in this case, don't you think?"[7]

It would appear so. That voice, judging by the numbers, rings out across the country. When Gary Gates, a demographer at the UCLA law school, looked into 2008 statistics for the *New York Times*, he found some 250,000 children under age eighteen being reared by 116,000 same-sex couples.

Five years earlier, McKinley's voice at the kitchen table was filled with pain. Something was wrong with her family; something was missing. Her parents tried to explain how the law wouldn't let them marry, but their words brought no solace.

"Does that mean you're splitting up?" McKinley asked.

"No, not at all," came the answer. "We're the same strong family we've been and always will be. We're married in our hearts."

The look on McKinley's face that morning reminded Dawn and Jen BarbouRoske what they already knew—what the majority of Americans would someday come to accept. Married in their hearts was not enough.

CHAPTER TWO

||||||||||||||||||||||||||||||||||||||||||||||||||||||||||||||||||||||||||||||||||

Right and Wrong

A s Matt McCoy entered the statehouse in March of 1998, he knew it would be a difficult day.[1] Before leaving his desk on the senate floor the night before, McCoy, in his first term representing a blue-collar district on the south side of Des Moines, noted that House File 382 had been readied for debate. The bill was three pages long but would change chapter 592.2 of the Iowa Code in only one significant way. The new wording to be added to the statute read simply: "Only a marriage between a male and female is valid."

McCoy, a Democrat, sighed. He already had served two terms in the Iowa House before his senate election in 1996 and had concluded then that nothing could stop Republican lawmakers from restricting marriage in Iowa to a man and a woman. He heard the arguments for change again and again. They had begun in 1993 when the Hawaii Supreme Court sent tremors through the country. Three years earlier, three same-sex Hawaiian couples had challenged the state's ban on same-sex marriage and, shockingly, won the case. Dire predictions followed. Allow same-sex marriage in one state, and it would be legal everywhere under Article IV — the full faith and credit clause — of the U.S. Constitution. Conservative and evangelical groups with strong Republican ties were insistent. This must be stopped immediately.

What those opponents failed to acknowledge was that no clear answer existed regarding the clause's impact on recognition of marriage. Many legal scholars had concluded the constitutional clause governing how states dealt with conflicting laws had never been used to force one state to accept a marriage performed in another. For example, states forbidding interracial marriage weren't required to recognize interracial marriages from other states. That changed in 1967, but only after the U.S. Supreme Court ruled unconstitutional all state laws banning interracial marriage. While states could accept marriages from other states as a courtesy, nothing in the Constitution required it.

"For some years now, the press has fecklessly repeated the claim that the full faith and credit clause will require every state to recognize same-sex marriages," Andrew Koppelman wrote in his 2006 book, *Same Sex, Different States: When Same-Sex Marriages Cross State Lines.*[2]

Similarly, Ralph Whitten, in a *Creighton Law Review* article published in 2005, pointed out just how wrong those claims were when they were made: "The subject of same-sex marriage has produced a seemingly endless set of preposterous ideas about why the full faith and credit clause requires states to give effect to marriages performed in other states."[3] Other scholars, mostly conservative, insisted there should be no chance of having same-sex marriage recognized under any circumstance. If states or even the federal government wanted to prevent same-sex marriages from being recognized, they had the right to do so.

But by 1996, poll-watching Republicans noticed the public's discomfort with the Hawaii decision and began pushing the antimarriage agenda as hard as they could. That realization hit home in Iowa when antigay and religious groups, including the American Family Association, the Eagle Forum, and the Christian Coalition, staged a "National Marriage Protection Rally" just two days before the presidential caucuses. The rally featured an appearance by actor Charlton Heston, who introduced Texas senator Phil Graham as "the next president of the United States" but said nothing about same-sex marriage.

The rally, held in part to keep Hawaiian same-sex marriages from being recognized in other states, included several presidential candidates signing a "marriage protection resolution." Said candidate Alan Keyes, "If we accept the homosexual agenda, which seeks recognition for homosexual marriages, we will be destroying the integrity of the marriage-based family." Fellow presidential hopeful Pat Buchanan, a leader in the Republican Party's "culture war," declared same-sex marriage to be part of the "false God of gay rights," saying, "There is no equality between what

has been sanctified by God and what is fundamentally wrong."⁴ Before
the night was over, all the Republican candidates—eventual presidential nominee Bob Dole, former Tennessee governor Lamar Alexander, and
Steve Forbes included—either signed the pledge or promised to sign it.
Only Indiana senator Richard Lugar, who did not appear at the rally, declined.

Much of the party's effort stemmed from the Hawaii decision, but Republicans also were smarting over President Bill Clinton's 1993 executive
order to implement the so-called Don't Ask, Don't Tell military policy.
Then there were the HIV and AIDS epidemics. In 1992, the problem had
made headlines when professional basketball star Earvin "Magic" Johnson acknowledged he had become infected with the HIV virus, and U.S.
tennis champion Arthur Ashe said he had contracted AIDS from a blood
transfusion. Ashe would die the next year.

Statistics from the Centers for Disease Control show the AIDS epi-
demic peaking in the mid-1990s. From 1993 to 1995, 257,262 cases were
reported, up from 202,520 between 1988 and 1992 and from 50,280 the
previous six years. While incidents of AIDS increased to 264,405 between
1996 and 2000, deaths plummeted to 59,807, compared to 159,048 deaths
from 1993 to 1995.

Against that backdrop, McCoy had been elected to the Iowa House
for the first time. Though most of his constituents were either registered Democrats or Independents, many were also blue-collar workers
of Italian descent. What's more, the vast majority were parishioners of
St. Anthony's Catholic Church just south of downtown Des Moines and
within sight of the Iowa statehouse. The neighborhoods were solid middle
class with average annual incomes around fifty thousand dollars. Nearly
50 percent of the population lived in married family households with the
average home valued in the range of $150,000 to $170,000.

When it came to voting on the legality of same-sex marriage, McCoy
knew what those folks expected from him. The polls left little doubt.
While nearly 75 percent of Iowans opposed same-sex marriage, the other
25 percent were split between no opinion and acceptance.

As a result, McCoy joined his fellow house Democrats when they stood
meekly to the side in 1996 while the Republican majority passed its first
attempt to restrict marriage. The bill flew through, 86–11. McCoy had

voted for it, yes. But he knew something else. The Democratic-controlled senate would never consider it.

"What difference did it make?" he thought at the time. "The Republicans get their bill; the Democrats don't move it any further, and nothing changes. My vote doesn't matter."

McCoy was a rising political star, and he knew it. Married with a young son, he'd attended Catholic high school and had strong family ties in Des Moines. Classmates had even taken to calling him "Governor." No way was he about to stand up publicly against this kind of legislation. Why side with anything remotely related to helping homosexuals—including their civil rights? Politically, nothing good could possibly come of it. The Democratic legislative leaders had been blunt about it in their meetings: Don't fight it. The Republicans will bring it up for debate, but don't say a word. Don't give them a juicy headline. Don't give them one more excuse to call us extremists. Just get out of the way. Go down quickly. Go down quietly.

McCoy also knew the stories about how Iowa politicians were treated when there was the slightest hint they were gay or lesbian—or even supportive of equal rights. Inside the legislative halls, the stories about two former Democratic state representatives, Norman Jesse and Dan Johnston, were almost legend. People who knew them knew they were lovers. But neither man would acknowledge it publicly. "It really wasn't anyone's business," Johnston said years later when asked why they hid their relationship. It lasted until Jesse's death from lung cancer in 2000.[5]

Johnston had served one term in the Iowa House, but at the same time had been lead counsel in successfully arguing the landmark freedom of speech case—*Tinker v. Des Moines School District*—through the U.S. Supreme Court. From 1977 through 1985, Johnston had served as Polk County Attorney.

Jesse also had become well-known as one of the few state legislators who could change votes just by speaking on the floor of the house. His humor could be wicked. In a January 31, 1978, speech endorsing state ratification of the Equal Rights Amendment to the U.S. Constitution, Jesse bludgeoned house opponents of the amendment for "appealing to all that is worst in society. . . . To raise specters of men and women having to use the same restroom facilities . . . is a ridiculous thing. We are going to have both—one of each," Jesse stormed.[6]

But some of the other stories weren't so funny. After Des Moines police leaked to the local newspaper that a grand jury investigation had targeted then county attorney Johnston, he had been forced to lie about his homosexuality at a news conference. Police claimed Johnston had reduced a drunken driving charge against a male defendant because the two were involved in a sexual relationship. Charges were never filed after evidence was presented that Johnston's office had reduced the charges when the defendant had agreed to become a confidential informant in another police investigation. But that meant nothing to members of Des Moines police, who routinely placed Johnston under surveillance in an effort to catch him in a homosexual act. He eventually left the state to escape the harassment.

Jesse was voted out of office in 1980 (after the Republican candidate simply accused him of being gay) and refused to talk about it. The final straw had been when Jesse's opponents printed leaflets that claimed he was gay and distributed them in church parking lots the weekend before the election.

McCoy understood the history. In 1996, openly gay Iowans couldn't win anything politically. There was also the campaign of Des Moines businessman Rich Eychaner, who ran twice for the Republican nomination in Iowa's Fourth Congressional District. Acknowledging from the beginning he was homosexual, Eychaner lost both times. Just a year before McCoy's election, well-respected Des Moines lawyer Jonathan Wilson had been voted off the Des Moines School Board after twelve years. Wilson had been targeted by the same group that would stage the precaucus rally that attracted the 1996 Republican presidential candidates.

Wilson's major offense, according to his conservative critics, was taking part in an effort to include information about sexual orientation in the school's health development curriculum. The false charges had been leaked from a school employee to an evangelical activist who claimed school officials were attempting to hide it from parents. The result was a whisper campaign that Wilson was homosexual. After several weeks of controversy, Wilson, who had been advised by Des Moines police to wear a bulletproof vest in public, acknowledged his sexual orientation with his ex-wife and grown children sitting nearby. In the school board election campaign that followed, Wilson raised and spent sixty thousand dollars, all for nothing. He finished a distant third in the race behind two Christian Coalition–backed candidates.

With that sorry slice of history in the back of his mind, McCoy cast his 1996 vote in favor of marriage restrictions. By 1998, nothing had changed—except for the Iowa legislature, which was now under complete Republican control. That bill was going to pass no matter what. McCoy rode the elevator from the statehouse basement to the third floor of the capitol knowing a final vote would come before the end of the day. He also knew he would vote for the law again and would carry the shame for more than a decade.

Janelle Rettig heard her phone ringing but was in no mood to answer it.[7] The former staff member for Iowa congressman Jim Leach had already heard the bad news, and the last thing the feisty Republican wanted to do was relive it. The U.S. House had given its final approval to the Defense of Marriage Act by a veto-proof 342–67.

She and her partner, Robin Butler, had watched closely as Republicans, who took control of congress in 1994 for the first time in more than forty years, capitalized politically on the issue of same-sex marriage. Particularly impressive was how they'd cornered Clinton into signing the federal Defense of Marriage Act during his 1996 presidential reelection campaign. Introducing DOMA and leading it through the U.S. House was Georgia congressman Bob Barr, an Iowa native. Republican majority leader Bob Dole, running against Clinton for the presidency, ushered it through the Senate. The bill defined marriage for federal purposes as between a man and a woman only. If any state approved same-sex marriage, the federal government was forbidden to recognize it. DOMA also permitted states to deny recognition of any same-sex marriage permitted in another state.

Clinton's decision to sign the measure into law clearly had been political—designed to keep Republicans from continuing their election-year attacks on him for removing restrictions on gays and lesbians serving in the military through "Don't Ask, Don't Tell." He signed the federal DOMA into law late at night and issued a statement in which he tried to walk the tightrope between generally opposing discrimination against gays and lesbians and specifically enacting a discriminatory law against them.

Rettig understood the politics well but felt helpless. She and her partner had wanted to marry for years and believed they had a right to do so no matter how others felt about it. In fact, in 2003 the couple would marry in Toronto after both had medical scares. The province of Ontario had recognized the legality of same-sex marriage in June 2003 — two years before all of Canada would. Robin had been diagnosed with breast cancer; Janelle had contracted a severe case of Lyme disease on a camping trip. "We just decided we didn't want to die as strangers in the eyes of the law," Rettig would tell friends.

The women had met thirteen years earlier as sorority sisters at Knox College in Galesburg, Illinois. They both had an intense interest in politics but from decidedly different viewpoints. Butler, a Houston native, was a liberal Democrat. Rettig, a native of rural western Illinois, gravitated to the Republican Party in her teens and cemented her views while at Knox. "I fell in love with Robin from the start," Rettig recalled. "But she broke my heart when she graduated and went on to Chicago. I always say she went to sow her oats."

During their time apart, Rettig, after a brief teaching and athletic coaching career, entered politics, first working on U.S. senator Robert Dole's 1988 presidential campaign, then becoming an assistant to an Illinois Republican state lawmaker. She later joined Jim Leach's staff in Iowa City. By that time, Rettig had reunited with Butler, who had just earned a master's degree at DePaul University. Butler had moved to Iowa City to get a doctorate degree, which was when the couple settled down together. Butler would eventually get a job in city government while Rettig remained with Leach's office until leaving to open a gift shop.

"Jim never cared about political affiliations," Rettig said, "And, of course, he knew Robin and I were a couple." But now Leach, a moderate Republican, was on the telephone. Knowing why he was calling, Rettig told Butler she didn't want to talk to him. After the women looked at each other for a moment, Butler placed the phone in Rettig's hand and walked away.

"Jim, how could you vote for that bill?" Rettig said.

"I know you and Robin are upset with me," Leach responded, in Rettig's version of the conversation. Leach then explained his thinking, concluding that voting for DOMA was the best way to go despite what it meant. Gay and lesbian groups like the Human Rights Campaign told Leach and others that the important measure to them was the Employment Non-Discrimination Act, which would prohibit inequity based on sexual orientation.

"I can't believe you bought into that," Rettig replied. The two talked a little while longer, but soon there was nothing left to say. Rettig remembered only one other thing from that conversation.

"Jim was crying," she said. "So was I."

There is an axiom among Iowa statehouse reporters: "Right and wrong are determined solely by twenty-six votes in the senate and fifty-one votes in the house"—the constitutionally required majorities for legislation to become law.

Jeff Angelo, a young conservative from southwest Iowa, was about to vote, in protest, against something he thought was right.[8] That's because the bill didn't go far enough to suit him and his side didn't need his vote. When the secretary of the senate opened the voting machine after less than ninety minutes of debate on House File 382, Angelo, who led the effort to ban same-sex marriage in Iowa, punched the red "no" button on his desk, sat back, and watched the big electronic board light up green with "yes" in defense of traditional marriage.

Angelo's objection was simple. Just before the final vote, Democrats (with the help of a few Republican sympathizers) attached a guilt-laden, feel-good amendment to the bill—a request to study other forms of domestic partnerships for gays and lesbians. Just study them, mind you. Nothing more.

"A waste of time," Angelo thought to himself. "No way will they ever do that." But rather than let this bloodless little courtesy slide, he was so far to the right on the issue that he was ready to blow up any amendment that would keep the door open even a crack for civil unions. The winning side obviously didn't need his backing. By voting no, Angelo wasn't supporting same-sex marriage. Anything but. Casting his protest vote while trying not to sneer, he settled in to watch the show. What could be more entertaining, he thought to himself, than seeing a roomful of weak-kneed

Democrats vote against same-sex marriage. All he needed was a tub of popcorn.

"Liberal hypocrites," he said under his breath. "Look at them. They don't even have the guts to vote their conscience." It was a harsh, yet fair, indictment. Many of Angelo's colleagues on the other side of the aisle, many of those "liberal hypocrites," had the same disdainful thoughts. Angelo loved it. Though most of the Republican lawmakers truly believed in the sanctity of traditional marriage, he couldn't say the same about the Democrats who voted for DOMA. Those self-appointed champions of civil rights had no excuse. Yes, a few from the rural districts were probably reading the polls and feeling no qualms about restricting marriage to a man and a woman: Jack Kibbie from northwest Iowa, for example, and Dennis Black from nearby Newton. They didn't want to irritate their constituents and might have even agreed with them.

Angelo would also be correct when it came to any consideration of giving gays and lesbians the opportunity to enter into civil unions. Months later, legislative leaders released a list of studies to be conducted during the summer break. Civil unions weren't on the list, and no one explained why. The issue was never studied.

No one understood the political climate — and the opposition of Republicans like Angelo — better than McCoy, who wanted to be anywhere that day but in the senate chamber. As he had in the house, he refrained from engaging in debate and walked in to vote at the last possible moment. While voting, he sensed eyes watching, tongues wagging, and colleagues wondering what he might do.

As McCoy voted to join conservative Republicans in defending the sanctity of traditional marriage, he noticed he wasn't alone. Voting with him was state senator Tom Vilsack, who would later be elected Iowa's first Democratic governor in thirty years and subsequently appointed U.S. secretary of agriculture. As governor, ironically, he appointed four justices to the Iowa Supreme Court who would undo what he and McCoy helped the Republicans accomplish that day.

Final score: Ayes 41; Nays 9. A few days later, the Iowa House gave final passage. Three weeks after that, Governor Terry Branstad signed it into law — less than a month after Jen and Dawn BarbouRoske battled to bring their daughter McKinley into the world.

Years later, after his life had changed dramatically, McCoy would finally learn to stop kicking himself. Still, he remained haunted by the memory, saying, "It was the most regrettable vote I will take in my life."

Three months later, Janelle Rettig watched the returns from the 1998 Democratic primary election go up on a screen inside the Johnson County Building. Her first vote in a Democratic primary had turned out well. Her good friend Kim Painter had just been nominated by Johnson County Democrats to run for county recorder—an essentially ministerial record-keeping position that included responsibility for the issuing of marriage licenses. With her win that night, Painter was a lock to become the first openly gay or lesbian nonincumbent elected to a public office in Iowa. But Rettig felt even better when she noticed what had happened in the Democratic primary for governor. Mark McCormick, a former Iowa Supreme Court justice, had received eleven more votes (out of seven thousand cast) in Johnson County than Tom Vilsack. Vilsack would narrowly win nomination for governor but would lose in what some Iowans call "the Peoples' Republic of Johnson County."

As Rettig stood quietly reading the results, a Vilsack supporter approached. "Isn't it terrible Tom lost here?" the supporter asked.

"Naw, it's not terrible," she responded. "I voted against him. He's a lying son of a bitch. I won't vote for a politician who lies to me." She told the supporter that Vilsack had assured her in a personal e-mail that he would vote against House File 382. Moments later, Rettig found herself nose to nose with Bob Dvorsky, an Iowa state senator and cochair of Vilsack's Johnson County campaign. Dvorsky was angry and derisive. Rettig's response was profane and to the point. "Get out of my face. I'm not even a . . . Democrat. . . . I will vote for whoever I want."

On August 31, 1998, weeks after the confrontation, Rettig, Butler, and a few others met with Vilsack at Dvorsky's home. The governor-to-be had heard about the confrontation and wanted to clear the air. Butler, who wrote five pages of notes from the session, now calls it a "tail between the legs meeting." The couple said they heard Vilsack acknowledge that his vote had been motivated solely by the politics of running for higher office. According to Butler's notes, Vilsack, after conceding he was unfamiliar with gay and lesbian issues, said he couldn't explain his vote "without being brutally honest." The notes record Vilsack saying the vote was "wrong" and calling it "the toughest vote in the Iowa legislature because [I] knew if it were up to me, [I] would vote the other way." They also documented Vilsack using the phrase "political cowardice" and suggesting that Republican opponents had pushed for the senate vote as a means of creating a campaign issue against him because they knew he would be running in a statewide election. Butler's notes quote Vilsack as saying "[there is a] difference between a candidate and governor. I understand that's not satisfactory to many people in this room."

Reflecting years later, Vilsack said he didn't remember describing his vote as cowardice but said the meeting provided him with "help and assistance in understanding the gay community. As a small-town lawyer, it wasn't something I had a great deal of direct experience with."[9] Vilsack also said he didn't remember voting to restrict marriage to a man and a woman.

"I honestly don't remember that vote," he said. "I don't know why I did but, to me, what is relevant is what transpired after I became governor and the steps I took to fulfill the commitment I made at that meeting in Sue's and the senator's house."

Rettig said she remembered Vilsack's comments that night mostly because she learned one thing. "I realized we needed to stop acting like victims," she said years later. "And that if we acted like victims, the politicians were going to walk all over us. I no longer cared about being tolerated. I wanted my rights."

CHAPTER THREE

Near the Truth

The expression of the idea, that men are, by nature, possessed of equal rights, contains the germ of that great idea, which embodies the sentiment of universal brotherhood, in which we feel that we are all equal in the exercise of whatever nature has bestowed upon us."[1]

Wﾠith those words, David Bunker, a two-term state legislator and delegate to the Iowa Constitutional Convention of 1857, initiated a long history of legal commitment to protecting equal rights and individual liberties for all people within the borders of Iowa. Bunker was among thirty-six delegates—twenty-one Republicans and fifteen Democrats—assigned to the difficult task of rewriting the state's constitution at a time of racial unrest and rumor of civil war.

Iowa, like most states at the time, was in conflict over the various issues of equality, education, suffrage, temperance, and the rights of corporations, which dominated the business of the young rural agricultural state struggling to establish its foundation. The state had even banned the operation of certain banks—known as "banks of issue"—because depositors had lost their money as a result of bank failures. The convention became necessary only eleven years after Iowans had adopted the state's first constitution in 1846. Dissatisfaction with that constitution was abundantly evident on the day of its adoption when 9,492 voters approved it and 9,036 didn't—a majority of only 456 votes.

In 1855, the Fifth Iowa General Assembly agreed to put the question of another constitutional convention on the ballot at the request of Governor James Grimes, who insisted there was not a "single valid argument" against allowing voters to decide if the state's constitution needed change. In response, Iowans voted overwhelmingly, 32,790 to 14,162, calling for a constitutional convention to be held, indicating that both Democrats and Republicans were greatly dissatisfied with the 1846 document.[2]

Of the delegates who convened in the bitter cold of January 1857, only nine had been born in the Midwest. Six had moved from New England, eleven from the mid-Atlantic states, and ten were natives of slave states. Only four of the delegates had participated in the territorial government and only five in state government. Bunker, a farmer from Washington County, was one of the few delegates who had been a voting member of the Iowa territorial legislature as well as the Iowa House by the time the convention was held.

As in most states in the 1850s, the issues of slavery and racial equality permeated Iowa's political conversation and landscape. Much of northeastern and east central Iowa was considered antislavery; the rest of the state was dominated by Jacksonian Democrats, who supported the so-called black codes approved by the territorial legislatures prior to statehood. Those codes limited public education to whites, allowed only white males to vote, required only white males to register for the militia, and banned blacks from testifying as witnesses against whites. Interracial marriage also was prohibited. Though the 1844 convention delegates had even briefly banned all blacks and mixed-race people from settling within Iowa's borders, this measure was reconsidered and rejected. In any case, voters later rejected the 1844 constitution, forcing the second convention in 1846 as a prerequisite to obtaining statehood. But even given the prevalence of racism in the state, the Iowa judiciary took up the cause of personal liberty and equality based on the state's overall opposition to slavery.

On July 4, 1839, Iowa started down the path of protecting civil and human rights in the case of *In the Matter of Ralph (A Colored Man) on Habeus Corpus*.[3] That's when the Iowa Territorial Court, in its first decision ever, ruled that a former slave could not be returned to slavery, even after he had failed to make good on an agreement with his former owner to purchase his freedom. In 1834, Ralph had persuaded his owner, J. Montgomery, to accept an agreement giving the enslaved man his freedom. The agreement required Ralph to pay Montgomery $550 (the equivalent of about $13,750 today) plus interest. It also allowed him to leave Missouri for the Iowa territory, where he would earn money to pay for his freedom by working in the lead mines in Dubuque. But when Ralph failed to pay Montgomery, the slave owner sent bounty hunters to capture the slave and return him to Missouri. That scheme failed, however, when a local farmer, Alexander Butterworth, witnessed the capture and complained to a local judge, Thomas Wilson. Wilson immediately issued a writ of habeas corpus stopping the bounty hunters and directed the matter to the territorial supreme court. In a remarkable example of judicial efficiency, the court heard Ralph's case and issued a ruling on the same day.

Chief Justice Charles Mason — who would become a leader for the Iowa Democratic Party and, as candidate for governor in 1861, would support the constitutional rights of the South while opposing secession — rejected the slave owner's claim, based on the language of the Missouri Compromise of 1820. The legislation, crafted as a compromise between proslavery and antislavery factions in Congress, prohibited slavery above the parallel of 36 degrees, 30 minutes within the United States, with the exception of the proposed boundaries of Missouri. While the act was intended to allow slavery not only to continue in parts of the U.S. but also to grow into future states, Mason's reading of the law made it clear that slavery no longer existed in the Iowa territory for anyone who lived there:

> The language of the act of 1820, in relation to the district of country in which this territory is embraced is, that slavery therein "shall be, and is hereby, forever prohibited."[4]

Mason said the court could reject the slave owner's claim only because he had given his permission to the slave to live in a free state. Mason further wrote:

> The master who, subsequently to that Act, permits his slave to become a resident here, cannot afterwards exercise any acts of ownership over him within this territory. The law does not take away his property in express terms, but declares it no longer to be property at all. . . .
>
> When he applies to our tribunals for the purpose of controlling, as

property, that which our laws have declared shall not be property, it is incumbent on them to refuse their co-operation. When, in seeking to accomplish his object, he illegally restrains a human being of his liberty, it is proper that the laws, which should extend equal protection to men of all colors and conditions, should exert their remedial interposition."[5]

Despite that ruling, Iowans, though decidedly antislavery, remained as severely divided over racial equality as any state in the union. In 1851, the Iowa legislature approved a bill sponsored by William G. Haun, the Kentucky-born proprietor of a distillery and grist mill, to forbid blacks and those of mixed race from settling in Iowa and to require that they leave the state within three days to avoid arrest and fine. But antislavery lawmakers pulled a fast one. They required that, before going into effect, the legislation had to be printed in a Mount Pleasant weekly newspaper, the *Iowa True Democrat*—a publication affiliated with the antislavery Free Soil Party and owned by an abolitionist schoolteacher, Samuel Howe. Howe refused to publish the law, raising a substantial question of enforceability because the law wasn't included in the Iowa Code of 1851.[6] Howe decried Haun's bill as a monstrosity that transformed Iowa into a "slave holding state." He added, "When we take into consideration this new law . . . we think our legislature serves the Devil . . . with more alacrity than even their slave holding lords could desire."[7] Howe's refusal to publish the law, plus an apparent ambivalence among most Iowans, resulted in the law becoming more symbol than regulation as it went largely unenforced until its repeal after the Civil War.

But it was against that divisive background that Republicans and Democrats convened the constitutional convention. Jacksonian Democrats, whose party dominated national politics with the claim that its chief goal was to save the country from civil war, were pitted against Republicans, a party still in its infancy but growing strong in the North with its slogan "Free speech, free press, free men, free soil."

Republicans had shown growing strength despite the 1856 presidential election defeat of Republican John Fremont by Democrat James Buchanan. Iowa, which had named its far southwest county after Fremont in 1847, was one of four midwestern states to join seven New England states to cast its majority of presidential ballots for Fremont, who had gained fame as a military officer before entering politics. Although Fremont lost to Buchanan, Republicans' strength in Iowa had grown with the consolidation of several antislavery parties into one and the election of James Grimes, a Burlington lawyer, who would serve as governor from 1854 to 1858 and as a two-term U.S. Senate member.

Grimes had called for the constitutional convention mostly to debate ways to increase the young state's economic development, which up until then depended on out-of-state money and credit. But race and equality commanded a substantial amount of the convention's time: more than two hundred pages of the convention's debate journal (one-thousand-plus pages) are devoted to slavery equality issues.[8] Those issues included removing the term "white" from the existing constitutional guarantee of public education for Iowa children, permitting blacks and other minorities to testify in court proceedings involving whites, and approving black male suffrage—an issue that would, much like the debate over same-sex marriage, put Iowa in the forefront of a national debate. On one side were Republicans, who opposed slavery and argued freed slaves, particularly if they owned property, and others were entitled to many, if not all, of the legal rights of citizenship. On the other side were Democrats—most of whom agreed that slavery was wrong but maintained that freed slaves should not be allowed into Iowa, should have few, if any, civil rights, and, at minimum, be separated from the white population whenever and wherever possible.

Amos Harris, a state lawmaker from Appanoose County, spoke for many of his fellow Democratic delegates when he insisted he opposed slavery but didn't want freed slaves moving into Iowa. He said he would defend the rights of minorities already in the state. In a searing debate over whether freed slaves should be allowed to settle in Iowa, Harris said the state should not be "a hospital for the worn out Negroes of the South."[9] He further declared,

> I am proud to think that the party to which I belong is the white man's party and seeks to promote the interests of the white man. I believe that this country and this Government legitimately belongs [sic] to the white man, and when the two races cannot live together

in harmony, upon an equality, I would give the ascendency to the white race.[10]

The conflict between these two sides broke out early in the convention over amending Article I, Section 1, of the 1846 constitution. The question related mostly to the debate over allowing blacks to give court testimony against whites. Democrats opposed expanding a specific judicial right to allow testimony from blacks, but Republicans devised a compromise giving the party to a court case the right to use any person as a witness. But before that could be addressed, the question of man's natural right to equality had to be debated. The section that topped the 1846 constitution's bill of rights read at the time:

All men are by nature free and independent, and have certain in-alienable rights, among which are those of enjoying and defending life and liberty, acquiring, possessing, and protecting property, and pursuing and obtaining safety and happiness.[11]

Just days into what would become a thirty-nine-day convention, David Bunker proposed unsuccessfully that the term "independent" be removed and replaced by the word "equal." "This may appear to be a very unimportant amendment," he said, according to the convention's journal,

but it appears to me, that we should endeavor to get this bill of rights as near the truth as we can. My object . . . is simply to declare that men have certain equal rights, instead of declaring that all men are independent. I wish simply to declare the great truth, that men are, by nature, perfectly equal in the use of whatever Nature's God has bestowed upon them.

Bunker also pointed out that this amendment, like many others to be debated, would have a lasting effect on Iowa. "I believe that every action of this Convention may produce an influence for good or evil in all coming time."[12]

While Bunker's egalitarian argument fell on deaf ears at first, eventually the Republican majority decided to adopt Bunker's amendment. Fewer than thirty days after the initial defeat of Bunker's amendment, the convention revisited the issue; and Bunker again led the effort with an expanded justification for the change. He said that because the convention was using "our bill of rights" to lay down

> a kind of geological, or rather theological substratum upon which to build our government, it would be proper for us to get that as nearly correct as possible. It occurred to me that it was not absolutely true in the nature of things that all men were, by nature, *independent*, but I supposed it was true that by nature each man had equal rights, whatever power might restrain him from the exercise of those rights.[13]

In response, Harris, the Appanoose County Democrat, made an argument similar to one to be used in the political and legal battle over same-sex marriage 150 years later. His personal review of state constitutions at that time, he told the delegates, had disclosed that the term "independent" had been "used oftener than any other form of expression, in attempting to define that particular right."[14]

A similar argument would be repeated in state after state following the 1993 Hawaii *Baehr* decision, in which opponents of same-sex marriage claimed it was necessary to restrict marriage to a man and woman in order to deny recognition of same-sex marriage if it ever became legal in any individual state. The argument gained strength from 1996 through 2008, when forty states had either approved a constitutional amendment or legislation banning same-sex marriage.

Marriage equality opponents uniformly would insist that their intent was not to discriminate against homosexuals but simply to legislatively preserve an important cog of American culture—traditional marriage. Put another way, same-sex couples should be denied their equal right to marry civilly for what the majority perceived to be a greater good.

In his final argument against Bunker's amendment, Harris related that same view when he said, "The word 'independent' expresses what we desire to express, better than any word we can make use of." He continued,

> We are simply desiring, as I understand it, to give some expression to what we conceive to be the rights of man, politically if you please, naturally if you desire to have it so. It does not matter particularly

which we are speaking of. Our rights must be limited politically, because we all compromise something in coming together."[15]

On a party line vote, Bunker's proposed change to Article I, Section 1, was adopted. Iowa chose equality:

All men are, by nature, free and equal, and have certain inalienable rights among which are those enjoying and defending life and liberty, acquiring, possessing, and protecting property, and pursuing and obtaining safety and happiness.

That choice would have a lasting effect on Iowa's politics and legal system over the next 152 years.

The impact began in 1868 when a twelve-year-old black girl from Muscatine claimed to have the right to attend the same grammar school as the white children in her neighborhood.

If John Edwards, a lawyer from Chariton, Iowa, in the mid-1800s, had been a baseball player today, the term "journeyman" would have fit perfectly. If he were a politician today, his opponents would have called him a "carpetbagger."

Edwards, born in Louisville, Kentucky, on October 24, 1805, spent much of his adult life getting elected to public office, despite little formal schooling and refusing to live in states where slavery was permitted. Admitted to the bar in Indiana, Edwards began his political life when he was elected as a state representative to the Indiana legislature at age forty. At that time, he illustrated his abhorrence of slavery when he freed the slaves he inherited from his father's Kentucky estate and provided them with property from that estate on which to live. After moving to California three years later, he was elected an *alcalde*—a position established during the Mexican government's control of California that encompassed the roles of mayor, judge, and regulator of a city. Records don't indicate in which California city Edwards and his family lived, but his tenure was brief: the United States took over the province in 1848, and it became a state in 1850.

Three years later, after losing his first wife, with whom he had seven children, Edwards moved to the Lucas County seat city of Chariton in southern Iowa. There he married his second wife (and had three more children), practiced law, and began his Iowa political career.

Edwards's role in changing Article I, Section 6, of the 1846 Iowa Constitution, unlike David Bunker's fight over Article I, Section 1, drew little attention and even less comment. At that time, Section 6 read simply that "all laws of a general nature shall have uniform operation." According to the journal of the debates of the Constitutional Convention, Edwards proposed expanding and clarifying the section on the thirteenth day of the convention. He proposed it should read:

> All laws of a general nature shall have a uniform operation. And the General Assembly shall not grant to any citizen, or class of citizens, privileges or immunities, which, upon the same terms, shall not equally belong to other citizens.

After proposing the amendment, Edwards was asked for an explanation of the purpose of the change. He replied:

> Its object is contained in a nut shell, and is merely this: It is to prevent the General Assembly from granting any privileges or immunities to any citizen or class of citizens, that it would not be willing to grant to any other citizen or class of citizens upon the same terms. It is to prevent the Legislature from granting exclusive privileges to any class of citizens.[16]

Immediately after his explanation, the change to Section 6 was adopted and was not considered again during the convention.

Without debate on the issue, just what Edwards was attempting to accomplish and why are difficult to ascertain. Still, many legal scholars interpret the language in Section 6 not as an attempt to require state government to provide equal protection under the law to its citizens, but rather as an attempt to prohibit state lawmakers from approving legislation giving individuals or businesses willing to use bribery or kickbacks an advantage over a competitor. After all, the language in Section 6 was adopted in 1857, when Iowa still had a number of black codes in effect, including a ban on black suffrage and a ban on educating children who were black or of a mixed race. At the same time, distrust of banks, corporations, and the railroads permeated much of the country.

In late 1857, that distrust would be confirmed by the financial panic that began after a hurricane off the coast of North Carolina sank a California ship carrying thirty thousand pounds of gold from the San Francisco Mint. Major banks had been counting on the gold to cover growing losses from poor investments. Within days of the wreck, a New York branch of the Ohio Life Insurance and Trust Company went bust, setting off bank failures across the country, rising unemployment, a major stock market decline, and a national depression that wouldn't end until the Civil War.

In addition, scholars point out that the Fourteenth Amendment was adopted after the Civil War and was designed to protect blacks from being deprived of their civil rights by governmental action. Iowa, along with several other states, including Indiana and Oregon, chose to prohibit the government from granting special privileges to individuals or businesses—a populist Jacksonian precept at a time of deep distrust of the practices of big business.

Alexander Clark had moved to Muscatine in 1842 after learning to become a barber. Born in Pennsylvania to freed slaves, Clark had lived in Cincinnati, Ohio, where he was educated and then trained in haircutting, but moved to the Hawkeye state where he became known for his advocacy of civil rights and his success as a businessman. Eventually, Clark would become the second black ever to graduate from the University of Iowa Law School; the first graduate was his son. Clark also would be appointed U.S. minister to Liberia by President William Henry Harrison and would die in that country while serving at his post.

At the time, Muscatine and Mount Pleasant, sixty miles apart in southeast Iowa, had become population centers for blacks—many of them freed slaves—and those of mixed race. By 1867, Alexander already had become one of the state's most influential voices promoting equality of the black population. He, along with Thomas Motts, had led efforts in various legislative sessions to repeal Iowa's black codes and to advocate for black suffrage.

That year, his daughter, Susan, attempted to enroll at an all-white neighborhood grammar school. The Muscatine Board of Education denied her admission. Like many districts with black or mixed-race children, Muscatine had established separate schools for minority children, but Alexander Clark objected because no school of that type was available to her. In addition, he claimed the instruction in the minority schools was inferior to that of the white school.

Like the other equal rights issues, the question of school integration had prompted a major and sometimes ugly fight during the 1857 convention. The state's first constitution didn't specifically limit public education to white children, but one of Iowa's black codes prohibited black and mixed-race children any public education opportunity.

Almost from the beginning of the convention, Republicans pushed to eliminate most of the black codes and to require the state to provide education to minority children even if it meant in separate schools. Delegates clashed again and again over the issues limiting most rights to white Iowans—whether it was the right to vote, testify in court, serve in the legislature, or join the militia. Finally, with no apparent agreement in sight, there came a compromise. Republicans, led by Rufus L. B. Clarke of Henry County, offered to place a second referendum before Iowa voters in conjunction with the ratification referendum of the proposed new constitution. The question to be asked in the second referendum was whether the word "white" should be dropped from the constitution.

Clarke, along with other Republicans, had argued for elimination of racial restrictions within the constitution but was under no illusion of the likely outcome of the second vote. "Mr. Chairman," Clarke told the convention delegates on February 23, 1857. "I do not expect a majority will vote for it; sir, I wish that the State was in such a condition that we could vote for the resolution with an expectation of success." Clarke said that the time had not yet come when voters "would throw aside this childish timidity, this worse than foolish prejudice, that leads them to imagine innumerable evils that might fall upon them." He also made a brash prediction.

> I tell you, sir, as there is a God in Heaven, the principles I this day advocate, *shall* yet triumph in Iowa. . . . The day is coming when the people of this State shall not be afraid to carry out to the letter, the true intent and spirit of every iota of the true democratic creed."[17]

The convention approved the holding of the additional referendum, which, as Clarke had predicted, would fail by a large vote later that year. Yet the delegates refused to include a racial restriction in Article IX, Section 12, of the constitution, regarding public education through common schools. In a debate over whether the constitution should mandate that education be provided to "all youth" or "all white youth," delegates rejected imposing a racial restriction despite objections from some delegates who claimed it would lead to interracial marriage and procreation — then termed "amalgamation."

George Gillaspy, a Democrat from Ottumwa, decried the possibility of integrated schools during debate of his amendment to limit public education solely to white children.

Put your white children in the country, upon an equality with the negro, in the schools or the social circle, and I undertake to say that it is the very thing to lead to amalgamation. Teach them that the colored population are just as good as they are by nature, and equal in every sense of the word, and that's the inevitable consequence.[18]

In response, Republican delegate William Penn Clarke (no relation to Rufus L. B. Clarke) of Johnson County characterized Gillaspy's arguments as an appeal to prejudice. "What are they?" he asked.

Are they based upon reason, founded upon truth, or are they the veriest appeals we have had to prejudice in the convention? Does the gentleman say he is willing to put a clause in the constitution refusing to give any of God's creatures living upon our soil, an education? . . . Is he willing to say that any other class of men, not belonging to the Anglo-Saxon race, shall be excluded from the privileges of education?[19]

Republicans, including both Clarkes, assured delegates that the question of school integration would be left to the local districts. Said John Parvin, another delegate:

In districts where the whites are willing that the colored children should be educated in the same schools, let them come in; but in cases where there is so much prejudice that they prefer that they shall be educated in a separate place, let that be required.[20]

In short order, the delegates rejected Gillaspy's amendment on a 22–10 vote, then quickly approved Article IX, Section 12, directing the Board of Education to "provide for the education of all the youths of the state through a system of common schools."[21] The vote was the same, 22–10.

Twelve years later, the Iowa Supreme Court would impose its first test of the meaning of those words with a result that would be startling for its time. But it wouldn't be the only example in 1868 of Iowa forcing the country to rethink racial prejudice and confront it head-on with change.

By 1868, Iowa Supreme Court justice Chester C. Cole already had become a figure of controversy within Iowa. New York–born and educated at the Harvard Law School, Cole arrived in Des Moines, Iowa, in 1857 with his wife, Amanda, from Kentucky, fearful of the secession movement in the South and looking to establish a law practice. Almost immediately, Cole entered the world of Iowa politics by obtaining a Democratic Party nomination for the Iowa Supreme Court in the election of 1859—an election he would lose.

Five years later, in 1864, Cole, who had become a Republican as a result of the Civil War, was appointed to the supreme court by Governor William Stone following legislative expansion of the court from three members to four. Stone chose Cole, who later founded two Des Moines law schools—one that would be transferred to the University of Iowa in Iowa City and one that would eventually be established at Drake University in Des Moines. He was selected as a reward for spending substantial time traveling through southern and southwestern Iowa during the turbulent year following President Abraham Lincoln's Emancipation Proclamation in 1863.

Cole's task, as assigned by Governor Samuel Kirkwood, a strong Lincoln supporter, was to assure southern Iowans they need not concern themselves about the proclamation or heed conspiracy theories of local Copperheads, who were hoping for a peace agreement with the Confederacy. Kirkwood, later known as "the old war governor," had helped oversee 76,000 Iowa men as volunteers for the Union Army and, in 1863, the formation of the Sixtieth U.S. Colored Infantry Regiment, nearly one thousand black soldiers. Cole fulfilled his task by spending much of 1863 and part of 1864 traveling throughout the southern portions of Iowa talking with farmers and townfolk concerned more about the possible loss of the war than about attempting to make peace with the Confederacy.

As Union victory became apparent, Cole returned to Des Moines as one of the Republican Party's leading lawyers and received his appointment to the supreme court, a position he would be elected to a year later. The victory had a dramatic impact on Iowa's politics — so much so that the Democrats, who had dominated the state's politics for more than half the nineteenth century, were down to just ten seats in the legislature. What's more, Republican William Stone had been elected governor in 1863 and reelected in 1865.

Republicans began to clamor for the removal of various restrictions on racial equality. Black suffrage was top on the list of many Republicans including Cole, who would enter the debate after the 1864 federal election by urging adoption of a constitutional amendment — Resolution 4 — to permit black males to vote.

The drumbeat for a constitutional amendment had its birth, according to Robert Dykstra's book *Bright Radical Star*, at the Iowa Republican Party's 1865 convention. There, Congressman Hiram Price and newspaper editor Ed Russell, both of Davenport, forged an agreement on Resolution 4 that demanded the issue be considered a centerpiece of the Republican platform. Following the convention, Republican candidates, including Stone, exerted their electoral muscle by vanquishing their Democratic opponents, who had run under the banner of the Union Anti–Negro Suffrage Party. That victory led Stone and other Republicans to push for a suffrage amendment on the 1868 ballot.

Chester C. Cole entered the fray over suffrage, later describing himself as "probably the first man of influence in the state to put himself . . . publicly on record in favor of this then unpopular measure."[22] Under the new constitution, any amendment would have to be approved by two different legislatures before being placed on the ballot. That meant the earliest the amendment could be considered was 1868. Cole disclosed his support for black suffrage in a June 1865 article written for the *Des Moines Register*. Cole offered that, though black suffrage would help freed slaves in their home states to thwart a defiant white majority, granting suffrage in Iowa was more a matter of respect for what black Iowans had done for the Union in the Civil War.

Cole viewed black suffrage partially as a *quid pro quo* arrangement. If black soldiers could use their skill and bravery in combat for the Union, they were qualified to vote. "That skill and bravery, which has character-ized their use of bullets against our enemies, ought to be received as suf-ficient proof of their ability thus to use the ballot also."[23]

But Cole pointed to another reason for Iowans to adopt the constitu-tional amendment — its impact on the nation. Until then, only five New England states, including Massachusetts and Vermont, permitted black males to vote. Those constitutions had never imposed a racial restriction on voting. If the federal government was going to insist on black suffrage in the South, they needed to adopt it in the North as well. Cole said Iowa should help lead the way to become the first midwestern state to approve the change. He wrote in the *Register*,

> The *moral influence* of correct action in Iowa will be potent for good upon the national cause. . . . Let her be *first* in the great act of po-litical progress . . . to secure complete victory in the struggle for equality.[24]

Three years after advocating suffrage, Cole wrote the supreme court de-cision that would eventually be hailed as one "of the signal black triumphs in court [that] preceded the ratification of the Fourteenth Amendment."[25]

Alexander Clark had hired a local Muscatine lawyer to represent him and his daughter in their fight with the Muscatine school board. But that local lawyer, David Cloud, also happened to be a former Iowa attorney general. Cloud and a partner had been hired years earlier by Thomas Motts, an-other prominent black Muscatine businessman and civil rights advocate, to represent him in a dispute with white owners of a local hotel. Cloud's key witness in the *Motts* case had been a black man, whom defense law-yers, citing Iowa's black codes, demanded could not testify. But Cloud had won in district court with the black witness's testimony included in the record and again in 1856 before the Iowa Supreme Court.

Now, years later, Cloud's argument before the Iowa Supreme Court for Susan Clark was straightforward. The state constitution guaranteed that all youth, regardless of color, would be educated. Susan Clark was entitled to attend her neighborhood school with white children because other minority schools were inferior and too far from her home. What's more, Iowa's bill of rights declared that "all men are, by nature, free and equal." Cloud also pointed out that the state statute governing the education of children had changed over the years. First, beginning in 1846, education services had been limited to white children. Then, state law changed to allow black children to attend separate or integrated schools with the unanimous approval of the entire district. Finally, state law changed again, and those changes were silent on the issue of race.

Lawyers for the school district insisted that state law still gave the district discretion to establish segregated schools and that the school had offered to provide Susan Clark with a teacher and facility that met her educational needs. Cole, in writing the 3–1 majority opinion, dismissed the school district's claims by suggesting that the constitution and state law required Susan Clark to be able to attend the school she chose when no other was available to her. Cole wrote,

> If the legislature [has], by first denying admission of colored children to common schools, and then by admitting them only upon unanimous consent, denied all discretion to the school board as to the admission of colored children, such discretion is equally denied when the legislature [has] declared, pursuant to a constitutional requirement, that *all the youths* of the State shall be admitted to the common schools.[26]

He also pointed out that if the children of black families could be treated in such a fashion, then the district board would have the "same power and right to exclude German children from our common schools, require them to attend (if at all) a school composed wholly of children of that nationality, and so of Irish, French, English, and other nationalities."

Cole said neither the Iowa Constitution nor existing state law permitted that kind of discrimination. "Our statute does not, either in letter or in spirit, recognize or justify any such distinction or limitations of right or privilege on account of nationality," he wrote, adding that the sanctioning of such limitations was contrary to the tendencies and policies that constituted what was American: "the common purpose to perpetuate and spread our free institutions for the development, elevation, and happiness of *mankind.*" If the court allowed this, it "would be to sanction a plain violation of the spirit of our laws . . . , [and] would tend to perpetuate the national differences of our people and stimulate a constant strife, if not a war of races."[27]

The court issued Cole's majority opinion on April 14, 1868—eighty-six years before a similar decision was reached by the U.S. Supreme Court in its landmark civil rights decision, *Brown v. Board of Education of Topeka*. On November 3, 1868, Cole and other Iowa Republican leaders were rewarded for their support of black suffrage as well. Reversing the referendum vote in 1857 that kept racial classifications within the constitution, Iowans, an estimated 87 percent of them Republicans, voted overwhelmingly to become the first midwestern state to remove all racial restrictions from the voting franchise. Joined by Minnesota weeks later, the two states would be the only two in the nation to grant black suffrage before the ratification of the Fifteenth Amendment to the U.S. Constitution in 1870.

Cole's tenure on the Iowa Supreme Court was marked by two other landmark civil rights decisions. In 1869, Cole was among the court members who refused to review a district court judge's decision to allow Arabella Mansfield, born Belle Aurelia Babb, to become the first female lawyer within the United States.

Mansfield, who was born in 1842 on a farm near Burlington, had become a teacher after studying at Iowa Wesleyan College in Mount Pleasant. After marrying, she studied law at her brother's law office and passed the bar examination. District court judge Francis Springer, who had presided over the Iowa Constitutional Convention of 1857, certified her membership to the bar, despite a law requiring that only white males be permitted to take the examination. Springer's conclusion was that "the affirmative declaration that male persons may be admitted is not an implied denial of the right to females."[28]

Mansfield would not practice law, choosing instead to teach and focus on the women's suffrage movement. But Springer's decision—as well as the Supreme Court's decision not to reverse it—again contradicted what was considered the accepted jurisprudence at the time. Just three years later, however, the U.S. Supreme Court upheld an Illinois law prohibiting women from practicing law on the grounds that such a prohibition was a reasonable judgment for the Illinois legislature and its courts to make.

CHAPTER THREE

In 1873, the Iowa high court then confronted a second question in the battle over the issue of "separate but equal." Emma Coger, a schoolteacher of mixed race in Quincy, Illinois, was traveling on the SS *Merrill* to return to her home after visiting in Keokuk, Iowa. Coger had initially attempted to purchase a ticket providing her with first-class accommodations, including meals at the ladies table in a cabin of the steamer. Rebuffed by company officials citing the fact she was of mixed race, Coger eventually obtained a ticket that provided her with a cot, but not meals on board.

As the dinner hour approached, Coger sent a chambermaid to purchase a meal ticket for her only to discover on the maid's return the words "colored girl" written on it. After Coger inquired about the meaning of the inscription, a boat clerk informed her that she would be required to take her meal at a table set up outdoors along the guards of the boat or "in such place where the clerk saw fit."

Coger demanded a refund and received it. She then enlisted a male passenger to purchase for her a different meal ticket. No restrictions were written on that ticket. When mealtime arrived, Coger entered the dining cabin and sat at the ladies' table. Immediately, white passengers and boat officials demanded she leave the cabin. Coger refused, and the boat captain was summoned. He demanded she leave. When Coger refused again, the captain had her removed forcibly, resulting in broken dishes and a slightly injured boat official. Defense witnesses claimed that Coger's response had been less than genteel, saying she used "abusive, threatening, and coarse" language, which Coger denied.

Chief Justice Joseph Beck, who wrote the court's majority opinion, described Coger's response to her removal from the cabin:

> Certain it is, however, that by her spirited resistance and her defiant words, as well as by her pertinacity in demanding the recognition of her rights and in vindicating them, she has exhibited evidence of the Anglo-Saxon blood that flows in her veins.

But Beck also conceded that "neither womanly delicacy nor unwomanly courage has anything to do with her legal rights and the remedies for their deprivation."[29]

Those, Beck wrote, emanated clearly from the first words of the Iowa

Constitution—the same words David Bunker had proposed almost apologetically sixteen years earlier in his successful attempt to have the constitution be "near the truth":

> This principle of equality is announced and secured by the very first words of our State constitution which relate to the rights of the people, in language most comprehensive, and incapable of misconstruction, namely: "All men are, by nature, free and equal." . . . Upon it we rest our conclusion in the case.

Beck's fifteen-page opinion also cited the *Clark* school decision as precedent that the "doctrines of natural law and of Christianity forbid that rights be denied on the ground of race or color."[30]

"In our opinion the plaintiff was entitled to same rights and privileges while upon defendant's boat . . . , which were possessed and exercised by white passengers," Beck wrote.

> These rights and privileges rest upon the equality of all before the law, the very foundation principle of our government. If the Negro must submit to different treatment, to accommodations inferior to those given to the white man, when transported by public carriers, he is deprived of the benefits of this very principle of equality.[31]

In reaching the *Clark* and *Coger* decisions, the Iowa Supreme Court took its place as one of the most progressive states in the U.S. on the issue of civil rights. Both decisions preceded the 1896 U.S. Supreme Court decision in *Plessy v. Ferguson*—the infamous court decision that upheld the constitutionality of state laws requiring racial segregation in public accommodations under the doctrine of separate but equal. With almost identical facts to those presented in the *Coger* case, the U.S. Supreme Court, on a 7–1 vote, viewed a Louisiana statute requiring segregated public accommodations as a matter of acceptable public policy, not a violation of the rights of a minority race. And, instead of understanding the fervor with which Emma Coger attempted to protect her rights on that steamboat, Justice Henry Billings Brown dismissed the contention that blacks were being subjected to "a badge of inferiority."

"If this be so, it is not by reason of anything found in the act, but solely because the colored race chooses to put that construction upon it," Brown wrote.[32]

The decisions of Constitutional Convention delegates in Iowa's bill of rights in 1857 laid the foundation for the Iowa Supreme Court to declare "separate, but equal" in education and public accommodations a violation of the state constitution. Those cases were instrumental 152 years later in leading the court to its equal protection analysis overturning Iowa's law restricting marriage to a man and a woman.

The convention's journals disclose a heated and coarse debate over an issue of equality as it was considered then and illustrate the deep division within the state's populace. Such was also the case starting in 2003 when a district court judge in northwest Iowa made a fateful decision.

CHAPTER FOUR

Two Women

District court judge Jeffrey Neary took a seat at his desk just before 8 A.M. and waited for the parade of lawyers to march through his chambers.[1] On November 14, 2003, it was his turn to deal with the routine work of his northwest Iowa judicial district. Each day one judge was required to spend an hour serving as judicial traffic cop. Dozens of lawyers from greater Sioux City troop up to the Woodbury County courthouse chambers with briefcases full of motions, requests to continue hearings, child support or divorce petitions, and just about every other legal document known to mankind.

Neary had been sworn into office in January after a career in private practice and as a sometime public defender. He knew "order hour," as it was called, would be a blur. It wasn't unusual for him to hear between thirty and fifty cases per sitting. Given the time constraint, each one would receive a cursory review at best. That meant giving the lawyers what they wanted—quick, routine judicial action—before moving on to the next case.

The workload wasn't overly burdensome that day. Time was just about to run out when Neary noticed Sioux City lawyer Dennis Ringgenberg standing in his office. A respected family law professional, he handed the judge a divorce petition.

"I've got a decree and stipulation here," Ringgenberg said. "It is all agreed to."

As the judge looked through the petition, he heard Ringgenberg say there were no children involved and that the couple had stipulated to a division of the property and assets. The date on the filing of the petition was August 1. Neary hurriedly reviewed the document by going to the last page, making sure no children were involved and the rest of the petition was in order. After signing the petition, he flipped the pages back over and glanced at the title: *Kimberly Jean Brown v. Jennifer Sue Perez.*

"I think these are two women, or at least it looks like it," Neary said, looking up at Ringgenberg.

"They are," the lawyer replied. He went on to explain the two women were Sioux City residents who had gone to Vermont and joined in a civil union after the state legislature there had approved it. The couple then returned to Sioux City but decided to separate after living together for a short period.

Ringgenberg has declined to talk publicly about whether he relayed the special circumstances of the case to Neary at the beginning of the petition review but insists that, as a general matter of principle, he mentions special circumstances to judges when warranted. If Ringgenberg told Neary the divorce petition involved two women as he handed him the petition, the judge says he didn't hear it. Years later, Neary said he knew he was holding a keg of dynamite and, by signing the paper, had lit the fuse.

He knew Iowa had prohibited same-sex marriage since 1998, but what about this kind of case? Neary believes he could have stopped the petition from being filed then and there and prevented the explosion either by telling Ringgenberg to draw up another order setting aside his original decision and signing it or by calling the clerk of court's office and instructing the staff to refuse the petition if Ringgenberg tried to file it. But as he contemplated what he should do, Neary thought about the nature of the request. Essentially, the couple was asking for a dissolution of a legal partnership valid in another state. As far as he knew then, the only way to do that in Iowa would be through the state's dissolution of marriage statute.

Two long-standing legal principles also entered Neary's mind. First, the U.S. Constitution's Article IV, Section 1, guarantees that "Full Faith and Credit shall be given in each State to the public Acts, Records, and Judicial Proceedings of every other State." He also thought about how judges generally are required to defer to the legal acts of other states under the concept of "judicial comity." Both principles have been essential in enabling the federal and state governments to interact with each other and allowing states that might have differing statutes to simply get along.

"I believed at the time and I do to this day," Neary said years later, "that those two legal principles allowed me to do what I did. I wasn't recognizing or creating a same-sex marriage, but only recognizing that Vermont had created this relationship; and the only way to dissolve it at that precise moment was through our divorce statute."

After reviewing the petition one last time, Neary handed it back to Ringgenberg. "OK, you can go ahead and file this now. But I know this is going to cause problems," he muttered as Ringgenberg walked out the door. "We're probably going to be on the front page of the paper." Saying little, the lawyer took the petition, walked to the clerk's office, filed it, and waited to see what would happen next. Not that he didn't have a really good idea. Neary had done his duty. Another routine petition had been served. But this time, the dynamite was about to explode.

Under Iowa law, divorce petitions are sealed until finalized. The second state in the U.S. to adopt no-fault divorce in 1970, Iowa mandates that neither party is allowed to cite wrongful behavior of the spouse unless it is to challenge child custody or property division. Disclosure of any information to a third party about the legal proceeding up to that point is punishable by up to a year in jail and one thousand dollars. The law also mandates that both parties must wait at least ninety days after the initial filing before they can receive a final decree. That's why the petition had been filed August 1 and brought to Neary in November.

For years, the Woodbury County clerk of courts office kept the finalized divorce petitions in a file as a favor to the local *Sioux City Journal*. Each week, the newspaper's courts reporter would go through the file, take notes on each petition, and get the names, city of residence, and place of marriage. The reporter would then prepare a list of divorces that would run in agate type similar to the paper's listings of bankruptcies, marriage licenses, and real estate sales.

When Nick Hytrek, the courts reporter for the *Sioux City Journal*, began going through the divorce petitions filed a few days after Neary's decision had been made, he had no reason to believe he would find anything out of the ordinary.[2] Hytrek knew the odds of any news rising out of the process were slim unless the divorce involved a public figure or official from the area. But even then Hytrek knew his editors weren't all that interested in using newsprint for routine stories. The object of the game was finishing the weekly agate-list housekeeping as soon as possible and getting back to a more worthwhile task. This time, however, Hytrek saw something curious. A divorce decree involving a Kimberly and a Jennifer?

"Is this what I think it is?" he asked, turning to a nearby clerk.

"Yes, it is," the clerk said with a smile.

Hytrek looked at the back page of the petition to see who had signed off on it.

Jeffrey Neary.

How can a judge end a relationship the state doesn't recognize in the first place? In an Associated Press story, December 31, 2003, the president of the Christian conservative Iowa Family Policy Center sought perspective in a deadly disease simile: "It's like a doctor saying you're cured of cancer when you never had cancer."[3]

Even Neary, in an interview with Hytrek, made it clear he wasn't all that sure himself. "My thought is treat it like a contract or partnership and dissolve it. I know that's a broad look at it," said the judge to the reporter. "I don't know what's right or wrong here."[4]

Hytrek's first story on the divorce ran on December 6, 2003, more than three weeks after the decree was filed. The headline in the *Sioux City Journal* played up the Iowa angle: "Divorce Granted to Lesbian Couple Doesn't Mean Iowa Accepts Union." For days, the story lay dormant. Hytrek expected some controversy, but none bubbled up — until a story appeared the following week on the *Des Moines Register*'s front page under the headline: "Iowa Judge OKs Lesbian Divorce."

Neary's uncertainty and his legal explanation stood in direct contrast to the explosion of opposition that erupted. Within days, a group of lawmakers, most of them social conservatives from the northwest corner of the state, did more than speak out against the judge's decision. With the help of antigay groups and at least one church, they responded by filing a lawsuit demanding that the Iowa Supreme Court overturn the decision.

They called Neary an activist, policy-making judge and vowed to oust him in the 2004 retention vote. Under state law, newly appointed judges are on the ballot in the first general election after serving a year. After that, they face retention once every six years, compared to the supreme court's once every eight.

Just as Massachusetts had just become the first state to permit same-sex marriages, the social conservatives predicted Iowa would become the state where same-sex civil unions and marriages go to die. The claim was somewhat similar to the argument during the 1857 Constitutional Convention debates against allowing freed slaves to move to Iowa. Some even said Neary's decision would be used by advocates to force same-sex marriages despite Iowa's DOMA.

Taking it all in from her Des Moines law office two hundred miles away, Sharon Malheiro picked up the phone to see if she could help.[5] The more she saw, the more she believed this was it—the case that would convince important marriage-equality proponents, inside Iowa and out, that the heart of the heartland might indeed be the place to make the next big push. Malheiro had been touting Iowa for years, but few listened. As a partner in one of Iowa's largest and politically influential law firms, she had built a substantial part of her employment-law practice representing gays, lesbians, and transgenders.

She had landed at the Davis Brown Law Firm after spending two years as a clerk for Iowa chief justice Louis Lavorato and another ten years before that as a newspaper editor in Des Moines. She had deep roots in Iowa and knew its political dynamics well. Those credentials were just what it took to get into Davis Brown. Founded in 1929, the firm's reputation and most recent success had been built primarily by two men—a former chair of the Iowa Democratic Party and a prominent Republican. Together Arthur Davis and Harlan "Bud" Hockenberg built a practice specializing in politics and political influence that often stretched far beyond state lines. Davis had been the Democratic Party chair; Hockenberg, the Republican heavyweight. But the firm also had Stephen Roberts, a longtime member of the Republican National Committee.

Intrigued by the Sioux City divorce case, Malheiro called Dennis Ringgenberg and offered to help him defend the decision before the supreme court. Ringgenberg made it clear his client, Kimberly Brown, didn't want any more publicity; and a challenge before the supreme court would certainly draw even more attention. He also pointed out that neither Brown nor Perez had been named as defendants in the lawmakers' case. In addition, at Neary's request, he had made substantive changes in the original order nine days after the filing of the lawsuit challenging the decision.

Troubled by the wording in the original petition and seeking to clarify his position, Neary had consulted with family-law attorneys who had handled the breakups of same-sex couples in other Iowa jurisdictions. His decree now said that Brown and Perez had entered into a civil union in Vermont and that he had no specific authority to grant dissolution of the civil union under the Iowa law governing divorce. But the judge also issued a declaration of fact to be used by Brown and Perez that said the union should be recognized as terminated, that both individuals were now single, and that all property had been divided with agreement of both parties. Years later, Neary justified his decision: "This state recognizes termination of contracts made out of state as well as divorces. I didn't see any point in making an exception to it since there was no dispute between the parties."

Opponents of the decision insisted that the judge's amended decree, as well as his original decision, should not be allowed to stand for a variety of reasons. In response and without any opposition, the supreme court agreed to hear the case. With the original plaintiffs not interested in defending the case, Malheiro decided she and any other legal groups representing the interests of those in the LGBT community should put together a defense of Neary's decision in amicus briefs and arguments. For her, this case was an opportunity to convince activists outside the state that Iowa was the perfect place to stage a legal battle for marriage equality.

Of this Malheiro was also convinced: support from a national civil rights group like Lambda Legal would be essential. Even without a trial, costs could easily top six figures; too steep a tab for a local advocacy group, much less any one plaintiff couple. Plus, there would be time and cost in finding gay and lesbian couples in Iowa willing to become plaintiffs challenging the law. In all, it would be a major undertaking—requiring expertise, money, and a creative approach, not to mention an ability to withstand the kind of controversy it would generate.

In law school, Malheiro had been drawn to civil rights issues while also developing an expertise in media and communications law. Part of it was personal. She is a lesbian. In 2005, Malheiro would help to form One Iowa, an LGBT advocacy group. When she began her practice, she went public with her own sexual orientation and threw herself into the gay and lesbian rights movement. That led to her relationship with Lambda Legal Defense and Education Fund, the well-financed national civil rights group out of New York City. Every now and then the New York headquarters or the Chicago branch would call and ask for help, and she would do whatever she could.

Most of the early cases she handled involved people who wanted to change the sex designation on their birth certificates. Eventually, that led to difficult legal questions involving property, estates, adoption, and health care for gay and lesbian couples. During that time, she kept telling Lambda officials they were wasting time and money jumping from one coast to another to fight their marriage-equality cases. Take a look at Iowa, she kept saying. The state has been a civil rights champion. Check out the constitution and the history. Look at all the precedent-setting, forward-thinking supreme court decisions that date back to territorial days. Consider the makeup of the current court.

"How come you guys always want to fight for marriage equality in California and New York?" Malheiro would ask the Lambda bosses, only half in jest. "California and New York are not the norm. The people are crazy out there. If you're looking for a state to do a civil rights argument on a constitutional issue, Iowa is the place."

But Lambda officials were not easily persuaded. Much of their reluctance was the result of a failed attempt early in Iowa governor Tom Vilsack's first term to provide a small but important step to protect gays and lesbians employed in state government. On September 14, 1999, Vilsack had issued an executive order prohibiting discrimination based on sexual orientation or gender identity in government. As a Democratic state legislator, Vilsack had voted like almost everyone else to limit marriage to a man and a woman in 1996 and 1998. As governor, however, he issued the order prohibiting job discrimination based on sexual orientation or gender identity.

Predictably, Republican legislators rebelled, filing a lawsuit challenging Vilsack's authority. In late 2000, a district court agreed with the challenge. Unexpectedly, Vilsack, wanting to avoid a supreme court precedent, declined to appeal, leaving Lambda doubting that protection or expansion of the rights of gays and lesbians in Iowa had much support. But now, thanks to the divorce litigation in Sioux City, Malheiro was convinced she had the case to show Lambda that Iowa was receptive to gay rights. The focus, she believed, was the question of harm. Who was damaged by a lesbian couple's divorce? Brown and Perez, the divorcees, were the only ones entitled to challenge the case; and they were happy with Neary's decision. Another trip to the courthouse was not in the plan.

And how could the conservative opponents of Neary's decision prove harm? Malheiro was convinced the opponents would lose. By fighting this case, she believed, Lambda would see once and for all that the Iowa Supreme Court might view marriage equality favorably. Malheiro also believed Lambda's legal expertise could make the difference in arguing the case. After all, Lambda had been litigating gay and lesbian rights cases since the early 1970s and had managed several recent key victories. It had argued successfully before the U.S. Supreme Court to overturn a Colorado constitutional amendment preventing homosexuals from obtaining protected status in 2002 and to declare laws criminalizing sodomy between consenting adults to be unconstitutional the following year.

"Finally," Malheiro said as she picked up the phone and punched in Lambda Legal's number. "This might get them interested."

||||||||||||||||||||||||||||||||||||||||||||||||||||||||||||||||||||||||||||||||||||

CHAPTER FIVE

Legal Trifecta

Republican House Speaker Chris Rants didn't even have to ask. He already knew what Chuck Hurley wanted.[1] The leader of the Iowa Family Policy Center wanted a meeting with Rants as soon as possible.

The topic: how to get a constitutional amendment ensuring same-sex couples would never legally marry in Iowa. As far as Hurley was concerned, this was a matter of urgency for the Republican-controlled legislature. The Iowa Constitution had to be changed as quickly as possible. After the groundbreaking 2003 decision by the Massachusetts Supreme Court to permit the marriage of a same-sex couple and a few weeks before the opening of the 2004 legislative session in Iowa, Rants agreed to meet with Hurley.

What neither realized was that several events—legal and political—in 2004 would mark a major turning point for both opponents and proponents of marriage equality in Iowa. Nor did they know that by year's end, those events would set into motion the legal battle over the constitutionality of Iowa's law restricting marriage to one man and one woman.

An even-mannered, low-key lawyer and lobbyist for the Iowa Family Policy Center, Hurley had served with Rants in the legislature. After a brief career in the Iowa House, he became one of the public leaders in the effort to bring conservative Iowa evangelicals into power as major players in Republican Party politics. When Hurley arrived for the meeting, Rants, a conservative Republican from Sioux City, contemplated the irony of the meeting place. Members of the Iowa Supreme Court and staff had recently moved out of the Iowa statehouse into new digs across the street. Given the shortage of office space in the capitol building, legislators were happy to say good-bye. The court members were just as thrilled to say hello to the sparkling 123,000–square foot Iowa State Judicial Building, built in the classic Beaux-Arts style at a cost to taxpayers of more than thirty million dollars. Rants had moved the Speaker's office from the third floor of the statehouse behind the house chambers to Chief Justice Louis Lavorato's old office on the second floor. He would use the court's former conference room—where they debated their decisions—to meet Hurley.

"Funny us meeting here," Rants mused. Funny because that's where Hurley insisted the Republican leadership begin the process of amending Iowa's constitution, making sure marriage remained between a man and a woman and out of the court's hands. Just a few weeks earlier, the supreme court of Massachusetts had decided the state constitution required Massachusetts to permit the marriage of a same-sex couple. Unlike Iowa in 1998, Massachusetts had not enacted a Defense of Marriage Act. But a Massachusetts lower court had upheld the state's right to restrict civil marriage licenses to opposite-sex couples.

Chief Justice Margaret Marshall, writing for a plurality in the court's 4–3 decision, saw it differently. She said refusing to provide civil marriage licenses to same-sex couples was incompatible with the state's constitutional protections of personal freedom and equality. Marshall also dismissed the opponents' claim that same-sex marriage would change the institution of marriage. She wrote:

> Here, the plaintiffs seek only to be married, not to undermine the institution of civil marriage. They do not want marriage abolished. They do not attack the binary nature of marriage, the consanguinity provisions, or any of the other gate-keeping provisions of the marriage licensing law. Recognizing the right of an individual to marry a person of the same sex will not diminish the validity or dignity of opposite-sex marriage, any more than recognizing the right of an individual to marry a person of a different race devalues the marriage of a person who marries someone of her own race. If anything, extending civil marriage to same-sex couples reinforces the importance of marriage to individuals and communities. That same-sex

couples are willing to embrace marriage's solemn obligations of exclusivity, mutual support, and commitment to one another is a testament to the enduring place of marriage in our laws and in the human spirit.[2]

Marshall's opinion, despite its eloquence, set off a storm of controversy—not only in Massachusetts, where the debate would continue for another five months before the court required licenses to be issued to qualifying same-sex couples, but also throughout the country.

Hurley told Rants he wanted to take no chances in preserving Iowa's law banning same-sex marriage. He feared the Massachusetts decision would (1) encourage gay and lesbian legal and activist groups to begin looking at states like Iowa to challenge their DOMAs and (2) encourage the Iowa Supreme Court to overturn the law. Both men understood that the Iowa law's constitutionality had barely been considered, if at all, during its passage. Rants couldn't remember whether lawmakers had even requested an opinion from the house legal counsel about its constitutionality or if the Republican caucus had discussed its legality. Not that those questions really mattered much to legislators, who generally viewed such matters as outside their jurisdiction. A frequent legislative rejoinder to questions about constitutionality went like this: "My job is to pass laws. It is up to the courts to decide if they are constitutional."

Rants, an assistant Republican leader in 1998 when the law was approved, remembered one other thing in particular: very few people opposed it. Why, even Tom Vilsack had voted for it, and he was currently sitting in the governor's office. Now just five years later, the Massachusetts decision had ignited controversy all over the country. Anti–gay marriage groups, many religiously affiliated, were indignant about what one court had done.

Imagine the indignation, Rants reflected, if it ever happened here. He was well aware that back home in Sioux City, district court judge Jeff Neary, a Democrat appointed by Vilsack, was already under vicious attack by social conservatives for dissolving the civil union between Kimberly Brown and Jennifer Perez. The speaker had heard talk that a bunch of legislators from around Sioux City were about to file a lawsuit, and he knew conservative groups would target Neary in his retention election next November. Up to this point, Rants thought, same-sex marriage hadn't been much of an issue in Iowa. No one had really challenged the law except a few liberals nobody cared about with nothing to lose, and things remained quiet. Now, because of the Neary decision and the Massachusetts decision, there was controversy and emotion, particularly coming from conservatives and evangelicals—which couldn't possibly hurt Republicans going into a presidential election year, particularly with President Bush's popularity sliding as a result of the war in Iraq.

Back in 1998, Iowa's DOMA had passed simply because most people still believed marriage between a man and a woman was a sacred, untouchable tradition that protected children. Polls showed nearly two-thirds of Iowans opposed same-sex marriage, though half the population also thought same-sex couples probably should have the same legal rights as married couples. Your religion, particularly if you were one of Rants's caucus members, told you same-sex marriage was immoral. If some people had difficulty voting for the restrictions, that wasn't a big deal. Those folks also knew what the polls showed.

Did some legislators vote for DOMA because they hated gays and lesbians and simply wanted to make sure they never could marry? To be sure—but they weren't in the majority, and most of them were smart enough to keep their mouths shut. But now a couple of judges, including one in Iowa, had handed Republicans what appeared to be a political slam dunk—an issue to use not only to raise money but also to keep their solid majorities in place and to bedevil Governor Vilsack during his final two years in office.

"There came a point in time when we just thought the politics were on our side," Rants remembered later as he talked about his meeting with Hurley. "It absolutely was a winning issue for us. It was an issue we didn't pick to use, but when it was laid before us, we knew the public at the time was overwhelmingly on our side."

Rants told Hurley he agreed the constitutional amendment against same-sex marriage had to be passed. Several lawyers over the years had mentioned to him that if the law ever got to the Iowa Supreme Court, it probably would be declared unconstitutional. But there was a hitch. Amending Iowa's constitution is a difficult task. A joint resolution, not subject to veto by the governor, must be approved by two successive but different legislatures. Only then can an amendment be placed on the ballot. As a result, voters wouldn't get a chance to act on a resolution, if approved in 2004, any earlier than November 2006. And the necessary initial resolution had to start in the Iowa Senate. The Republicans had a 29–21 majority there, but Rants knew instinctively there would be trouble getting the resolution through. Three moderate Republicans—Mary Lundby, Don Redfern, and Maggie Tinsman—were likely to vote against it. That meant the other twenty-six Republicans had to vote for it. This time, little or no help would likely come from the Democrats.

Part of the change had been spawned by Republicans outside Iowa. President George W. Bush attacked the Massachusetts decision in his 2004 State of the Union speech, in which he said "activist judges, however, have begun redefining marriage by court order, without regard for the will of the people and their elected representatives."

Bush, in declaring his opposition to same-sex marriage, urged consideration of amending the U.S. Constitution mandating marriage remain between a man and a woman. "If judges insist on forcing their arbitrary will upon the people, the only alternative left to the people would be the constitutional process. Our nation must defend the sanctity of marriage."[3]

With the 2004 presidential election approaching, Democrats viewed Bush's attack as another round of ammunition to be used by those wanting to oppose his reelection. While gays and lesbians weren't a large enough constituency to make or break an election, they had begun to assert themselves with financial support within the Democratic Party and make demands on the party structure. Bush, his popularity already declining with the U.S. involvement in Iraq, could now be attacked as an opponent of equal rights for gays and lesbians and as a friend of far-right Christian groups. Yes, there would be backlash, but that is what civil rights battles are all about: moving forward, then holding on to as much ground as possible when the backlash hits.

In San Francisco, Mayor Gavin Newsom, in answer to Bush's attack in his State of the Union address, began issuing marriage licenses to gay and lesbian couples until the California Supreme Court told him to stop. By that time, San Francisco officials had married four thousand same-sex couples. The San Francisco "Winter of Love" inspired local officials in New York, Oregon, and New Mexico also to begin issuing licenses. Before it was over, an estimated seven thousand same-sex couples had married, only to see their marriages later voided.

The sudden burst of activity drew attention from national media. A national debate was now under way that showed no signs of stopping. News stories related to same-sex marriage became daily fare on TV and in the newspapers. At the same time, *Will and Grace*, a situation comedy about a gay man living with a straight woman, continued to grow in popularity. Mainstream America, while still reluctant to accept same-sex marriage, was becoming more comfortable with gay people. The news stories, television depictions, and political unrest were having an impact. Polling data prepared by the Pew Research Center for the People and the Press show that same-sex marriage grew as an issue of substantial public interest during the period. In 2003, the Pew poll disclosed that 19 percent of respondents reported following the issue "very closely." By March of 2004, the number had grown to 29 percent.

In Iowa, residents remained steadfastly against same-sex marriage. An Iowa poll taken in September 2003 showed 65 percent opposed. A contrary indicator was the 49 percent who supported equal rights for gays and lesbians. Another was the 41 percent of Iowans ages eighteen to thirty-four supporting same-sex marriage, not to mention the 64 percent supporting equal rights for gays and lesbians. There were also rumblings that a gay Democratic state senator, slowly coming out to his colleagues, was recruiting support for his belief that a constitutional amendment was an overreach by the Republican majority.

"We knew it would be close in the senate," Rants remembered years later, "but I thought we'd get the votes. So it was smart to start there. I knew the house would have no trouble passing it. The politics were too good for us."

Camilla Taylor, an attorney for the Lambda Legal Defense and Education Fund, picked up her office telephone.[4] On the other end of the line was Des Moines lawyer Sharon Malheiro. For years, the two had been working together on various cases involving LGBT legal issues in Iowa, but now Malheiro had an idea she thought would appeal to Lambda.

"There's this judge up in northwest Iowa." Over the next few minutes, she recited the facts of the Neary case and informed Taylor that a group of state legislators had filed a lawsuit directly to the Iowa Supreme Court to overturn the decision. Malheiro went on to explain that neither Dennis Ringgenberg, who represented one of the women, nor the office of Iowa attorney general Tom Miller would oppose the legislators' suit. This seemed like a good time to join forces on a case that needed defending.

Taylor, the national marriage project director for Lambda Legal, acknowledged she had heard about the case. Actually, Iowa had been on Taylor's mind a lot. In her view, Iowa clearly had become a candidate for the first midwestern state to challenge a statute limiting marriage to a man and a woman. She already had been contacted by a number of gay and lesbian couples wanting Lambda to file a lawsuit, including Janelle Rettig and Robin Butler. Now, the Neary case would provide Lambda with an opportunity to learn firsthand about the state, to make contact with potential plaintiffs, and to learn about the Iowa Supreme Court. She agreed to help argue the case, and on April 19, 2004, Malheiro filed her application to represent Jeffrey Neary's decision as a friend of the court.

As the two lawyers concluded their discussion, Malheiro sensed Taylor's growing interest in Iowa. Although she had been urging the group to consider the state as a place to file a lawsuit, she also knew a major obstacle lay ahead. They had to stop the passage of a constitutional amendment limiting marriage to a man and a woman. If they didn't, Lambda's interest in Iowa would cease, and with it would go any chance of getting the law overturned—ever.

Janelle Rettig knew what was at stake, too. She and her wife, Robin Butler, didn't have Taylor's Chicago number on speed dial at first, but that soon changed. Whenever they could, they would urge, cajole, and plead with the Lambda Legal attorney to help them overturn Iowa's DOMA. Sometimes, at the end of the day, Rettig would leave a simple phone message: "Our liberties we prize, our rights we will maintain." It was the Iowa state motto. But Taylor made the organization's reluctance clear. The threat of opponents plugging a statutory ban into the Iowa Constitution had to be overcome if her organization was to attack the state marriage ban. Already, Lambda officials could see growing sentiment among conservative Republicans throughout the country pushing, like legislators in Iowa, for constitutional amendments. Taylor had to consider how a lawsuit would affect her opponents' momentum over the two years it would take to get the amendment resolution to the voters. She knew that a lawsuit filed in Iowa in 2004 could work against them by giving their opponents more reason to get going on the amendment.

"We can't file a lawsuit," Taylor told Rettig and Butler. "We don't want to make things worse in the legislature. If we file suit and it prompts passage of a constitutional amendment, we will have set the community back. It's important for us to be sensitive to political context." And yet the Lambda attorney didn't completely rule out the possibility of a lawsuit. She'd already received approval to help Malheiro fight the action against Judge Neary. The Iowa Supreme Court was in no hurry to hear the case and decided to set oral arguments for January 2005. A long wait.

What's more, going to court over a same-sex marriage ban was a whole different situation. Despite the Massachusetts decision, lawsuits challenging marriage laws had been a losing proposition across the country. Another loss would be even more devastating. Lambda had to be sure and needed more time. "We are just going to watch very closely to see what happens in the legislature," Taylor told the couple.

Unknown to most, she already had started doing research on Iowa's history and legal traditions. What impressed her was the willingness of the state's judiciary to break new ground and uphold civil rights even when other courts all the way to the top were making contradictory decisions on the same topics. Discussions with Iowa historians further impressed the attorney. Iowa was clearly a state willing to protect the rights of minorities.

She also knew about the Iowa Supreme Court's recent decision in a taxation case that made the state even more attractive as a place to make a legal challenge. In a 5–2 decision, the court stunned state leaders by ruling for the second time that three racetracks—a horse track in Des Moines operated by the Racing Association of Central Iowa (RACI) and greyhound tracks in Council Bluffs and Dubuque operated by two other nonprofit license holders—had been taxed illegally at a higher percentage rate than Iowa's riverboat casinos. Legislators had imposed higher taxes on the financially troubled tracks to overcome riverboat opposition to table gambling and slot machines at the racing facilities. Deciding that different tax rates for different gambling operations made no sense, the court declared them unconstitutional. The price tag for the decision was high—$112 million in refunds owed to the tracks, which had been paying as much as 36 percent tax on gross gambling revenues compared to the riverboats' 20 percent. Even more interesting was the timing. The Iowa court reached its decision after the U.S. Supreme Court had ruled the original tax scheme legal under the federal Constitution.

Taylor, who had received her undergraduate degree at Yale and her law degree at Columbia, immediately understood the potential significance of the decision as it related to Iowa's same-sex marriage ban. The court had considered whether the legislature had imposed a tax on the tracks improperly under Article I, Section 6, of the Iowa Constitution. That section provides that "all laws of a general nature shall have a uniform operation; the general assembly shall not grant to any citizen, or class of citizens, privileges or immunities, which, upon the same terms shall not equally belong to all citizens." This was the passage John Edwards had so easily persuaded fellow Constitutional Convention delegates to approve in 1857.

As expected, the court had used a rational basis analysis, which supposedly gives legislatures a huge benefit of the doubt in determining whether a law is constitutional. Put simply, when reviewing cases involving social and economic legislation, courts generally let a legislature do what it wants, even when the justification for "classifying" a group for different treatment isn't strong. That often amounts to the definition of right and wrong in the Iowa legislature: twenty-six votes in the Iowa Senate and fifty-one votes in the Iowa House. But in this case, the court decided, remarkably, that the legislature's justifications for levying different tax rates on tracks and riverboats—to promote river communities, to provide tax certainty to riverboat operators, and to protect the financial condition of riverboats—neither achieved the stated purposes nor were rational. For example, the court asked, how could a different tax rate promote river communities when two cities, Council Bluffs and Dubuque, had both riverboat casinos and greyhound race tracks? As a result, the court ruled that while the legislature often deserved the benefit of the doubt, this time it didn't. Different tax rates for different gambling operations simply didn't make sense. From the majority opinion,

Our prior cases illustrate that, although the rational basis standard of review is admittedly deferential to legislative judgment, it is not "a toothless one" in Iowa. . . . Indeed, this court's meaningful review of social and economic legislation is mandated by our constitutional obligation to safeguard constitutional values by ensuring all legislation complies with those values.[5]

Taylor knew immediately the RACI II decision provided an excellent first signal that a lawsuit challenging Iowa's ban on same-sex marriage could be successful. If the legislature had to tax businesses equally in the absence of a compelling reason to do otherwise, didn't it have to recognize marriages between people of the same sex just as it did marriages between people of the opposite sex, in the absence of a compelling reason to do otherwise? Until then, state court decisions upholding same-sex marriage bans, like the one in New York, had used rational basis. In those cases, the courts, without examining the justifications, ruled that legislatures could deny marriage to some citizens because they believed that those bans protected the tradition of marriage, encouraged procreation, and provided children with an optimal environment.

"Those courts discarded all of the reality," Taylor recalled later. "They said it was common sense, intuition that a child needs a Mommy and a Daddy to fare well, which is completely an embrace of stereotype and bias in such an irresponsible way. It was an abrogation of what a court is supposed to be about. New York was one of the worst." But the Iowa Supreme Court, in the RACI II case, provided Taylor with evidence that at least one court was ready and willing to examine critically the legislative justifications for treating similar groups differently—and that it had enough courage to do what the court thought was right despite its possible impact. In particular, Taylor liked the fact that the Iowa court was willing to come to a different conclusion than the U.S. Supreme Court, even if it cost the state as much as $112 million in collected tax money.

"We needed to have a type of analysis under the lowest level of review applied to the equality guarantees of the state constitution that actually had some kind of meaning," she said. "We also knew that the (RACI) decision had deprived the state of some revenue and that, too, took some backbone." Still, Taylor wondered whether that willingness would extend to gays and lesbians. After all, Governor Vilsack had refused just a few years earlier to fight for one of his own first executive orders, which prohibited discrimination based on sexual orientation or gender identity within state government. His failure to appeal a lower court decision in a Republican lawsuit challenging the legality of the order had led many to question his commitment to various gay issues.

Taylor thought a vote on a constitutional amendment in the legislature would tell her and her bosses a lot about the political climate in Iowa. In a memo to her bosses in March 2004 she said, "Iowa is the obvious midwestern choice" if the "strongest factor in our selection of a state" is preventing a constitutional amendment from passage. Taylor already had heard that there was growing opposition to the resolution and that it stood a good chance of defeat in the Iowa Senate.

They would watch and wait.

Meanwhile, Rettig and Butler, already well versed in political organizing, began their fight against the constitutional amendment. The battle began with little fanfare in February 2004, two weeks after the introduction of a joint resolution in the Iowa Senate. The resolution called for an amendment to the constitution, saying "only a marriage between a man and a woman shall be valid or recognized in the State of Iowa." Rettig e-mailed friends and acquaintances, asking them to forward the information to their friends and acquaintances. "We really didn't think we would win," she later recalled, "but we had to do something to make sure they knew who they were hurting."

Added Butler, "We decided we weren't going to be victims anymore."

Rettig's initial e-mail went out to nearly seventy people and included a list of legislators' e-mail addresses as well as a plea to support a lobbying effort. "Even if you really don't care about marriage rights," she wrote, "allowing the legislators to vote on this in darkness is harmful to all gay, lesbian, bisexual, transgendered allied Iowans."

The response, Butler recalled, was strong. "I don't think legislators had ever seen people e-mailing them and lobbying them against this as much as our folks were." Over the next two months, Rettig e-mailed weekly updates to the growing number of recipients who had joined the effort. Before long, she had accumulated nearly three hundred e-mail addresses of gays, lesbians, and their supporters. The new supporters did more than spread the word. They also helped plan and stage lobbying efforts and media events.

Among those on the list were Jen and Dawn BarbouRoske, Chuck Swaggerty and Jason Morgan, Bill Musser and Otter Dreaming, Ingrid Olson and Reva Evans, and Katherine Varnum and Patricia Hyde — five of the six couples who would become *Varnum* plaintiffs nearly two years later. "We didn't know it then," Rettig said later, "but Lambda found almost all the plaintiffs from our mailing list."

In late February, she heard that media outlets had been calling county recorders throughout the state to ask if same-sex couples had been requesting marriage licenses. Since few requests had been made over the years, Rettig said, some outlets decided it was an indication that same-sex couples in Iowa did not wish to be married. Her solution was simple. Give the media a staged example of same-sex couples asking for marriage licenses. And what better place than the Johnson County recorder's office, where Kim Painter, a lesbian, was in her first term.

Rettig e-mailed her friends two days before the demonstration, saying she expected eight to ten couples to join them in the recorder's office. What happened next surprised even her. With some ten television cameras from around the state watching every move, forty same-sex couples arrived at the recorder's office, each with a witness and the thirty-five-dollar marriage license fee. "I couldn't believe what I was watching," Rettig remembered. "We'd packed the place, and everything went perfectly."

As each couple approached Painter, who stood behind the office counter, a small group of Butler's friends would start singing "Chapel of Love," the old Dixie Cups hit. "Goin' to the chapel and we're gonna get married . . . ." When a couple asked for a marriage license, Painter would read from a script: "Due to the Iowa Code of the State of Iowa, marriage is only allowed between a man and a woman, and I am not allowed to issue you a license." Then she would repeat the drill for the next couple, and the next. Later, Painter would describe her refusal as painful, but necessary. As an officeholder she had upheld the law despite her conviction that the same-sex marriage prohibition was "un-American and unconstitutional. I believe our legal and judicial system will reach that conclusion one day."[6]

Among the applicants were Jen and Dawn BarbouRoske, who viewed their participation as a necessary protest for their daughters, McKinley and Breeanna. Both needed to see their mothers standing up for them, Dawn would tell friends. "For us that's been crucial," she said. "Stand up and be proud about who you are. We want to make the best world for us and our kids and for others. An education campaign or any day event in town we're available. Just ask."

As Matt McCoy walked to caucus with the other twenty Democrats of the Iowa Senate, there was no getting around what he was feeling: absolute, total fear. Everyone knew what the meeting would be about; each Democrat would talk about the Senate Joint Resolution 2002, the resolution to amend the constitution to ban same-sex marriage. The Democrats recognized that a final vote was coming, and they wanted to discuss strategy and tactics. McCoy knew he would be the center of attention. Much of the news of the first three months of the 2004 legislative session had centered on the question of whether the constitutional amendment would be approved. But McCoy, other Democrats, and several gay and lesbian groups, including Rettig and Butler and their friends, had determined that this vote was not going to be 1998 all over again. If they were going to go down in defeat this time, they were going to make as much noise as possible.

Demonstrations and lobbying on both sides of the issue became weekly events in the statehouse. Supporters of the constitutional amendment argued simply that a law wasn't enough to protect traditional marriage and procreation, particularly given the Massachusetts decision. Opponents of the amendment adopted a simple mantra: The law restricting marriage to a man and a woman is more than enough. The Iowa Constitution should not be used to discriminate against anyone or any group.

From the beginning, senate Democrats didn't believe they could stop the resolution from passing. Republicans, under the leadership of majority leader Stewart Iverson, had a commanding 29–21 majority—more than sufficient to get the twenty-six votes necessary. What most of them didn't know was that several Republicans were deeply troubled by the proposal. One was Senator Mary Lundby, a tough-minded moderate from a working-class district near Cedar Rapids. Lundby, who died of cervical cancer in 2009, had a reputation within the senate as one of the few legislators willing to compromise. At least three other things were noteworthy about her: she had a gay son, Daniel, who would one day become a state legislator; she couldn't stand Iverson; and she and Janelle Rettig were good friends. When Rettig worked for Jim Leach, Lundby would lend her her convertible for use in parades.

Years later, state representative Daniel Lundby said his mother understood she was endangering her political career if she voted against the constitutional amendment. "She prayed. She meditated. Her decision was simple. Women and others subjected to discrimination in the past would be subject to even more of it in the future. She didn't believe the Iowa constitution should be used like that," he said.[7]

With the vote approaching, Rettig contacted the senator about the constitutional amendment and learned she would probably vote against it. Without naming names, Lundby hinted that other Republicans might also be willing to oppose it. She also had little time for Democrats who seemed to be vacillating.

"I'm so goddamn angry at the Democrats right now," she told Rettig. "They need to get their act together." In response, Rettig ramped up the e-mailing effort by expanding the number of Republican and Democrat legislators on the list for lobbying. She also implored those on her mailing list not to think this was a lost cause.

A month before the final debate, the activist learned the Republicans had lost another vote. Senator Maggie Tinsman voted in committee against the resolution, contending that a constitutional amendment was unnecessary. Tinsman, who would lose in a Republican primary challenge in 2006 partially because of her opposition, had spent time thinking about the issue because she considered it unsettling.[8] As part of her research, she read every amendment to the Iowa Constitution and found something she thought remarkable. "The amendments all grant something. This amendment took away something," she said years later. "I just didn't believe that our constitution should be used that way."

Now, possibly only two votes down, Rettig began to think there might be a chance to block the Republican-backed resolution. Even the senate majority leader acknowledged to reporters after the committee vote he wasn't sure whether the proposal would be approved. "I don't know where the votes are," he told reporters.[9]

For Rettig, a big question was whether the Democrats would take a caucus position against it.

Since his 1998 vote to restrict marriage to a man and a woman, McCoy's life had changed dramatically. Serious addiction problems with alcohol had forced him into rehabilitation, where he found the courage to acknowledge something he'd known even back in 1998 — he was gay. Now, six years later, divorced and sober, McCoy was in a different place, speaking to the senate's Democratic caucus about his life and his opposition to the resolution. Most, if not all, of them already knew he was ready to acknowledge his sexual orientation. McCoy had spent a good part of the 2004 legislative session meeting individually with members of the Democratic caucus to explain his decision. He also met privately with Vilsack but had no intention of going public. If people asked, he would acknowledge it without going any further. The last thing he wanted was to be known as Iowa's "gay" legislator.

SJR 2002 was something different, however. He had voted for the law in 1998 and had felt shame ever since. Now, he would tell his caucus why the constitutional amendment was wrong and provide his colleagues with a firsthand account of why gays and lesbians were opposed. It was also the first time he would address a group and talk about his sexual orientation.

"Look, I am as scared as anyone that I am not going to be able to get reelected," he told them. "And a lot of people think I should have just gotten out of politics immediately. But I have decided I am not going to do that. I have people to represent and I have things to say in representing them." McCoy described how senators, both Republican and Democratic, had come forward individually to voice support and ask about his life. One had been Lundby. Another was Dennis Black, who voted to restrict marriage and was being pummeled at home to vote for the constitutional amendment. Though Black had grave misgivings about voting against the amendment, at least now he better understood what it was like to be gay.

But as McCoy addressed the caucus, he noticed a wave of sympathetic emotion welling up among his colleagues. The story of his battle with alcoholism and the slow and painful struggle to accept his sexual orientation had struck a chord with almost everyone, including several members from swing districts.

"I think they thought I was pretty fragile because I didn't hide my emotions when I talked," McCoy said later. "They didn't know I was a whole lot less fragile than I had been before I went through rehab."

Senate minority leader Michael Gronstal said that, while he had voted in 1998 for the Iowa DOMA, he also disapproved of using the constitution to discriminate against any group. He mentioned his daughter and how she had changed his mind about his initial vote. He told the story of how he watched his daughter Kate listen to a group of older male conservatives talk about their opposition to same-sex marriage before joining the conversation. As Gronstal remembered it, his daughter told them, "You guys don't understand. You've already lost. My generation doesn't care."

Kate's words brought Gronstal back to his 1998 vote and how he had come to change his position. He told them he couldn't see why anyone should be allowed to vote on the civil rights of another. "I don't think we want to go down that road ever," he said. Then, Jack Kibbie, a veteran senator from a conservative northwest Iowa district, spoke briefly, but pointedly. Kibbie had voted to approve the Iowa bill limiting marriage to a man and a woman in 1998 but said placing the same restriction in the Iowa Constitution went too far. "I probably should vote for this if you just look at the numbers in my district," he said. "But I didn't go halfway across the world to Korea to fight for freedom, then to come back here and deny it to a bunch of people."[10]

After the caucus, Rettig talked to Gronstal about what had just happened. He told her that no Democrat would vote for the amendment. It was up to the Republicans to get it passed.

Rettig said later that McCoy's decision to talk about his homosexuality had prompted the caucus — even those with deep reservations about same-sex marriage — to support him. "Matt's coming out was really important," Rettig said later. "To have one of your own be gay and have that in your caucus. You'd have to sit with a colleague then say to him he wasn't worthy of protection."

Rettig and Butler sat nervously but quietly at their Iowa City home as they listened online to the senate's debate on SJR 2002. As she listened and waited for the final vote, Rettig kept in touch with Gronstal and Lundby by telephone. Both told her it was looking good; they just might stop the resolution from passing. The only problem was making sure all votes would be cast. "People were still trying to dodge the vote, and we actually had to make it difficult for them to leave," Rettig remembered. "They sure were using the bathroom a lot."

For two hours, legislators debated the necessity and the importance of the resolution. Ken Veenstra, a northwest Iowa conservative and sponsor of the measure, argued for passage. "It's a constitutional amendment that I believe most Iowans would agree with, and I want them to have that choice. To defend [marriage] is crucial to the future of our society."[11]

Jeff Angelo, who had had the luxury of voting in 1998 against the statute because his vote wasn't necessary for passage, knew this time was different. He would vote for it. "The power to have this debate is being taken away from us by courts across the land," he argued.[12]

And this time Angelo would not have the opportunity to sneer at his opponents' hypocrisy. Like his conservative colleague, McCoy would not only vote his conscience this time but would also voice his opposition to the proposal from the senate floor, calling it "meaningless, mean-spirited, discriminatory legislation."[13]

In response, Veenstra directly addressed McCoy and alluded openly to his homosexuality. Until then, the subject hadn't come up in a public debate. News reports would declare that Veenstra had outed McCoy on the senate floor. "I was insulted by it," McCoy said. "I really was. But I didn't say anything. I knew better than to respond. That told me we had a real shot."

When the senate voting machine opened, McCoy punched his red "no" button and looked up at the board. He and the rest of the Democrats had assumed all along there would be twenty-six votes in favor—all of the Republicans in the chamber. Then he noticed Lundby voting no and Don Redfern, a moderate Republican from Cedar Falls, doing the same. Then Maggie Tinsman's red light went on. Suddenly, an audible gasp shot throughout the chamber. Doug Shull, a former corporate executive from nearby Indianola, had also voted against the amendment. Though he knew McCoy's family well, Shull had spoken with no one, including McCoy, about his vote.

"I was shocked, just shocked," McCoy said. "You could hear it. It was like, my God, we are going to win this thing."

The final vote was 24 yes to 25 no. The measure, having failed to receive the necessary twenty-six votes, was declared to have lost in the senate. In Iowa City, Rettig and Butler held each other and cried. Rettig called Lundby to thank her. She called Gronstal to remind him to remain vigilant; the Republicans would try it again. "We have never been stronger," Gronstal told her. "We finally got backbone. We are united."

Years later, Robin Butler reflected on what had caused such a change in just a short six years. She said the decision by gays and lesbians to fight publicly for their rights had forced a number of state lawmakers to reconsider their views. "I think it was just saying that you have the right to vote the way you want," Butler said. "But we had the right to tell people how you voted. They knew we weren't going to be quiet anymore. They knew things were going be different from then on."

After the vote, Republican leaders said the defeat was just a temporary setback. And, besides, they added, the November election will take care of the swing Democrats who were now on record voting to keep same-sex marriage out of the constitution. Believing they would have stronger legislative majorities in the near future, the Republican leadership, including House Speaker Rants, decided to forgo any further attempt to push for a constitutional amendment in 2004. They felt confident that legislative votes in 2005 and 2007 would put the issue on the ballot in 2008.

But then something happened they didn't expect. Despite the reelection of President George W. Bush and the passage of eleven state constitutional amendments restricting marriage to a man and a woman, Iowa voters veered in a different direction. Voters in Arkansas, Georgia, Kentucky, Michigan, Mississippi, Montana, Oklahoma, North Dakota, Oregon, Ohio, and Utah approved constitutionally restricting marriage to a man and a woman. Oklahoma took it one step further, making it a misdemeanor crime to issue a marriage license to a same-sex couple.

In Iowa, voters returned Republican U.S. senator Charles Grassley to another term as well as four incumbent Republican congressmen and one Democrat. But, in another example of the state's political cross-dressing, voters turned on Republican state lawmakers. Veenstra, who led the effort for a constitutional convention, was voted out by Republicans in a primary.

In the general election, meanwhile, the GOP also lost three legislators who had voted for the constitutional amendment. In addition, the Democrats picked up two open seats previously held by Republicans. Every Democrat who voted against SJR 2002 and ran for reelection won. As a result, Republicans lost majority control in the senate. For the next two years, the senate would consist of twenty-five Republicans and twenty-five Democrats. Nothing would pass the senate without the Democrats' approval.

As of November 2004, the drive to adopt a constitutional amendment was dead for at least another two years. Gronstal, who would share the leadership of the senate, vowed to reject any attempt to bring the measure up again in the 2005 and 2006 sessions. With that legislative session not voting on the constitutional amendment proposal, it meant the legislatures convening in 2007 and 2009 would have to approve it before it would be become eligible for a vote. As a result, the earliest a vote could be taken on a constitutional amendment would be six years down the road in 2010. That gave Camilla Taylor and Lambda Legal ample time to prepare for the next big test — challenging the constitutionality of DOMA before the Iowa Supreme Court. But the election of 2004 had created another problem within Lambda. The passage of the constitutional amendments in eleven states had created a firestorm within gay and lesbian activist groups. Many blamed Lambda's legal actions in various states for fueling the opposition and paving the way for their passage, not to mention the defeat of John Kerry in his bid for the presidency.

Taylor got a message from her bosses: no lawsuits until further notice — and that includes Iowa.

CHAPTER SIX

Old Farts and Rosa Parks

L arry Hoch and David Twombley could barely contain their excitement. So this is how it feels to be on the right side of history.[1] The
"Old Fart Couple," as they called themselves, parked their car at
the Polk County Administration Building in downtown Des Moines and
headed inside. Like five other same-sex couples in November and December of 2005, they strolled into the recorder's office to apply for a marriage
license. They knew their requests would be rejected, but that was part of
the fun. Unlike the protest Janelle Rettig had staged in February 2004,
this action was about more than dramatizing gay and lesbian couples'
desire to marry. The lawyers had sent Hoch and Twombley there to help
pick a fight with Polk County recorder Timothy J. Brien over whether they
should be allowed to marry in Iowa.

Hoch, sixty-three then, and Twombley, sixty-four, figured their fighting days were over. Not so. Four months earlier, political junkie Hoch
had been surfing the Internet for the latest news when the phone rang.
It was Camilla Taylor, a top lawyer for Lambda Legal. After all of Sharon
Malheiro's and Janelle Rettig's lobbying, the defeat of the constitutional
amendment to ban same-sex marriage had finally persuaded the organization to take up the marriage-equality battle in Iowa. Taylor was calling
from the Midwest regional office in Chicago. Introducing herself to Hoch,
she began a conversation that would change his and Twombley's lives.
Would Hoch and his partner of twelve years consider becoming plaintiffs
in a case challenging the constitutionality of Iowa's marriage laws?

In many ways Hoch and Twombley were as good as married. Each included the other in his will and held power of attorney in health-care decisions. They shared a joint checking account. But as Jen and Dawn BarbouRoske discovered around the same time, it wasn't enough. As the years passed, the more vulnerable they felt. For example, if Twombley died, Hoch would receive none of the normal spousal death benefits, and Twombley had a nice pension.

Listening to Lambda's lead counsel in this lawsuit, Hoch realized something. He and Twombley weren't the first couple the organization had contacted. In fact, they might have been the last. Several Des Moines area couples had been approached but declined for a variety of reasons, mostly because of the attention the case would attract. Much of the legal work had already been done. This stage in the plaintiff hunt was about finding the perfect mix of couples. When Taylor asked Hoch if they were interested in being considered, he didn't have to think about it. "Oh, absolutely," he said.

"But don't you think you'd better talk to your partner first?"

Hoch laughed. "He'll go along with the idea. He'll do whatever I say. Would we qualify?" Taylor wasn't ready to make that call, but Hoch didn't mind. He never figured the world would view him as the Rosa Parks of gay marriage — or any other civil rights champion, for that matter. The comparison has a few holes, but the thought made him smile. Parks was forty-three when she refused to give up her bus seat in Alabama. He was thrilled just to be considered — and intrigued. *Why me? Why David?*

It didn't take long to figure it out. He and Twombley would represent the old guard, the pioneers who still remembered the way it used to be. When they were coming of age in the 1960s and 1970s, many still viewed gay people as perverts, freaks, and even sex criminals — not just the general public but legislators, law enforcement officials, the media, and the medical profession as well. Then there was the couple's appearance, history, and everyday-American personas. When the average citizen summons images of the annual lesbian, gay, bisexual, and transgender (LGBT) pride parade, Hoch and Twombley are rarely the participants who pop to mind. Hoch, in fact, laughingly calls himself "as straight a gay person as ever was." Before they retired, Larry and David were schoolteachers who simply wanted what all straight people seemed to have. They wanted the right to marry the person of their choice.

Hoch and Twombley were each at least twenty years older than any of the other plaintiffs. Unlike the rest, they'd spent the vast majority of their lives in the closet.

Growing up, Twombley realized early he was different from most of his friends. He never cared much for the little boys' games they played. And he wasn't the Cub Scouts type. When, as a young adult, he finally discovered part of that difference was his sexual identity, he kept it to himself. Twombley knew there was no way he would change and doubted he would ever act upon it.

In those days, some men were simply "lifelong bachelors" or "not the marrying type." That's just the way it was. To compensate for the hole in his world, Twombley became an overachiever, filling his life with challenges that would require him to focus on everything other than his sexual orientation. He earned bachelor's and master's degrees in music education from Drake University. The clarinet performances and contest judging kept him active and involved. His achievements included a pilot's license and distance running that led to twenty-one marathons, three of them at the famous race in Boston. But something was missing: the opportunity to love openly and marry.

Though Hoch also became an educator after college, nearly everything else about his situation was different from Twombley's. A middle-school math teacher for thirty-two years in the lower Hudson Valley of New York state, he was slower to accept the truth. Hoch knew who he was supposed to be — teacher, husband, father of two. Not only was he the son of a Methodist minister, but he also married one. Hoch was thirty-nine when he married and forty-one when he and his wife had their first child. He says he never had a homosexual encounter before or during his marriage and spent too much of his life pretending to be straight. He realized something was wrong before he was even married. On the day of his wedding, Hoch peered into the mirror while dressing for the ceremony and said, "I hope I can pull this off."

He and his wife eventually discussed his attraction to men. Though they were open and honest about the situation, they had to know deep down their relationship was doomed. Still, they remained married for ten years, hoping he could change, trying to make it work, but failing to pull it off. In 1992, Hoch and his wife separated. Two years later, they were divorced. Their daughter offered a frank but accurate take on the dissolution. It would have happened anyway, she told her father. "Even if you were straight, you and Mom never would have made it."

Without knowing one another, Hoch and Twombley went public ten days apart in August of 2000. Each broke the news first to a brother.

As Twombley drove to that meeting, nervous sweat dripped from his hands onto the steering wheel. When he arrived, he walked through the door, opened his mouth, and let the truth come tumbling out. The reaction surprised him: "I'm still your brother and I love you." Long ago, the brother and sister-in-law had exchanged suspicions, so this unveiling was no surprise. Both had long since accepted who he was. When Twombley told others he was gay, about half said he wasn't telling them anything they hadn't already assumed. The rest of his friends and relatives said something like, "You are? Oh. OK."

A student of Twombley's in Osceola, about an hour south of Des Moines, wasn't so accepting. The young man said his teacher was going straight to hell. Another student, Joel Fry, was a bright kid, a talented high school trumpet player. Mature and reliable beyond his years, he also had a keen sense of humor. Teacher and student hit it off right away.

At the time, Twombley owned a 1992 Cadillac Allante. It wasn't unusual to get requests from kids who wanted to take it for a spin. He kept saying no—until Fry asked if he could borrow the car to escort a date to prom. How could he refuse? They'd known and respected one another since Joel was a seventh-grader. On the big night, Twombley snapped a picture of Joel and the Cadillac.

Fry went on to earn a master's degree in social work at the University of Iowa and become a Republican state representative and assistant house speaker. He and his wife became foster parents with four children of their own. Years later, when Twombley gave Fry the photo with the Cadillac, the former student placed it on his desk at the statehouse.

After Twombley came out, he felt he owed Fry an explanation. They talked for forty-five minutes, hugging afterward, but Fry was clearly disappointed. He couldn't understand why someone—especially someone he so liked and admired—would choose such a lifestyle. Twombley has never been able to shake the memory. Fry joined the house in 2010, just in time to try to amend the state constitution to prohibit same-sex marriage and civil unions. Twombley e-mailed him asking for a meeting to discuss Joel's position. It had been ten years since he'd come out to his student, but the warmth was still there. Joel was gracious and respectful, telling Twombley how much his old band teacher had meant to him. The young state representative said he knew Twombley was still the same person he'd looked up to as a teenager. He talked about how conflicted he'd been ten years before and how he couldn't understand why one of his role models had "chosen that path."

Twombley told Fry it wasn't a path. "I no more chose my orientation," he said, "than my eye color." Fry still wasn't sure about that part, though he did say he was beginning to change his thinking on the matter. Twombley wasn't expecting a total reversal, but he wanted to know how Fry would feel if one of his four children were gay. Fry couldn't answer that question. Later in an essay for a local LGBT breakfast club, Twombley wrote, "I am sure he thinks that their 'Christian' upbringing would prevent this. Now he knows that didn't work for me."

When it was time for Hoch to tell his loved ones the truth, he arranged a meeting with his brother. "I have been thinking about this for quite some time," he began, "and it's important I tell you something. I have known for many years that I'm gay, and I'm in the process of coming out."

The reaction from Hoch's brother was slightly different from the response Twombley received from his sibling: "Are you sure?"

"No," Hoch replied in exasperation. "I just made this up. Of course I'm sure."

After giving his little speech, Hoch broke down and cried off and on for the next twelve hours, which wasn't like him. When Twombley heard about that a few years later, he knew exactly what his partner was talking about. The two had been living parallel lives a thousand miles apart. It took Twombley twelve tries before he could finally tell someone his secret without crying.

Hoch didn't know it at the time, but hearing the gravity in his voice over the phone, his brother and sister-in-law thought he might be dying of cancer or some other terrible illness. Learning about it later, Hoch laughed. Had he been dying, he would have skipped the meeting and simply picked up the phone.

Old Farts and Rosa Parks

Twombley and Hoch found each other in September of 2000 in an on-line chat room for men insecure with their sexuality. Each was new to this life. Neither, they say, had been romantically or physically involved with another man. The chemistry became quickly apparent. After trading e-mails, they finally met in person. On Easter Sunday in 2001, they held a private commitment ceremony on a Florida beach. The following year, when Vermont became the first state to allow civil unions, Larry and David traveled to New England to avail themselves of the new law. Four years later, retired from teaching, Hoch left New York, spent a year looking for a place in Des Moines, and started a new life.

At the time of the commitment ceremony, neither saw it as a dress rehearsal for the real thing. And certainly, neither dreamed Hoch would someday spend an hour on the phone talking with a lawyer about a lawsuit demanding the right to marry.

After that initial phone call, four months passed before they heard from Lambda again. Then the phone rang; it was Taylor, who had finally received permission to proceed with the lawsuit after nearly nine months of waiting.

"We made the cut!" Hoch said.

"Yes," Taylor replied with a laugh. "You made the cut."

On November 29, 2005, the Old Fart Couple set off for the county recorder's office to apply for a marriage license. They weren't the first plaintiff couple to make the trip. That distinction belonged to the Barbou-Roskes, who drove from Iowa City and back with, as planned, nothing to show for it.

As David and Larry approached the entrance, ready to be turned down, they were joined by a diminutive woman in her midseventies. Her name was Carol Leach, and she had agreed to be their witness. They'd met in North Carolina at a national United Methodist convention of reconciling congregations, which encourage and enable people of all sexual orientations to take part in the church. The convention had not only attracted some six hundred Methodists intent on keeping their congregations open but also lured a group of protesters, including some from the local Ku Klux Klan.

Twombley noticed Leach at breakfast and, being the "outgoing one," introduced himself. It was hard to miss her. You don't see many people in the Great Smoky Mountains wearing "Des Moines" T-shirts. As they talked, Twombley was surprised to learn Leach and Hoch attended the same Methodist church. The three quickly became friends. Later she would mention her gay grandson. When they joined forces again in downtown Des Moines, Hoch looked at Leach and smiled, thinking to himself, "This is about the last person you'd ever expect to be an in-your-face activist." Approaching the counter, she stood between the two men.

"May I help you?" asked the attendant.

"We'd like to apply for a marriage license," Hoch said.

The clerk looked puzzled. Her expression seemed to say, "And the groom is . . . ?"

Leach quickly came to the rescue. "I'm the witness."

"Ohhhh," the woman said after a pause. "Excuse me. I have to talk to someone about this." The "grooms" and their witness stood at the counter and watched the attendant walk to a nearby cubicle to discuss the request with a supervisor. Before long, everyone in the office seemed to be scurrying toward Polk County recorder Tim Brien's office.

A few minutes later, the woman from the cubicle approached the counter. "We're very sorry," she said. "But it's against the law in Iowa."

Hoch played dumb. "Oh," he said, "I thought it was legal here."

As the three headed toward the door, the woman at the counter stopped them. Two same-sex couples requesting a marriage license within a period of six days? Something was up here. Sensing the makings of a parade, the woman said, "I know I shouldn't be telling you this, but I'm all for it myself. I hope this works out for you."

Leaving the building, Twombley tried to wrap his mind around what had just happened. "Am I really doing this?" It seemed so out of character—not only consenting to become plaintiffs but actually *wanting* to play such a contentious role. When they were becoming teachers, coming out would have been professional suicide. But nothing was stopping them now. After all those years in hiding, worried they'd lose their jobs if the wrong person discovered the truth, they were ready to face the public scrutiny they had tried for so long to avoid. "The noose," Hoch said, "is no longer around our necks."

Before going public, Twombley had kept a mental log to help him remember what he'd told whom about his situation. Hoch had taken it a step further, writing it all down. Finally, hundreds of miles apart, both decided this was no way to live. Both had spent most of their adult lives maintaining secret identities. Now, after all these years, they had agreed to subject themselves to fierce public scrutiny, not to mention the ridicule and scorn they had managed to avoid for so long. Out for four years now, Twombley understood what this meant. "Enough is enough," he said. "Somebody has to take a stand."

Two hours to the east in Iowa City, Dawn and Jen BarbouRoske had been thinking the same thing. Six days before Twombley and Hoch visited the county recorder's office, the BarbouRoskes had become the first of the six plaintiff couples to be turned down.

If it weren't for the law, they would have been married long ago. Almost from the moment they met in the summer of 1990, Jen Barbour and Dawn Roske, both in their early twenties at the time, knew they would someday marry. It was a wonder they met at all. Jen grew up in Illinois and enrolled at the University of Iowa, where she earned a nursing degree. Dawn grew up in Florida and graduated from the North Carolina School of the Arts with a degree in technical stage direction. Their paths finally crossed when each moved to the small college town of Grinnell, Iowa. Jen took an assignment at the local hospital as a nursing assistant while working toward her license. Dawn became assistant technical director in the Grinnell College theater department, where she helped students learn to build scenery.

Both knew immediately they were meant to be together. They still joke about the day they saw each other for the first time—meeting on a softball field. Isn't that where all lesbian relationships begin? As it happened, the team was made up mostly of Grinnell College faculty wives. Jen and Dawn were too shy to speak to one another that day, but their reticence wasn't for lack of interest. Dawn got out of the car, saw Jen playing catch, and that was it. Before long, Jen was asking Dawn, "Oh my gosh, where have you been?" In their first softball game together, Jen dislocated a knee and had trouble operating the stick shift in her car. Dawn helped her get home and up the stairs to her apartment. They have been together ever since.

The two come from different backgrounds. Jen's mother and father both had doctorate degrees—he in English, she in nursing. Dawn had conservative blue-collar roots. In high school, she was more interested in playing softball and other sports than socializing. Dawn also was involved in community theatre. Though acting wasn't her specialty, she enjoyed building sets and solving problems for the directors and designers. When Dawn took her love of theatre to Winston-Salem, she became the first member of her family to go to college.

For both Dawn and Jen, there was never one specific red-letter moment when they realized they were gay. Self-recognition came over time.

The other kids would tease Dawn about being a tomboy, and she didn't fight the image. She was a headstrong kid who didn't much care what people thought. On the morning of picture day in third grade, her parents sent her to school in a nice new dress. Young Dawn, however, threw on something more to her liking and slipped out of the house. In her photo, much to her parents' surprise, she's wearing a floppy-collar blue shirt with a burgundy suit that could have come from her brother's closet. The photo remains one of her favorites.

Soccer was Jen's big sport in high school, but she played softball, too. She remembers hearing her softball teammates talking about another player who was supposedly "interested in a girl" so "don't get too close to her." Jen never dated boys. The first girl she officially dated was from another high school. Anybody she happened to bring home was introduced to family as a "good friend." Despite the rumors, she mostly kept her sexual identity to herself. Jen was a happy, bright, well-adjusted kid who never felt the need to be someone she wasn't. As others learned the truth, Jen seldom felt alone or abandoned. She knew she was a solid person with parents who would love and accept her no matter what.

That knowledge was put to the test the day her mother found a note from Jen's girlfriend that made everything a little too clear. Jen's mother was upset—not so much for what the note said about Jen the person but for what it said about the mother-daughter relationship and the big secret never shared. When Jen's mother pictured the journey ahead, she thought about how difficult Jen's life would be as a gay person. She thought of the milestones and mainstream life passages her daughter would never experience. How much bigotry and discrimination would she face? Jen's mother wanted to help her through it all, but how?

Now, as a mother of two girls herself, Jen understands. It would kill her, she says years later, to be so totally oblivious to what's going on with someone you love so much. Like most parents, she looks at McKinley and Bre and wants to know who they are and who they'll turn out to be.

A few months after Dawn and Jen met, Jen gave Dawn a ring she'd made in high school, and Dawn proposed marriage. A year after meeting, the couple moved to Iowa City, where Dawn pursued a master's degree in production stage management. Then in 1994, they moved again. But before leaving for Northern California, they had their names legally changed. After three years together, Jen Barbour and Dawn Roske became Jen and Dawn BarbouRoske. They celebrated with a big party and a "name-change cake." The celebration was their way of showing they would do everything they could to prove they were more than partners. They were also a family.

In California, Jen went to work at Alta Bates Medical Center. Dawn became a stage manager for the San Francisco Opera. After California passed a new domestic partnership law, they were among the first to sign on. It was a step in the right direction, but it wasn't a marriage license. Though they wanted to spend the rest of their lives with one another and have children together, the BarbouRoskes also knew it wouldn't be easy. Seventeen months before McKinley was born, their first attempt at donor insemination ended in miscarriage.

As if that wasn't devastating enough, Dawn's brother added to the anguish. After their father encouraged him to reach out, Dawn's brother sent a card with a flower and a letter expressing his sympathy. But the letter didn't stop there. Dawn's brother concluded it was just as well; the baby was better off with God than with two lesbian parents. Brother and sister haven't spoken to one another in over seventeen years. Dawn's grandparents, meanwhile, have yet to acknowledge she has children.

Yet family friction wasn't what frightened Jen most. After the first pregnancy, doctors diagnosed a blood-clotting disorder that accounted for the ministrokes she suffered as often as twenty times a day. The medical professionals laid it out for them: give pregnancy another try if you wish, but beware of the perils. Not only would the next baby likely be premature, but Jen also could be putting her life in jeopardy. The possibility of a massive stroke could not be ruled out, the perinatologist at Alta Bates warned them. Having this baby, he said, would be a challenge on the order of climbing Mt. Everest. That's when Jen and Dawn decided they would name their child after the highest peak in North America.

When Jen was diagnosed with the clotting disorder—a tongue twister known as antiphospholipid antibody syndrome—they had gone to the Stanford medical library and learned everything they could about the condition. They had talked to the doctors and to another mother who went through the same thing. They waded through all the latest literature and research, which advised them to wait the length of the previous pregnancy before trying again. They drew comfort from the studies that said the chances were small that Jen's medical problems would be passed onto her offspring. And the doctor said they knew more about Jen's condition this time and were better prepared.

One of the treatments would involve an injection of the anticoagulant heparin into Jen's abdomen twice a day. Jen remained undeterred. She knew about needles and blood work. She had a solid team behind her. Her mother was a delivery nurse and a midwife.

Dawn wasn't as gung ho about the idea, and she had no trouble relaying those concerns, telling Jen point-blank this do-over was a crazy idea. Dawn knew how the microclots and ministrokes debilitated her partner. Whenever they struck, it took all the strength Jen could muster just to stand. The last thing Dawn wanted was the most important person in her world giving her life to give birth. There were alternatives, including adoption.

The perinatologist had similar thoughts: Two potential birth mothers. One miscarried early and has a history of serious medical problems that could affect the second pregnancy. The other is healthy, with a clean slate. "Are you sure this is how you want to go about it?"

Absolutely sure. Jen believed she was meant to have this child and was able to convince Dawn. It was decided. Having a child was worth the risk. After Jen became pregnant with McKinley, she would attach herself to a monitor, record the fetal heartbeat, and leave it in a voice mail for Dawn. "Here she is," Jen would say into the phone. They did that as often as possible, vowing to love this infant every minute of every waking hour.

When anyone asked whether they were waiting until the big day to learn whether Dawn was carrying a boy or a girl, they smiled and said no. Because nothing was certain, they wanted to know everything they could. Every new day, every moment of this pregnancy was a bonus and a blessing, and they would take nothing for granted. In fact, they could not take anything for granted. Because they were not married, they could not assume that they had the rights of other parents. They knew the hospital could keep Dawn away from McKinley because once, while they were visiting Texas and Jen had to be rushed to the emergency room with a sudden illness, the staff had stopped Dawn from going to see her partner. Nobody knew Jen's medical history better than Dawn, but it didn't matter. Against her wishes, she was sent to the waiting room.

Whenever the two traveled together, they took documents outlining Jen's medical condition. Whenever they were made to feel they weren't a real family, Dawn couldn't help thinking, "This wouldn't be happening if we were able to tell them we were married."

If keeping Jen and the baby healthy was an Everest-like challenge, the legal issues proved an even higher mountain to climb — one that would ultimately convince them to sue for the right to marry. For Dawn, having no biological connection to McKinley meant no parental rights and no legal protection. What would become of McKinley if something happened to Jen during the delivery? Would Jen's partner of eight years be legally frozen out of the child's life? Jen wanted Dawn to have legal custody of the baby should something happen to her, but under California law it was impossible for Dawn to adopt McKinley before she was born. In the end it would take a year to finalize the adoption. As part of the legal process, Jen would have to give up her parental rights — the necessary first step toward reasserting them along with Dawn. The price tag was six hundred dollars.

The two mandatory counseling sessions were designed to make sure Jen understood that she would not be the sole legal guardian of the child and why California law said she had to sign two seemingly contradictory second-parent adoption forms. One said she was giving up her parental rights, thus making the child an orphan eligible for adoption. Another said she would get those rights back moments later, at the same time that Dawn also acquired rights as McKinley's adoptive parent. Jen knew intellectually that terminating her parental rights was a temporary formality, but emotionally, the uncertainty troubled her.

The BarbouRoskes also had to pay three thousand for an intensive home study program to determine whether Dawn and Jen would be good adoptive parents. In their minds, they would turn out to be the best adoptive parents ever. The process struck them as unnecessary. That money would have given them a nice jump on McKinley's college savings. But it was law. Dawn had to go through a background check that included a trip to the county jail for fingerprinting. After all that, they couldn't wait to bring McKinley home but couldn't start the adoption process until she was born. They were able to make power-of-attorney arrangements for each other, but the second-parent adoption details had to wait. Most of the lawyers wouldn't even talk to them before Jen gave birth.

When McKinley showed up eight weeks premature on March 29, 1998, the hospital staff did its best to make sure Dawn was part of the process. The nurses let her cut the umbilical cord and gave her a wristband that said "Father," which gave her access to McKinley. The couple laughed good-naturedly at the plastic ID bracelet. The hospital did not have to do that. It was funny yet sad. How many times in the years to come would Dawn cross out the word "father" on one of McKinley's school forms? How many times would they have to check off "single" when that didn't truly explain their relationship?

After Dawn cut the umbilical cord, the nurses dried McKinley, wrapped her up, and let Jen hold her for a few moments. Then they swept her away, hooking her to a ventilator and a network of intravenous tubes in the neonatal intensive care unit. Four pounds, seven ounces at birth, the preemie was a scrawny little thing, but she seemed to be hanging tough. That was good because the race was on outside the maternity ward; and the adoption laws became the next of several hurdles to clear.

Once McKinley had arrived, Dawn wanted more than anything to be with the two people she loved most. After giving birth, Jen was given double anticoagulant doses while still dealing with four or five ministrokes a day. For several weeks, she required twenty-four-hour supervision. Dawn, meanwhile, couldn't stop thinking about the possibility of losing both Jen and McKinley. But with no legal ties to either, she had work to do. Her main role at that point was to act as their chief advocate. Her job was to find an adoption lawyer, and find one fast, who would draw up the documents that would protect Dawn's parental rights. It was no small task.

Before Jen checked into the hospital, she and Dawn compiled a list of twenty names and numbers of prospective attorneys. Dawn spent hours feeding quarters into a pay phone in the maternity waiting room, trying without luck to find a lawyer. When Jen was able to move out of her room, she eased into a chair in the maternity waiting room and watched Dawn work the pay phone, leaving messages and taking notes.

They had waited eight years to have this child. They wanted everything to be right. They had good jobs and a stable relationship. They were active in the community. They took the same last name. They did everything they could to prove their commitment as a couple. And now they struggled to find a lawyer who could help them ensure Dawn's rights as a parent. After hanging up the phone, Dawn would draw another line through another name and try again.

The few lawyers who did call back declined Dawn's request. The only one who didn't refuse was a family-law specialist in San Jose, who was thrilled to take the assignment. She wasn't gay but was passionate about the civil rights of all people.

And as the legal process began to move forward, Jen and McKinley both pulled through.

Eighteen hundred miles away, three days after McKinley was born, the Iowa Senate approved the Defense of Marriage Act. Two years earlier, President Clinton had signed the federal version, HR 3396, into law, saying, "I have long opposed governmental recognition of same-gender marriages and this legislation is consistent with that position."[2] The president added that no one should use the signing of this bill as an excuse for discriminating against others. To the BarbouRoskes and countless others, that seemed precisely the purpose.

If the governmental guardians of traditional marriage had their way, couples like Dawn and Jen BarbouRoske and their fellow plaintiffs in *Varnum v. Brien* would never marry. But this wasn't only about them. Changing the Iowa marriage laws was also about the kids. It was about McKinley and Breeanna and tiny Jamison Olson, son of plaintiffs Reva Evans and Ingrid Olson, who was born only a few months after the suit was filed.

By the time her parents signed on to challenge Iowa's defense of marriage law, McKinley BarbouRoske wasn't a kindergartner sobbing at the breakfast table anymore. In 2005, she was seven years old—a second grader who was beginning to understand why marriage equality was so important for everyone she loved. In the opinion of Lambda's Taylor, McKinley would turn out to be "the heart and soul" of the *Varnum* decision. With McKinley in the lead, the children and their rights would be central to the plaintiffs' case. How does the lack of marriage benefits for same-sex couples affect their kids?

It was as important a question then as it is now. The 2010 census reported nearly six hundred thousand same-sex couples living in the United States. Approximately 25 percent of those couples were rearing children who lacked many of the financial guarantees and protections, as well as the emotional benefits, enjoyed by children of couples in traditional marriages.

When, on November 23, 2005, Dawn and Jen BarbouRoske drove from Iowa City to downtown Des Moines, they had their daughters very much in mind. With identification papers in hand and witness in tow, they ducked into the office of the Polk County recorder and became the first of six same-sex couples to apply for a marriage license. Like the others to follow, the BarbouRoskes were politely told that state law would not permit the county to accept their application. The grounds for the case against DOMA had been established.

Signing on later as coplaintiffs were McKinley and Breeanna, who had joined the family as a foster child and was later adopted. Bre might have been too young to understand exactly what she was doing, but McKinley had the basics down.

To some opponents of same-sex marriage, she was little more than a prop to be used for an immoral cause. McKinley knew nothing about that. She simply wanted married parents, like most of the other kids. For the opponents who were all about protecting the children, well, meet McKinley. In elementary school, she was already learning to make the case for marriage equality. When one of the older girls had asked what it was like having two moms, McKinley said, "What's it like having a mom and a dad?"

The other girl had thought about it and replied, "I don't know. I guess we're exactly the same."

"You're right," McKinley said with a smile. "We're exactly the same."

McKinley understood why the kids were curious about her situation, and she was more than happy, with minimum prodding, to tell them everything they wanted to know. She'd say, "Hi, I'm McKinley, and I have two moms and no dads."

She never had had much of a filter. When it came to this child, there was no such as thing as the right place or time. When three-week-old Bre was placed with the BarbouRoskes in 2002, it was an uncertain time for the family. Dawn and Jen were remodeling their home — tearing the house apart to install hardwood floors — and had to find a temporary place to stay for a few days. Four-year-old McKinley made sure everyone within shouting distance got the latest update.

The family couldn't ride an elevator together or buy groceries without McKinley chirping, "Yeah, we don't know how long we're going to keep this baby, and we're living in a hotel." She wasn't shy about talking about her two moms, either. One of her good friends, an older boy named Miles, had some initial concerns.

"I'm a little confused," he said at first. "You have two moms and no dad?"

McKinley quickly explained the situation, and Miles soon became a good friend. When anyone got nasty, telling McKinley she was a "freak" or "going to hell" because of her family situation, Miles had her back. She didn't let it get to her, and she didn't tell her parents. Why give them something else to worry about? By the time she'd reached junior high school, where the kids were less accepting, McKinley had many allies among the students and teachers. She would stand up for them. They would stand up for her. When someone would say, "That's so gay," McKinley would jump in with her standard lecture:

> Seriously, saying "That's so gay" is not cool. If you're trying to come up with an insult, use something else. I have lesbian moms, and I've been fighting for their rights my whole life. So do not use *gay* as an insult. I don't go around saying "that's so hetero" to everybody.

Occasionally, her friends would notice her getting ready to fight back. They'd check the time and say, "Oh, oh. There she goes. Let this one slide, McKinley. We're going to be late for class. We'll handle it for you." And they would.

In November of 2005, Chuck Swaggerty and Jason Morgan from politically conservative Sioux City were next to be turned down at the Polk County recorder's office. Swaggerty and Morgan (later Swaggerty-Morgan) wanted two things in life more than anything else.[3] They wanted to be married to each other, and they wanted to have children. Jason is only slightly exaggerating, if that, when he says he knew he was gay from birth. "I can't remember a time I didn't know, and the feeling associated with it when I was younger was complete shame."

Though he and Chuck are now practicing Episcopalians, Jason took a detour. As a twelve-year-old, he joined the Jehovah's Witnesses, hoping God would eliminate his physical attraction to other boys. As a teenager, he suffered from depression and withdrew from social interactions, rarely taking part in school activities. When Morgan prayed, he didn't ask for patience or understanding. He asked God to make him straight. In his world, death was preferable to being gay. Like some of the other *Varnum* plaintiffs and many gay and lesbian teens, Morgan contemplated suicide. In high school, he watched a news report on the AIDS crisis of the 1980s. The disease seemed to affect everyone, including hemophiliac children. It was a gruesome, sad scene made worse by the comment of a member of the community he knew well, "Somebody should just put those people on an island and shoot them all." Morgan didn't say anything, but he couldn't stop thinking, "If he knew I was gay, would he believe I was fit to be shot, too?"

Morgan was a good kid growing up. No drugs or alcohol. Went to church regularly. Earned good grades. Dated girls as a teenager. At nineteen, Morgan even talked about marriage with a fellow Jehovah's Witness before realizing he would be living a lie and, possibly, ruining another person's life in the process. He tried hard to please his blue-collar parents and wondered how he could make them happy if he and some nice young woman didn't give them grandchildren. When Morgan was twenty-five, he told his sister everything. To his relief, she couldn't have been more accepting.

His mother was another story. She cried and said she had no idea he was gay. Jason believes she really did have an idea but was in denial. The grieving process didn't last forever. When the tears stopped flowing a week or two later, they were replaced by questions. One of them was, "How do you know you're gay if you've never had a boyfriend?"

Jason turned the tables. "You know *you're* not a lesbian. And *you've* never slept with a woman. Sleeping with someone doesn't mean you're gay or not. It's your orientation. And you know what your orientation is." His mother said she never thought of it that way and slowly became more comfortable with the reality of her son's sexuality. He had doubts about telling his father, a city bus driver. So did his mother, who was certain her husband would reject their son. Then what? She'd have to choose between husband and son, which, almost certainly, would mean the end of their marriage. And she did not want that. She told Jason not to tell his father. No problem there. "Believe me," he said later, "I was in no hurry to do that."

Fortunately, Jason's mother underestimated the breadth of her husband's love and understanding. "I know Jason," he told her, "and I know he wouldn't choose to be different. And I know people don't choose to be gay, so there's nothing we can do about it."

After his sister got the word, she would report back to Jason on the peculiar sentiments expressed by people who suspected others to be homosexual. "That guy seems gay," a cousin said, commenting on an acquaintance, "but you know he's not. Kind of like Jason. He seems gay but you know he's not. He's nice."

At first Jason asked his sister to refrain from telling anyone, but soon gave her the OK. When word got out among the relatives, a number of them (the women especially) shrugged and said, "Oh, I already knew."

Jason Morgan met Chuck Swaggerty in person in February 1998, the year DOMA passed in Iowa. Unlike Morgan, Swaggerty was bullied all through school in Wisconsin and dropped out because of the harassment when he was sixteen. He describes himself in those days as a "skinny little gay boy," the youngest of twelve kids raised by a single mom.

As they grew older, neither Morgan nor Swaggerty knew quite how they were supposed to proceed as gay men. They had no role models. Unlike Morgan, Swaggerty didn't just contemplate suicide growing up; he tried to kill himself three times. When he moved to Iowa with his mother at seventeen, he told her he was gay. She told him it was time to find a place of his own. It turned out to be for the best, but it wasn't easy. After Chuck started making friends in the gay community and feeling less isolated, thoughts of suicide went away. He began a relationship with another young man, which lasted six years.

Approaching his midtwenties, Morgan was too intimidated by the thought of actually going to a gay bar. He still didn't drink, and he wasn't even sure where to find such a place. Besides, the bar scene wasn't for him.

Still, he had no gay friends. Finally he summoned the courage to enter a chat room. That's where he met Swaggerty, who was living in Waterloo, three and a half hours to the east. They talked online for three months before deciding it was time to be friends in real life. Soon they were seeing each other, commuting back and forth every other week. Three months after that first meeting, Swaggerty moved to Sioux City to live with Morgan. Within weeks he asked Morgan to marry him. There was a catch, of course. It wasn't legal. Like the BarbouRoskes, they had to settle for being married in their hearts.

They also had to let their loved ones in on the relationship. Jason's mother knew about Chuck, but the plan was to break the news slowly to Jason's father. Stopping for a brief visit, they introduced Chuck to Jason's dad—without telling them they were a couple.

"He won't know you're my boyfriend," Jason said, "and he'll like you. Later, when he finds out we're together, it'll be okay because he'll already like you." The strategy worked. Afterward, Mr. Morgan asked Mrs. Morgan if Chuck was Jason's boyfriend.

Yes.

"Oh, he seems like a really great guy. I don't know what I was thinking, that he'd have blue hair or something. He seems like a real normal, nice person."

One of the interests Morgan and Swaggerty shared was a passion for restoring old homes. Over time, they turned their dilapidated, one-hundred-year-old foursquare into one of the marquee residences in the neighborhood. They received many compliments from the neighbors. On a Christmas tour of Sioux City homes in 2003, they connected with other gay people who shared the same interest in renovating stately old houses. Not long after, they were asked to take part in a movement to get the city council to pass a housing ordinance banning discrimination against LGBT people.

It was a tough time to be a gay person in Sioux City, a town of 85,000 whose congressman, Steve King, once labeled homosexuality a "self-professed" condition that cannot be "independently verified" but can be "willfully changed." This seemed to imply that people can pretend to be gay to receive preferential treatment. In 2004, the city council voted 4–1 against adding the words "sexual orientation" to the city's list of protected classes. Morgan and Swaggerty were part of a group that advocated for the proposal.

At one of the council meetings, a council member hauled out the slippery slope theory. Start granting special rights to gays, he said, and before you know it, you're talking about gay marriage. The mayor of Sioux City, Dave Ferris, went even further. The *Sioux City Journal* ran the following quote: "If I pass this ordinance and in ten years we see here what's happening now in San Francisco, I'd throw up my guts. I don't condone this lifestyle." Since then, Ferris told the newspaper he apologized within a week and a dozen times since. His words, he added, came at "eleven o'clock at night when emotions were running high. It had been a long day."[4]

Stunned by the open hostility, if not the vote, Morgan and Swaggerty joined with some other gay people and started the Café Community Alliance for Equality to inform and educate the community. By coincidence around the same time, Lambda Legal was holding a training session in Sioux City on how to speak to the media about gay rights and how to persuade city council members to act. After the meeting, Morgan and Swaggerty spoke with Lambda's Camilla Taylor, who said Iowa was ripe for a marriage-equality lawsuit. If it looks like a go, Swaggerty replied, give them a call. He and Morgan might be interested in taking part.

At the time, the couple had two foster children, biological brothers Ta'John and Reed, whom they were eager to adopt. In Iowa, children must live in the foster parents' home one year before they're eligible for adoption. Though the partners wanted to complete a joint adoption, they were told by the state on several occasions that would not be possible unless they were legally married. Adopting as two single parents often meant twice the expense and twice the red tape, but adoption was their dream.

As with the BarbouRoskes, however, the inability of Morgan and Swaggerty to marry undermined the family's security. If one of the two wanted to stay home with the foster kids while the other worked, the stay-at-home partner would not be covered by the employed partner's health insurance. If they were married, yes. For a while, in his job as a sales representative at the MCI call center in nearby Sergeant Bluff, Swaggerty received domestic partner insurance benefits for Jason. When the call center closed in 2006, he was out of work, which allowed him to stay home with the kids but left him without insurance. Morgan's policy at the bank didn't cover him.

There were other issues. When Swaggerty's mother died, Morgan's employers refused to give him bereavement time to travel to Wisconsin for the funeral. Leaving a message for his boss, Jason never heard back and wasn't sure what that meant. Would this be considered an unexcused absence? Yes. Would he still have a job when he came back? Yes, but a disciplinary black mark went on his employment record. It's unlikely this would have been a problem if Morgan and Swaggerty were married.

No issue, however, was more important to the Sioux City couple than children. While marriage was still only a fantasy, Morgan and Swaggerty opened their home. In 2005, they were in the process of bringing in biological brothers Ta'John and Reed, who were adopted in 2007. They would later be joined by Rain and Micah, also biological siblings, and then by Torrey. Some had special needs, which presents insurance problems for the single parent who stays home to care for them. Marriage would enable the stay-at-home partner to be covered by the employed partner's health insurance policy.

This was important because the partners were in demand. Sioux City is 85 percent white. In adoption as well as foster care, white couples are more likely to wait for white children to become available. Morgan and Swaggerty, on the other hand, willingly accepted minority and special-needs children. Whenever the Department of Human Services would tell them a high percentage of minority children were waiting for a home, the response was usually the same. "Give us whoever is next in line." Ultimately, the two partners would adopt five of their foster children. When the neighbors offered their thoughts and prayers, Jason and Chuck gladly accepted. They needed all the help they could get.

Next to visit the Polk County recorder's office were Reva Evans and Ingrid Olson of Council Bluffs on the western edge of Iowa. Evans, who grew up in the nearby town of Lenox, was pregnant at the time with their son, Jamison. The reason for their participation in the lawsuit was simple and straight to the point. They didn't want their child to grow up and ask his parents why they didn't go to bat for their family when they had the chance.[5]

Almost seven years after meeting, Evans and Olson commemorated their bond with a commitment ceremony in nearby Omaha. By the time they decided to have children, the two had been together for nine years. In her signed affidavit before the Iowa District Court, Evans described Olson as "the driving force in making the pregnancy happen," spending hours looking for the right donor, studying the procedures, "searching for the safest, most effective method," staying close to Evans every step of the way.

Late in 2006, when Jamison was six months old, he and his parents were returning from church when they were hit by another car. Olson rushed Jamison to the hospital. Evans followed her after dealing with the police. At the hospital, the staff had trouble understanding how a child could have two mothers. Being able to say they were legally married would have gone a long way in helping ease the confusion.

The two moms were excited about rearing Jamison in the former home of Evans's grandmother, whose first name was also Reva. She had lived in that house for sixty years. Across the street was Evans's mother. Nearby were dozens of extended-family members. "Family" was the key word. It was the most important thing in Evans's life. But having a child brought it home the way nothing else could: as lovely as a commitment might be, something was missing.

Even before Kate Varnum and Patricia Hyde Varnum were married, they had decided to have the same last name. That doesn't mean they asked to have it forever stamped on the front of a landmark court case. Why them? The lead-plaintiff designation could have fit any of the other couples.

They still aren't sure, but they have no complaints.[6] It was December 2, 2005. Kate and Trish had been the fifth of six couples to be turned away by the Polk County recorder's office after trying to apply for a marriage license. Before they headed back to Cedar Rapids, two hours or so from Des Moines, Camilla Taylor asked Kate if they'd like to become the lead plaintiffs. Though Trish had yet to legally change her name, it was in the works. She and Kate were trying to have a child, and they wanted to leave no doubt about their relationship.

Lead plaintiffs? What does it involve?

Oh, maybe a little more publicity, Taylor said. Just a little? The legal understatement of the year? "Probably the decade," Kate Varnum said, looking back years later. Both women now say it will probably always feel surreal to hear strangers talk about the "*Varnum* decision." At the time they became plaintiffs, however, neither was planning on becoming a civil rights champion.

During the day, Kate was directory assistance database manager for MCI. She'd lived in Iowa almost her entire life. Trish was an analyst at GEICO. She'd followed another woman to Iowa from Lubbock, Texas, where she grew up. When that fizzled, she met Kate online. Two months later, the woman Kate had been dating moved to Washington, D.C. Trish saw an opening and seized it. They had their first date in January of 2001.

Their backgrounds couldn't have been more different. Trish's father was adopted. Trish was adopted. When she and Kate later adopted Alex, the circle seemed complete. Trish's father was a country boy from west Texas, who spent most of his life working as a diesel mechanic. Her late mother was a Native American, who grew up poor and illiterate and died when her daughter was twenty-seven. Trish has a homophobic biological sister in Tulsa, who wants nothing to do with her. Her middle brother had disowned her long before he knew of her sexual orientation. Her father, despite the many roadblocks, still wanted what was best for his daughter. When Trish came out to him a few months into her relationship with Kate, there was silence on the other end of the line.

"Daddy," she said, "do you still love me?"

"Well," he replied, "let me ask you one thing. Does it change who you are?"

"No, sir. Not one bit."

"Okay then."

Kate's baby-boomer parents, in contrast, were politically correct before it was cool. The kids didn't play with GI Joes or Barbie dolls. Kate didn't have a Walkman growing up in Cedar Rapids, she had a "Walk-person." She wasn't a freshman in high school in Cedar Rapids, she was a "freshperson," who sometimes got a letter from the "mailperson." It was a nontraditional family, even for the times. When her father wasn't working with insurance companies doing medical billing, he was serving as a househusband and occasional elementary school "room mother." That was just before somebody in charge decided it might be a good time to change the name of the volunteer position to "room parent." Kate's dad enjoyed needlepoint and was the first Varnum not to farm. Kate's mom, meanwhile, spent more than thirty years as a traveling "salesperson." She also had a pilot's license. Rising to the level of rebellious in that household was no small feat. Growing up gay, as it turned out, was barely a blip on her progressive family's radar screen.

When Kate came out to her brother, he didn't respond. When she asked what was wrong, he shrugged. Nothing was wrong. "Kate," he said, "you could have told me you just bought new tires on your car." He was neither shocked nor dismayed. He was her brother, and nothing would change that.

Though the two families came from different worlds, almost everybody remained devoted to Trish and Kate and respectful of the life they share. When Trish's motorcycle-gang brother said good-bye, he told his sister, "Say hi to your old lady for me."

Trish and her old lady were members of the same Episcopal church Kate attended as a child. Around the time Massachusetts became the first state to legalize same-sex marriage, Trish and Kate decided to exchange rings at a Holy Blessing commitment ceremony at their church. Those plans evaporated, however, when the bishop of the Episcopal Diocese of Iowa told them some church members were against the idea. He offered some alternative settings. Kate didn't appreciate the timing. She and Trish had gone to great lengths to avoid controversy within the congregation by calling it anything but a wedding. The bishop apologized. Kate knew his intentions were good—he was trying to hold the flock together—but she didn't take it well.

So they rescheduled the ceremony at a park near Cedar Rapids. Another Episcopal priest performed the service as 120 or so looked on. At the reception later, Kate's father lifted a glass and provided one of the highlights when he said, "In another place and in another time, Trish would be referred to as my daughter-in-law. But in this time and in this place, I prefer to call her my daughter-in-love." It was a memorable moment on a rough ride. Both Trish and Kate had suffered from depression before they met. It will always be a battle, but Kate's mother noticed something else after Trish entered her daughter's life. The light, she said, was back in Kate's eye.

Before they could marry, Kate tried to get Trish's name on the home insurance policy, which couldn't happen until she was also on the deed to the house. And she couldn't be added to the deed without gift tax consequences. They both had living wills and durable power of attorney. In all financial matters, they were each other's beneficiary. But they still lacked the legal protection that came with the marriage contract.

The couple's attempt to have a child through donor insemination was unsuccessful. Both had medical issues that would make childbirth difficult and possibly even dangerous. Trish went to the doctor for tests. In most cases, the spouse is permitted to be present for the procedure. In this case, Kate was held up at the front desk.

"Nervous, undressed, and feeling vulnerable" in the examination room, Trish was growing more frustrated by the moment. Where was Kate? This is exactly why the couple had gone to the trouble of hiring a lawyer to draw up a power-of-attorney document. She was about to kick up a fuss.

"Doc," she said, "I'm about to piss you off."

He held up his hands. "She's on her way."

Good thing, because something was wrong. Due to a problem with the fallopian tube, a procedure using dye went awry, and Trish was in so much pain she couldn't communicate. Kate jumped in, telling the doctor to stop the procedure immediately. When he kept going, she grew more insistent. You must stop now. Finally, he did. Trish, doubled over in pain, hobbled away. The doctor said she was going to have a hard time getting pregnant and walked out.

That was troubling, but not as much as the thoughts running through Trish's mind: What if Kate hadn't been there? What if Trish can't ever be with her when it counts? Without a marriage license, there would always be more questions than answers. It was just one more reason they should be allowed to marry. Kate and Trish added it to the list.

A few years later, life is good. Kate, who stayed at home with Alex until he was three, has gone back to work. Their son recognizes the role his parents play in his life and theirs. Trish has been embraced by Kate's immediate and extended family. Best of all, everyone loves Alex.

Bill Musser and Otter Dreaming of Decorah, Iowa, met in June of 2001. A mutual friend who knew about their love of music and other common interests brought them together at a local café. The following year, they traveled to Vermont to take part in a civil union. It wasn't marriage, and it wouldn't carry much weight in Iowa; but it seemed like a step in the right direction that might even advance the marriage equality cause in some small way back home.

When Musser's mother died, he and Dreaming were stuck in Sioux City, almost three hundred miles away, with car trouble. "When I got word," Musser said in an interview with a local reporter, "Otter was great about everything—I don't know how else I would have gotten through it." After the visitation hours, Musser began introducing Dreaming to his family.

> That was a big thing for me. Maybe it was kind of an inopportune time, but I felt Otter was this special person to me, and I don't want to tell people he's not special. I wasn't going to lie. So I told people, "This is my partner, Otter."
>
> My family understood. So my mother's death was a life-changing event in many ways. Into all of this came the decision that we're not going to hide—we want to let people know, especially my family.[7]

Decorah is a lovely town of eight thousand in the rolling hills of northeast Iowa. It is the home of Luther College and the bald eagles that nest, feed, reproduce, and attract millions of online visitors who check out the live feed each spring and summer. Musser and Dreaming aren't quite as popular as the "eagle cam," but they were well-known in their little community even before they agreed to join five other Iowa couples to test the state's ban on same-sex marriage.

They had various jobs and played a number of roles in and around campus. Dreaming was church organist, piano teacher and accompanist, child-care provider, and English-as-a-second-language teacher. Musser graduated from Luther and later became a librarian there and elsewhere over the years. He played the bass fiddle in an old-time Scandinavian dance band that performed at the Kennedy Center for the Performing Arts in Washington, D.C.

Both are now involved in the Unitarian Universalist Church, which recognizes and even embraces same-sex marriages. Musser's family was Lutheran, a Protestant denomination that, on the whole, is not so accepting. His pastor growing up, however, was a "real source of consolation for a young person who had a lot of questions." In fact, Musser came out to the pastor, who stood by him, offering support and encouragement and giving him the confidence and will to be himself. "I can never say enough thanks for that person in my life," he said. "One person can make a difference — to move you in the direction and to not be afraid. Because it is fear, and fear is dangerous."[8]

For a while, however, Musser and Dreaming might have been best known around town for their local taxi business and the entertaining public conversations they held over the cab's radio. The discourse reportedly covered a wide range of topics, including grocery lists, dinner menus, and other vital Decorah news of the day.

Somehow they also found time to serve as foster parents for kids ranging in age from infants to eighteen-year-olds. Musser and Dreaming had many of the same financial concerns as the other couples — making important insurance, tax, health-care, and estate-planning decisions without the protection of a marriage contract. Still, as Dreaming said in his supreme court affidavit, his goal for them as a couple was to get married in a wedding instead of just playing in one.

On December 13, 2005, lawyers representing six committed same-sex couples and three of their children walked into the Polk County clerk of court's office. One carried a briefcase holding a twenty-page petition for marriage.

The case, known as *Varnum v. Brien*, had liftoff. The lawsuit argued that under the state's equal protection and due process guarantees, it is unlawful to bar same-sex couples from participating in civil marriage. According to the petition, the statute also denied the plaintiff children "equal access to the dignity, legitimacy, protections, benefits, support, and security conferred on the children of married parents."[9] The petition asked that Iowa Code, section 595.2(1)—the 1998 statute defining marriage as a union between only a man and a woman—be declared unconstitutional. The request was consistent with Iowa's history as a civil rights leader, going back to 1839 when the court ruled that a black slave from Missouri who crossed the state line could not be forced to return to a slave state. A century before the rest of the country allowed interracial marriage, Iowa broke the barrier.

In *Varnum v. Brien*, the cast was a carefully chosen ensemble of productive citizens with everyday lives and dreams who wanted only what society offered heterosexual couples. Lambda Legal had unearthed a wide array of prospects. Janelle Rettig and Robin Butler would have been worthy candidates for the A-list, but the two Iowa City women who prodded Lambda for years—"When are you coming to Iowa?"—had already married in Canada. Lambda had continually turned them down, saying not yet, not now. You don't want to make things worse in the Iowa legislature. If you file suit and it triggers a constitutional amendment prohibiting same-sex marriage, you could set back the cause another ten years. But the push for an amendment had failed, and the moment had come. Few understood it at the time, but the world was changing in ways that even Supreme Court justice Anthony Kennedy, McKinley BarbouRoske, or any of the plaintiff couples and their families could not have anticipated.

||||||||||||||||||||||||||||||||||||||||||||||||||||||||||||||||||||||||||||||||||

CHAPTER SEVEN

High Risk, High Reward

W hen district court judge Robert Hanson arrived at his fourth-floor office at the Polk County Courthouse, college football was on his mind.[1] It was December, and although his beloved Iowa Hawkeyes had finished the regular season with an acceptable 7–4 record, there was a catch. Now they would have to play the University of Florida in the Outback Bowl, and Hanson wasn't sure he liked their chances.

Though Iowa football was the big watercooler talk across the state on this day, the Hawkeyes would be only a momentary diversion for Hanson and anyone else in Iowa who paid attention to civil rights. In the judge's professional world, the real story on December 14, 2005, was the lawsuit, which had been all over the local news broadcasts and on the cover of the metro section of that morning's *Des Moines Register*. It appeared under the headline "Six Couples File Gay Marriage Lawsuit."

Five couples—from Iowa City, Cedar Rapids, Sioux City, greater Des Moines, and Council Bluffs—had requested marriage licenses at the Polk County recorder's office just a few weeks before the filing of the suit. A sixth couple, from Decorah, would follow just days after the filing. The recorder's office staff, citing Iowa Code, chapter 595.2, politely rejected each of the requests, thereby establishing the legal conflict necessary to proceed to litigation. The couples' lawsuit, prepared by Lambda Legal lawyers led by Camilla Taylor of Chicago and a local litigator from Des Moines, Dennis Johnson, said the state law restricting marriage to a man and a woman violated the state constitution's guarantee of equal protection and due process of law by drawing "impermissible distinctions based on sex and sexual orientation."[2]

Hanson knew he might get the case. For almost a year, he had been assigned to the civil docket. Just before lunch, Hanson checked his e-mails. Glancing at the inbox, he noticed a familiar name and clicked on "Same-sex couple marriage lawsuit." The message:

> I hope this does not land on your desk. My suggestion is to have a senior judge deal with it. Perhaps this just needs to get ruled upon so that those judges in ivory towers who feel entitled to salaries tantamount to those of Fortune 500 companies can wrestle with it. If anyone needs a media consultant, I am the one to contact. Jeff.[3]

Hanson and district court judge Jeffrey Neary knew each other well. The two had attended judge school together in Reno, Nevada, after their appointment by Democratic governor Vilsack and had developed a friendship. Like many judges across Iowa, Hanson regarded Neary as something of a judicial folk legend. His controversial decision two years earlier to grant a divorce to Kimberly Brown and Jennifer Perez attracted attention not only in Iowa but also nationally and even internationally. Yet no judge wants that kind of publicity. What made Neary remarkable was not just withstanding a legal challenge by a group of legislators but keeping his job in the process.

Throughout the fall of 2004, Neary, with the support of area lawyers both Republican and Democratic, staged a low-key but effective campaign in response to conservative leaders and evangelicals urging voters to oust him from office in his first retention election. Early on, few gave Neary any chance to stay on the bench. The majority of voters in his six-county district were among the most conservative Republicans in the state and wore their religious beliefs proudly and loudly. They also seemed very angry. Pamphlets and other direct mailings urging a no vote on Neary's retention began to fill mailboxes in the six counties. Yard signs sprouted early through the towns of LeMars, Sioux Center, Orange City, and Sioux City demanding a no vote. Radio advertising and even some television advertising did the same.

A political action committee headed by the son of Dwayne Alons, one of the legislators who challenged Neary's original decision, became his biggest adversary. Alons didn't do it alone. He had the help of national evangelical figures like James Dobson, founder of the national Focus on the Family organization, and Tony Perkins, president of the Family Research Council (FRC). Both organizations had been instrumental in supporting passage of the national Defense of Marriage Act and, according to the Southern Poverty Law Center, were connected with Dobson as a member of the FRC's original board of directors. Both organizations flourished in the 1990s with a stridently antigay and antilesbian agenda, earning the FRC a place on the Southern Poverty Law Center's hate group list in 2010. Dobson left the organization he founded in 2010, and Perkins remains as the FRC's president.

Dobson and Perkins appeared together in Sioux City just weeks before the 2004 retention election and urged the "Take a Stand for Marriage" crowd of an estimated five thousand to work and vote for Neary's ouster. "Now judges are telling us they want to redefine the definition of marriage," Dobson intoned to a standing ovation. "We say not in our lifetime."[4]

But the other side hadn't ignored Dobson's appearance. In a nearby parking lot, Chuck Swaggerty and Jason Morgan picketed the event. "We are letting people know we believe in marriage equality and equal rights for every American," Morgan said, as he carried a rainbow-colored flag.[5]

Neary himself had responded to Dobson's appearance by challenging the evangelical preacher to a discussion of his decision on the day Dobson came to Sioux City. Dobson never got back to him. "I am not an activist judge, and it is unfortunate that no one has taken me up on my offer," Neary said.[6]

His goal was simple. "I wanted to make sure every time this group or that group came at me, I had the opportunity to respond," he said years later. "To me that was the most important thing. I didn't want to campaign, but I was willing to explain what I did and why I did it."

Neary's strategy worked. He collected a 58 percent majority of more than 56,000 votes in the six-county district. Much of his support came from the area's lawyers, who urged voters to think carefully about what they were being asked to do. Area lawyer John Mayne, son of former Republican congressman Wiley Mayne, said,

> If challenges like these are successful, Iowa will be in danger of returning to the dark days of partisan election of judges in which party affiliation, religious beliefs, or a political stance on a social issue, rather than judicial qualification and integrity, determine who is elected.[7]

The following June, the Iowa Supreme Court ended the controversy, ruling that state legislators, led by Alons, lacked standing as taxpayers, lawmakers, married individuals, or members of the public. Chief Justice Louis Lavorato raised the question in oral arguments this way: "What injuries have you suffered?" Just as his former clerk, Sharon Malheiro, had predicted, the legislators had no answer other than to claim a general objection to the legal decision. Brown and Perez's divorce harmed no one.

Five months later, Lavorato cemented the court's view with a strongly worded unanimous opinion that denied the legislators' request by essentially telling them they should have minded their own business. Lavorato wrote:

> It would be strange indeed and contrary to our notions of separation of powers, if we were to recognize that legislators have standing to intervene in lawsuits just because they disagree with a court's interpretation of a statute.

The chief justice also provided another indication of what Lambda's Camilla Taylor was looking for as she considered filing the *Varnum* lawsuit: a willingness to stand up to political power. He further wrote:

> We fail to see how the district court's action in dissolving a civil union of another couple harmed in any specific way these plaintiffs' marriages, and for this reason they have shown no legally recognized interest or personal stake in the underlying action. The district's court action in terminating another couple's civil union did not injure these plaintiffs in a special manner, different from the public generally.[8]

Lavorato's decision, issued June 17, 2005, represented a third critical signal to Taylor that Iowa could be the place to break the judicial losing streak against same-sex marriage. The first signal had been the court's decision in 2004 on taxation in the RACI II case; the second signal was the Iowa Senate's refusal that same year to approve starting a constitutional amendment restricting marriage to a man and a woman. The fact that the Democrats would control the legislature at least until 2007 also meant a constitutional amendment couldn't be put before voters until the 2010 general election, which gave Lambda plenty of time to file a lawsuit and get a decision from the Iowa Supreme Court.

Taylor talked at length with Malheiro as well as Janelle Rettig and Robin Butler about the final decision to file the lawsuit. Though it would be six more months before the lawsuit would be filed, Taylor was confident *Varnum* would proceed. Malheiro's only thought was of the irony that a group of conservative legislators who challenged Neary's decision had prompted what was about to happen.

"I always give credit to Dwayne Alons," she said later. "Had those legislators left that case alone, I wouldn't have gotten Lambda Legal's attention. We can thank them for *Varnum*."

As Judge Hanson read his friend's message, he hit reply and tapped a quick note:

> I thought of you when I saw the article in this morning's newspaper. I also thought about the possibility it would end up on my docket. I'm not aware of it, but that's not to say it couldn't happen. If it does, I will worry about it then, and you'll be one of the first people I will call (although I won't admit it if asked. In fact, my line will be Jeff Neary? I don't know him. :)
>
> Seriously, I think your idea about assigning it to a senior judge would be a good one, but someone might also say, "Give it to Hanson—he's not up for retention for another six years!" So who knows . . . We did ask for these jobs, didn't we? Bob.[9]

It didn't take long for Hanson's prediction to come true. A couple hours after e-mailing Neary, Hanson's office telephone rang. Colleen Adams, the court administrator responsible for determining court assignments, wanted to talk to Hanson. "Are you sitting down?" she asked Hanson when he got on the line. "You've got the Varnum case."

He knew the next year or so would be one of the most interesting of his legal career.

When Dennis Johnson, local cocounsel for the *Varnum* plaintiffs, learned that Hanson had drawn the case, he didn't sigh. In fact, he smiled and thought, "He won't be afraid."[10]

A native Iowan, the judge came from a prominent family of lawyers. His father, William, had been a longtime federal judge in the Southern and Northern Districts of Iowa. His brother Tom is a prominent Des Moines trial lawyer, and his brother Jay and sister Cindy are also lawyers. In his senior year in high school, Hanson got a firsthand look at what it took to be a judge.

On March 28, 1974, William Hanson drew national attention when he overturned the conviction of a man accused of murdering a ten-year-old girl. Hanson ruled the suspect was entitled to a new trial after determining that during the investigation the police had violated the suspect's right to legal counsel.

Robert Anthony Williams, also known as Anthony Erthel Williams, an escapee from a Missouri mental hospital, had been convicted by a Polk County jury of murdering Pamela Powers on Christmas Eve 1968. Williams had kidnapped Powers from a local YMCA, where she and her family had been attending a wrestling match. Powers had disappeared after leaving her family to go to the restroom.

Police almost immediately targeted Williams, who had been observed leaving the YMCA hurriedly after a search for Powers had begun inside the YMCA. Williams's car was found the next day 160 miles east in Davenport, Iowa. Williams surrendered to Davenport police on the advice of a Des Moines lawyer the next day and was transported back to central Iowa by two Des Moines police detectives on the promise Williams would not be interrogated until he was in custody in Des Moines and could talk to his lawyer.

On the trip back to Des Moines—despite the promise—police detective Cletus Leaming began a conversation with Williams during which the detective urged Williams to lead him to Powers's body so she could have a "Christian burial." Williams, who had strong religious views, led police to where the girl had been buried near Grinnell about sixty miles east of Des Moines.

Williams's conviction was upheld by the Iowa Supreme Court on a 5–4 vote, but his lawyers took the case to the federal court claiming that Leaming's actions had amounted to an illegal interrogation in violation of Williams's right to have a lawyer present. In a decision that would be upheld narrowly by the U.S. Supreme Court three years later, William Hanson agreed, saying,

> This leaves the question of whether [Williams's] right to counsel was violated during that trip; the answer clearly is in the affirmative. . . . Petitioner not only had a right to counsel during the time in question, he actually had arranged for counsel. . . . The authorities used a ruse to obtain statements from defendant in the absence of counsel.[11]

Judge William Hanson's son Robert had received an undergraduate degree from Stanford in 1978 and a law degree from the University of Iowa in 1981. In Bob Hanson's short tenure as a judge, he had spent most of his time presiding on criminal cases, one of them quite notorious. The case—the trial of man accused of murdering a thirteen-year-old after being acquitted of killing a thirty-four-year-old homeless woman—provided an example of Hanson's commonsense approach to the law.

When prosecutors attempted to introduce testimony about the alleged previous murder, Hanson refused to permit it, contending it would prejudice the jury. Similarly, when prosecutors, after the man's conviction on first-degree murder charges, asked for two life sentences to be served consecutively, Hanson chose instead to sentence the man to two concurrent life sentences, saying, "In the court's view, there is nothing to be gained. He will be incarcerated for the balance of his life."[12]

Until his appointment to the court in 2003, Hanson had been in private practice in Des Moines. On the day of his swearing-in, he wore his father's black judicial robes.

Hanson's appointment only added to Dennis Johnson's optimism. Almost from the day Camilla Taylor had called out of the blue to ask him to join Lambda Legal's effort challenging Iowa's marriage law, Johnson knew he had a good case. The only question, he thought, would be whether the district court judge and, later, the supreme court had the courage to follow the law.

Taylor had sounded nervous when she called Johnson the first time during the spring of 2004. It was a cold call, but her research of Iowa trial lawyers led her directly to him. He had been solicitor general of Iowa, so he knew constitutional arguments. She learned from other lawyers that Johnson had a good reputation. He was an articulate, tenacious trial lawyer who could think on his feet.

"Have you heard of Lambda Legal?" Taylor asked.

"No, I haven't," Johnson responded, wondering what this call was about.

Taylor explained that she was in the process of building a case to challenge Iowa's ban on same-sex marriage and that much of the preliminary legal work had been completed. But she said the workload required for trial and an appeal mandated the assistance of local cocounsel. She added that while a final decision to proceed hadn't been reached, she was confident it was coming.

"Let me think about it," Johnson said.

Taylor suggested she send a memo outlining her thoughts on the case and why she thought it could be successful. Johnson agreed but had misgivings. First, he knew he'd have to work the case free of charge, or pro bono, which would require at least a review by the managers of his firm, Dorsey and Whitney. In addition, he knew possible conflicts with clients—particularly religious groups—would have to be resolved. But what really gave him pause was Taylor's reluctance to say what his role might be. Nearing retirement, Johnson liked the idea of taking the case but didn't want to be a paper pusher or end up working for a bunch of ideologues.

What bothered him least was accepting a case that would become highly controversial. Johnson understood that the plaintiffs' claims weren't frivolous and that they deserved to have the most competent and zealous representation possible. Like most lawyers, Johnson thought it almost required him to take the case. His misgivings eased significantly when Taylor's legal research memo arrived. In it, she outlined how Article I, Section 1, Section 6, and Section 9 of the Iowa Constitution had long been interpreted in Iowa civil rights cases dating back to the 1800s. Each section, she argued, would permit plaintiffs to make equal protection and due process arguments questioning whether restricting marriage to a man and a woman treated Iowa gays and lesbians unequally and deprived them of their rights to marry the person of their choice.

In addition, Iowa's long tradition of court decisions upholding civil rights gave the potential plaintiffs a historical argument that the supreme court would have to consider. Taylor pointed out that the recent RACI II decision as well as the 1999 decision in *Callender v. Skiles* provided insight into the willingness of the court to act independently of federal court precedent and to set its own course when analyzing questions of constitutional law. "The Iowa Supreme Court generally has treated gay and lesbian litigants fairly and has shown a willingness to expand state constitutional protections," she wrote.[13]

As Johnson read the memo, one thing became increasingly clear. "This isn't even a close case. This is a slam dunk."

Within a few days, he obtained clearance from his firm and called Taylor back to say he was on board. "I don't see how you can lose," he said. After hanging up, Johnson wondered whether he should have pushed harder for a better idea of his role. "Well, if I don't like what's going on," he told himself, "I'll deal with it later. This is worth arguing."

If Johnson thought the case against Iowa's marriage law was a slam dunk, Roger Kuhle, who would become Polk County's lead lawyer in the case, thought he was driving in for an easy layup.[14] Having argued nearly seventy Polk County cases before the Iowa Supreme Court, he saw immediately that his opposition had one big problem. Most of the decisions on the issue over the past forty years rejected the constitutional arguments cited by the *Varnum* plaintiffs.

The first case began in 1970 in Minnesota when a University of Minnesota gay activist, Jack Baker, and his partner, Michael McConnell, had requested a marriage license at the local county clerk's office. The clerk's office had rejected the request, setting up a case that went to the Minnesota Supreme Court. The court, despite acknowledging that Minnesota's marriage law made no reference to the sex of the spouses, concluded the law "employs that term [marriage] as one of common usage, meaning the state of union between persons of the opposite sex," adding later the implied definition "was as old as the book of Genesis."[15] This was the same argument Amos Harris had made against inserting "equal" into the Iowa constitution in 1857: why change the way things had always been done?

As for the claim by Baker and McConnell's lawyers that the law violated their constitutional rights—given recent federal decisions finding a right for an interracial couple to marry (*Loving v. Virginia*) and a right of privacy for couples within their homes (*Griswold v. Connecticut*)—the Minnesota high court said the claim simply held no weight: "We are not independently persuaded by these contentions and do not find support for them in any decisions of the United States Supreme Court."[16]

In 1972, the U.S. Supreme Court unanimously rejected the automatic appeal of Baker's case with a one-line rejection that same-sex marriage opponents would cite as precedent for the next forty years. "The appeal is dismissed for want of a substantial federal question."[17]

Yes, courts in several states had ruled the other way over the past twenty years: Hawaii (1993), Vermont (1999), and Massachusetts (2003) determined the restrictions on same-sex marriage in their state laws were unconstitutional, but only by narrow one-vote margins based on aspects of each state's constitution that could be distinguished from Iowa's.

True, Hawaii voters had also responded quickly by approving a constitutional amendment giving lawmakers the right to regulate marriage, while Vermont agreed only to permit civil unions. But those decisions would soon look way out of step as state appeals courts began upholding the sex restrictions in marriage laws. Arizona began the list in 2004 and would be followed by a series of appellate court decisions in 2005 and 2006 that added Indiana, Washington, Oregon, and New York to it. A 2006 court decision by the Eighth Circuit Court of Appeals, in whose jurisdiction Iowa was located, upheld the Nebraska constitutional amendment restricting marriage to a man and a woman.

As each case was resolved in favor of bans on same-sex marriage, Kuhle and Michael O'Meara, his boss in the county's civil division, felt increasingly confident. Both were convinced there was more than sufficient precedent to uphold the Iowa law. State courts like those in New York and Washington wanted nothing to do with the issue. The justices said they understood how the laws might discriminate against homosexuals, but given the controversial nature of the issue, courts should defer to the legislatures that adopted them. Public opinion, those courts said, must be considered, and judicial restraint had to recognize the reality that there was great debate over the issue.

Kuhle traveled extensively in 2006 to take depositions of expert witnesses on both sides of the issue, but he knew the decisions in New York and Washington provided what he considered to be the best argument for upholding the law: let the legislature deal with it. As Kuhle recalled,

> If you looked at New York culturally and the other states like Arizona, Nebraska, and Indiana, their rationales were obvious. If it was obvious for New Yorkers, how could it not be obvious to us that the law was valid? Regulating marriage has always been a matter of state law. It was just as plain as the end of your nose.

Kuhle and O'Meara, a former Catholic priest, had been expecting the lawsuit. Rumors about the filing of a challenge had circulated for several months in 2005. Then in late November a succession of gay and lesbian couples had visited recorder Tim Brien's office asking for a marriage license. Immediately, the two began to prepare for a sophisticated and lengthy litigation. Early on, Kuhle learned that Lambda Legal's extensive preparation had the Polk County attorneys at a disadvantage. Kuhle remembered,

> They were a decade ahead of us from the beginning, and that was way, way ahead of us. That became more apparent with their discovery. They were much more the sociologists than we were.

What was clear to Kuhle was that his opponents had a ready set of expert witnesses who had testified in court cases that, among other things, presented scientific studies justifying gay and lesbians adopting children and supporting the claim that most children raised by same-sex couples were as well-adjusted as those raised in traditional opposite-sex families. The plaintiff's experts would require him to quickly find some of his own.

Lawyers for both sides spent nearly eighteen months in legal research, filing various briefs as well as traveling extensively in the U.S., in Canada, and to Britain to take depositions of various expert witnesses. A major question addressed in those depositions was whether children growing up in families with same-sex partners were harmed in any way. One of Lambda Legal's expert witnesses had estimated that about 37 percent of the 5,800 same-sex couples in Iowa were raising children under the age of eighteen—a significant number.

Taylor's experts were well armed with empirical studies that indicated strongly that children grew up healthier and happier in families with two parents, but little statistical evidence indicated that those parents had to be of the opposite sex. In contrast, Kuhle relied on a mixture of experts who specialized in ethics, comparative religion, and government and who argued that children would be much better off in families with opposite-sex parents. But even he began to suspect, as he listened to experts on both sides, that the issue could probably be resolved if both sides weren't so entrenched. After taking the deposition of Nancy Cott, a Harvard professor whose expertise was on the history of marriage, the Polk County attorney wondered why the issue couldn't be resolved more amicably. As Kuhle later recalled,

> She had just talked to a legislative committee on the history of marriage relative to same-sex marriage. I asked myself if Iowa legislators would hear some of these people talk, would they be persuaded to allow it or be more dug in not to permit it? How would they go on this issue, if it wasn't so adversarial and now in the courts?

Camilla Taylor and Ken Upton, a Lambda Legal attorney based in Dallas, had been talking for weeks about taking a chance no one had tried before. It had a lot to do with young McKinley BarbouRoske. McKinley had captured Taylor's heart as the lawyer got to know the BarbouRoske family on visits to Iowa City. "She was always very busy writing in her notebook," Taylor remembered. "She was always making sure she was on top of what we were doing."

During depositions, Taylor was pregnant; she and her husband, Rusty, were expecting the first of their two children. Taylor would often sip Pepto-Bismol directly from the bottle she carried in her briefcase during that time. At one deposition, a defense expert witness, who argued that children should be raised by a man and a woman because of genetic differences, noticed Taylor was about eight months along. "One day you'll understand," he said, according to Taylor.

The story about McKinley's outburst at the kitchen table kept reverberating in Taylor's mind. "You aren't married?" the little girl had asked as her two moms watched the tears roll down her face. Then there was the story about a preschool administrator telling the BarbouRoskes their daughter couldn't talk about her lesbian parents in front of the other kids. Just how moving were those moments? Taylor thought. How are those not examples that McKinley is being injured by not having married parents?

Ken Upton also understood the potential significance of those two incidents and, like Taylor, the risks. None of the gay marriage cases to that point had asserted that children being raised by same-sex couples were injured by the marriage laws. In fact, the legal challenges consciously stayed away from the issue. The other side seemed to own the issue without having to prove a thing. But as Upton and Taylor deliberated, the benefits of including children in the lawsuit clearly began to outweigh the risks. Wasn't marriage about children? And why should children of same-sex couples not have married parents?

Hypocrisy ran through the county's argument, but no one was asking the question, Upton thought. "Okay, but what about our children?" he asked. "If marriage is about children, you need to look these children in the eye and say, 'Yes, marriage is about children, but not about you.'"

A July 2006 decision by a New York Court of Appeals panel, for example, had reversed a lower court decision overturning that state's DOMA. The court said the legislature could rationally have decided that heterosexual partners were more unreliable in having children than same-sex partners and thus needed the benefits of marriage as an inducement to "make a solemn, long-term commitment to each other."

> The Legislature could find that this rationale for marriage does not apply with comparable force to same-sex couples. These couples can become parents by adoption, or by artificial insemination or other technological marvels, but they do not become parents as a result of accident or impulse. The Legislature could find that unstable relationships between people of the opposite sex present a greater dan-

ger that children will be born into or grow up in unstable homes than is the case with same-sex couples, and thus that promoting stability in opposite-sex relationships will help children more.

Then, the appeals court added it would rely on intuition and experience to conclude that New York lawmakers could rationally believe "that it is better, other things being equal, for children to grow up with both a mother and a father."

> Intuition and experience suggest that a child benefits from having before his or her eyes, every day, living models of what both a man and a woman are like. It is obvious that there are exceptions to this general rule—some children who never know their fathers, or their mothers, do far better than some who grow up with parents of both sexes—but the Legislature could find that the general rule will usually hold.[18]

The New York ruling had angered Taylor and Upton, partly because Lambda Legal had represented the plaintiffs in the case; but they also noted that the court and every other court so far had easily dismissed the impact that the inability of same-sex couples to marry had on their children. Why shouldn't the court be required to see the face of a little girl who wanted her two mothers to be married? There also were McKinley's sister, Breeanna, and little Jamie Olson, the son of Reva Evans and Ingrid Olson. Chuck Swaggerty and Jason Morgan had become foster parents for a number of children and wanted to adopt them.

While Taylor and Upton agreed the three children should be added as plaintiffs, others weren't so sure. Upton had heard the complaints before. "These were the same people who were saying, 'Why Iowa? Why in the world are you making children part of your case? We always lose when children are part the case.' They just berated us," Upton said.

But one other lawyer agreed.

"That's brilliant," Dennis Johnson told Taylor when she asked him about amending the complaint to add the children.

Taylor said she understood there might be an issue of standing, which would require a showing that the children were actually being injured by not having married parents. Defense lawyers could argue that the children suffered no direct injury because the issue was whether a same-sex couple could get a marriage license—not whether children should have married parents. Ultimately, the team agreed that no judge would be able to rule that the marriage ban wasn't denying dignity, legitimacy, and all the other benefits that children of married parents are supposed to receive. They were added in an amended complaint, which was upheld by Hanson.

Like Taylor and Upton, Johnson also believed the addition of the children would put a human face on the plaintiffs' case. An effective lawsuit always tells a story, and the one about the children of same-sex couples stigmatized by not having married parents would surely resonate with Iowa judges. It would be up to him, Johnson knew, to make that argument to Judge Hanson.

Janelle Rettig and Robin Butler weren't going to miss this after all that they had been through. The two, along with friends and allies, had long battled for this chance to stand up for their right to marry. They had been leaders in the successful battle nearly three years earlier to keep a constitutional amendment restricting marriage to heterosexual couples off the ballot. Then, with the help of Taylor and her staff, Rettig and Butler had spent a substantial amount of time holding meetings, conferences, and seminars around the state to explain to Iowans and educate them about why gays and lesbians wanted to marry. The efforts had helped to lobby state residents to think about accepting marriage equality, but the two also knew that it would take years to overcome the opposition without a court victory.

As they walked into Judge Robert Hanson's courtroom on May 4, 2007, they waved hello to their Iowa City friends, Jen and Dawn BarbouRoske. Sharon Malheiro was there, as well as Camilla Taylor, the legal leader of the effort.

Rettig couldn't help but laugh to herself as she remembered the first time she had met Taylor two years earlier. The Lambda Legal attorney had agreed to participate on a panel about same-sex marriage at the University of Iowa. Part of her purpose was to explain why it was an important issue in legal terms, but she was also there to scope out the reaction she might get and to meet some of those individuals on the front lines of the struggle whom she had only spoken with over the telephone. Back then, Rettig and Butler had agreed to meet Taylor at a downtown hotel and walk to where the panel would take place on the Iowa campus. As they strolled through the downtown mall area, the lawyer noticed a series of similar small statues standing outside of various businesses.

"What's with this eagle?" Taylor asked.

Rettig laughed. "That's no eagle. It's Herky the Hawk, the university's athletic mascot." Everyone in the state knows that. While she explained, she realized a few lessons were in order. "This is never going to work," she thought. "Here's this New York lawyer in her high heels and power suit. You got a lot to learn about Iowa."

On this day, two years later, as the courtroom filled to capacity, the tension built. The hearing simply involved legal arguments on competing motions for summary judgment—a legal procedure used instead of a trial when the questions raised center on the law rather than on the facts of a case. No trial on the facts was necessary because each side agreed that no facts were actually in dispute. Marriage—whether between a man and a woman, two men, or two women—was a concept all the parties to the case understood. This hearing was about the law and whether the statute met constitutional standards.

Hanson had hinted broadly to both sides early on that summary judgment might be the best route to a decision, given that, no matter the outcome, one side would be appealing it to the supreme court. Each legal team, after dismissing the need for trial on the facts of the case, agreed that one hearing based on fifteen months of legal briefing, depositions, and argument would be sufficient.

Kuhle opened his argument on behalf of Polk County with an admonition echoing the decisions in New York and Washington. The debate over same-sex marriage didn't belong in the courts.

"It is our view that this case is really a separation of powers issue," he said. "This case is not properly before this court, not procedurally; but it's not properly before this court because it's a legislative matter."[19]

Quite simply, Kuhle argued, the *Varnum* plaintiffs were asking Hanson to do something that no court had ever done before—to find a fundamental right to same-sex marriage. "There is no dispute, I would submit, that marriage always has been between a man and a woman, a male and a female," Kuhle said, arguing Iowa law had been that way since statehood in 1846.[20] Again, he was echoing Harris's arguments from the 1857 Constitutional Convention, as well as the arguments of defenders of DOMAS elsewhere in the country: tradition is enough reason to keep the law.

Throughout his opening argument, the Polk County attorney hammered on three points relentlessly:

- First, that recent court cases in New York, Washington, Oregon, and Indiana "have all held that there is no fundamental right for two people of the same sex to marry."[21]
- Second, that Hanson should review the constitutionality of the law giving substantial deference to the legislature's right to view it as conveying "to our public that marriage is about the bringing together of a man and a woman for responsible procreation to found and a raise a family."[22] (This kind of deference was exactly what the state supreme court hadn't given legislators in the RACI II decision, one of the events that had given Lambda Legal reason to consider litigating gay marriage in Iowa.)
- Third, that the legislature, which had adopted the additional restrictions in 1998, was "the best body to review the wealth, the body of knowledge, of academic knowledge that's available to educate the legislature on what laws it might want to pass, how it might want to regulate marriage."[23] In other words, legislators should make laws, not judges.

"In all the litigation that's been had on this issue," Kuhle said, "we have learned that all of the states have always defined marriage as it's defined in Iowa."[24] At one point, he also raised the question of why six couples from Iowa had arranged to request licenses in Polk County and why Lambda Legal lawyers were involved in the case at all. Many critics of the case had raised the question, contending that this was nothing more than outside agitators attempting to disrupt the peace of Iowa by attempting to push an activist gay agenda.

"We've made our statements of what we think [this] effort is, why Lambda Legal is in this case today, why this case is in Polk County today. It is a test case," he said.[25]

As she sat in the audience, Rettig bristled but then thought about the demonstration in Johnson County in 2004 when forty couples had asked for marriage licenses. "They didn't come in here," she thought. "We not only asked them to come here, but we begged them."

Kuhle concluded by again raising the issue of separation of powers. "We would ask the court to not treat this case as an effort or an opportunity to legislate and to dismiss the case and allow the Iowa legislature to deal with the matter," he said.[26]

In response, Johnson, who would handle the oral arguments for the plaintiffs, attacked the county's case as "not a hypothetical question or an academic issue; this is a case involving real people"—not something Lambda Legal had ginned up in pursuit of an ideological agenda foreign to Iowans. "These people have real problems because the state of Iowa insists on treating them like second-class citizens," he said.[27]

In quick succession, Johnson rattled off the problems and complaints of Jason Morgan and Chuck Swaggerty, who couldn't get health insurance or family leave because they were an unmarried homosexual couple; of Jen and Dawn BarbouRoske, whose daughter McKinley had been told she would not be allowed to talk about her family in her preschool family-week unit because she had two mothers for parents; and of Larry Hoch and David Twombley, who were entering retirement together but could not receive spousal benefits under their pension plans or Social Security when one partner died.

"The examples could go on and on," Johnson said. "But the bottom line is this. It's definitely something that has a real harmful and adverse impact on my clients and other people situated just like them. It is wrong. It's unfair. And it is unconstitutional under the laws of the state of Iowa."[28] He then pounded on Kuhle's insistence that case law from other states should dictate the outcome of the case and that the legislature should have the final say.

"He wanted to talk about federal cases. He wanted to talk about lots of cases from other states. I almost thought he was going to completely forget about Iowa law until right at the very end," Johnson said.[29] As Kuhle hammered issues, so did Johnson. He argued strenuously that the county's position—that no court had found a fundamental right to same-sex marriage—was an attempt to avoid the reality of the right. It should be available to all people regardless of their sexual orientation. Just because

Americans had always done it one way did not mean that we should not do what was right, as Bunker had insisted in leading his fellow delegates to replace "independent" with "equal" in the state constitution in 1857.

"If there is a fundamental right to marry the person of your choice without government interference," he said, "then the government is violating that right when it says, we'll respect your right to marry the person of your choice as long as it's somebody of the opposite sex."[30]

Directly addressing the county's claim that the fundamental right to marry was based largely on history and tradition, Johnson cited an Iowa precedent countering that argument as well. In 1999, the Iowa Supreme Court broke considerable constitutional ground in *Callender v. Skiles* by finding that a man who had fathered a child with a woman married to another man had the right under Iowa's constitution to claim paternity rights over the objection of the married couple and the child. At the time, state law required that any child born to a married couple would be presumed to be the legitimate child of the couple regardless of paternity.

And, like RACI II, the Iowa court's decision in *Callender* ran completely counter to a ruling by the U.S. Supreme Court ten years earlier that decided natural fathers had no due process right to claim paternity. *Callender* had been approved on a narrow 5–4 vote, but its words provided Johnson with a key justification that crystallized his argument that the Iowa Constitution demanded that gays and lesbians be allowed to marry the person of their choice.

"Due process protections, however, should not ultimately hinge upon whether the right sought to be recognized has been historically afforded," Johnson said, reading from the decision. "Our constitution is not merely tied to tradition, but recognizes the changing nature of society."[31]

Johnson added the passage that the *Varnum* legal team would use again before the Iowa Supreme Court in its arguments to overturn the ban on same-sex marriages.

If we recognize parenting rights to be fundamental under one set of circumstances, those rights should not necessarily disappear simply because they arise in another set of circumstances involving consenting adults that have not traditionally been embraced. Instead, we need to focus on the underlying right at stake. The nontraditional circumstances in which parental rights arise do not diminish the traditional parental rights at stake.[32]

Johnson then said:

> That same analysis applies to the due process rights in this case of my clients. The fundamental right to marry extends to all Iowans, not just heterosexuals. The freedom of choice extends to allow them to marry any person of their choice, not just persons the State approves of."[33]

At the end of his presentation, Johnson summed up his view on the defense of marriage law adopted in 1998. He argued that the county could not prevail under Iowa's constitution because it couldn't prove that the law really achieved the governmental interests claimed as the reason for the passage of the law. Instead, Johnson argued that the law had been passed for one reason only.

> There was only one reason to adopt that one-sentence statute . . . and that was to make sure that gays and lesbians could not try to take advantage of the opportunities provided other people under the marriage statutes. They were a targeted group. That's an improper purpose, and it makes the statute unconstitutional.[34]

Judge Hanson put in a call to Denny Johnson's office around midafternoon on August 30, 2007. Almost four months had passed since oral arguments; the Labor Day holiday was approaching, and Johnson was in the process of leaving the office for the weekend to attend a wedding in Vermont. The judge asked if Johnson would come over to this office for a few minutes late in the afternoon. "I am going to give you the ruling before I release it to the press, and I want you to go over it," Hanson said.

When the attorney arrived in the judge's office, he found Kuhle already sitting in a chair in front of Hansen's desk.

"You won," Hanson told Johnson matter-of-factly as he handed him the sixty-two-page opinion. As the two lawyers thumbed through the decision, Johnson quickly recognized that the decision wasn't just a slam dunk. It was written almost as if Camilla Taylor, Ken Upton, and Dennis Johnson were the authors.

The judge had divided the opinion into several sections, including a lengthy list of statements of fact, which appeared to be taken almost verbatim from the plaintiffs' statement of material facts. That was mostly because Kuhle's filings had failed to challenge them, other than to deny the plaintiff's assertions for "lack of knowledge." Under the Iowa Rules of Civil Procedure, any objection to a plaintiff's statement of facts had to be accompanied by a citation from depositions or other documents within the court file supporting the objection. Hanson's decision said he could find no objection to the findings of fact that would prevent him from accepting the plaintiff's view.

Among the 119 findings of fact were the following statements:

34. As a result of their exclusion from the civil institution of marriage, Plaintiffs, their relationships, and their families are stigmatized and made more vulnerable in comparison to heterosexuals. Through the marriage exclusion the State devalues and delegitimizes relationships at the very core of the adult Plaintiffs' sexual orientation and expresses, compounds, and perpetuates the stigma historically attached to homosexuality, for them and all gay persons.[35]

40. Plaintiffs and their families are in just as much or more need of the rights, obligations, benefits, and privileges of marriage as heterosexuals and their families but cannot access them.[36]

57. Homosexuality is a normal expression of human sexuality. Although homosexuality once was classified as a mental disorder or abnormality, empirical research since the 1950s consistently has failed to provide an empirical or scientific basis for this view, which has been renounced by professionals in multiple disciplines.[37]

64. Iowa's interest in the welfare of children of lesbian and gay parents is as great as its interest in the welfare of any other children.[38]

So the undisputed facts of the case had persuaded Hanson to rule on behalf of the six couples. But the decision did more than that: Johnson realized that Hanson had ruled that the Iowa DOMA was unconstitutional under both the state's due process and equal protection guarantees, declaring the law could not meet strict scrutiny, heightened scrutiny, or rational basis.

To understand what these three terms mean in the law requires understanding the legal concepts of due process and equal protection. Hanson's ruling reflected changes made in the Iowa Constitution in 1857, as it applied to both equal protection, Article I, Section 6, and due process, Article I, Section 9. Like the change pushed by delegate John Edwards in amending the equal protection section, there was virtually no debate on adding a due process protection clause.

In the 1846 constitution, that section had been limited to a proscription of the right to a jury trial: "The right of trial by jury shall remain inviolate; but the General Assembly may authorize trial by a jury of a less number than twelve men in inferior courts."[39] But Republicans controlling the convention decided to add language that they acknowledged came directly from the Fifth Amendment of the U.S. Constitution: "No person shall be deprived of life, liberty, or property without due process of law."

Proponents argued that the state's constitution should reflect the due process requirement for two reasons. First, if it was good enough for the U.S. Constitution, it should be good enough for Iowa's. But, moreover, some believed adamantly that the federal Constitution applied only to the actions of the federal government, not the governments of the individual states. That problem was resolved with the ratification of the Fourteenth Amendment to the U.S. Constitution, but that didn't occur until 1868.

George Ells, the chairman of the convention's committee on the preamble and bill of rights, also urged the change as a possible way to nullify the application of the federal Fugitive Slave Law within Iowa. Adopted as part of the Compromise of 1850, the act required law enforcement officers to arrest individuals suspected of being runaway slaves or face a one-thousand-dollar fine (about thirty thousand dollars today). The act also denied those arrested the right to a trial by jury.

"We would be justified at this time, either by legal enactment or by incorporating provisions into our constitution, in protecting ourselves from its operation," Ells said of the federal law, echoing the 1839 decision of *In Re Ralph*. "I regard the Fugitive Slave Law as unconstitutional, because it does not give to man the right to defend his life and liberty by 'due process of law.'"[40] Days later, the amendment was adopted after a brief exchange of views and was not debated again throughout the rest of the convention.

Such is not the case more than a century and a half later. Due process, particularly substantive due process, remains one of the most hotly argued legal concepts within U.S. jurisprudence. The legal concept of "due process of law" has been split into two different principles. First, there is procedural due process, which is interpreted to mean a constitutional guarantee that any individual coping with a governmental action taken either criminally or civilly against him or her is entitled to a fair process before a court. Then there is substantive due process—the principle that any law found to be unreasonable, capricious, or arbitrary is unconstitutional even when no enumerated or specific constitutional right is found to have been violated.

Since the late 1800s, the concept or justification for what is called "substantive due process" has raged inside and outside the courts. The debate is heard most often in the argument between those who criticize the courts for "judicial activism" on issues they believe are better left to the democratic decision making of legislatures and those who believe that the courts have a legitimate interest in determining whether the purpose and consequence of a law is acceptable when judged against the underlying values of the constitutional principles of fairness and equality.

What Hanson heard during the oral argument between Kuhle and Johnson over Iowa's law restricting marriage to a man and a woman was a classic example of that very debate. Kuhle asserted that the issue should remain with the legislature because the historical definition and tradition of marriage had always been between a man and a woman. If there is a need to change the definition, Kuhle argued, it should be left to the democratically elected legislature, based on its judgment as well as public opinion. The fact that the rights of a minority group might be infringed upon was of less consequence than removing an important issue from the democratic process.

Johnson responded that the purpose and impact of the law amounted to the majority riding roughshod over the rights of a minority. Johnson pointed to the fact that the law stigmatized children like McKinley BarbouRoske, who were parented by a same-sex couple and, therefore, deserved to have married parents. In addition, he argued that the law subjected same-sex couples to a second-class-citizen status when it came to issues such as health rights, eligibility to inherit a spouse's estate or retirement benefits, or even tax relief.

Kuhle's and Johnson's arguments also applied to their dispute over whether the Iowa DOMA violated the state's requirement of equal protection—the legal concept that all persons have a right to be treated equally by the law both procedurally and substantively. As due process insists that laws not be applied arbitrarily, equal protection mandates, as a matter of fairness, that laws not treat people differently.

Kuhle argued that there was no unfairness in the law because homosexuals were not treated differently from heterosexuals. The restrictions of the law, according to Kuhle, treated all men and women alike. The only difference, he asserted, was that the state had defined marriage as only between a man and a woman, which had been the traditional definition of marriage. To permit a same-sex couple to marry would simply be redefining marriage—something that only legislators should do.

But Johnson countered that the correct way to analyze the law's constitutionality under equal protection was to determine the purpose of the law before anything else. "If you want to find out if a statute violates equal protection, first you have to look to the purpose of the statute," Johnson said. "If it serves an illegitimate purpose, the statute is unconstitutional." He pointed to the Iowa legislature's decision to restrict marriage to a man and a woman in 1998, which followed the court decision in Hawaii in 1993 that would allow a same-sex couple to marry there.

"You can't look at this statute and think there is any other purpose other than to exclude and target one minority group," Johnson said. "That is an illegitimate purpose."[41]

To make his decision, Hanson was required to select a standard of review among three—strict scrutiny, heighted scrutiny, or rational basis. The three-pronged hierarchy of standards is available to judges to weigh a governmental act, such as a law, against a constitutional right or principle. Put another way, each standard is a lens used by judges to examine the validity of the government's justification or interest in treating people differently under a law.

Before selecting the standard, Hanson would first have to determine whether the group challenging the law represented what is known as a "suspect" or "quasi-suspect" group. To classify a group as either suspect or quasi-suspect, a judge must determine that the group has been subjected historically to discrimination, that the defining characteristic is immutable, that the shared characteristic doesn't inhibit meaningful contribution to society, and that the group is powerless politically to protect itself.

If the group is determined to be "suspect," the judge is required to use strict scrutiny—the highest standard of analysis and most difficult for a government to meet. The courts have recognized that laws imposing restrictions or classifying groups, for example, on the basis of their race, national origin, or religion must be analyzed under strict scrutiny standards. If a law is to survive strict scrutiny, the government must show that the law is necessary to promote a compelling state interest and that no other less restrictive means is available to achieve that interest. Here the lens used by the courts is powerful and must reveal an obvious government interest.

If the group is determined to be "quasi-suspect," the judge is required to use heightened scrutiny—considered a less microscopic lens. To survive heightened scrutiny, those defending the law must show that it furthers a government interest by a means that is substantially related to that interest. Here the lens is moderately strong.

Laws placing restrictions or classifying groups on the basis of sex, for example, must be analyzed under heightened scrutiny standards. Sexual orientation has also become included as a defining characteristic for a quasi-suspect group in various legal decisions, including the early same-sex marriage decisions in Connecticut and Iowa.

Finally, if the group affected by the law is not found to be suspect or quasi-suspect, a judge is required to use rational basis as the standard of scrutiny. Under rational basis—the least microscopic lens—a judge must give substantial deference to the legislature's approval of the law and permit the law to stand if it can be reasonably related to a legitimate government purpose. Rational basis is also used generally when there is no fundamental right involved. Here, the lens must only reveal the government interest to be close enough to achieve the purpose.

Hanson specifically rejected Polk County's claim that "because no state Supreme Court or United States Supreme Court decision has declared same-sex marriage to be a fundamental right, this Court is precluded from finding the existence of such a right." He had proved Malheiro right in her belief that Iowa judges were not afraid to pursue their own course. Instead, Hanson, citing appellate court decisions dating back as far as *In Re Ralph*, observed that Iowa courts not only "have generally been at the forefront of preserving the civil rights of their citizens in areas such as race, gender, and sexual orientation" but that those constitutional protections "should not ultimately hinge upon whether the right sought to be recognized has been historically afforded."[42] Because we've always done it that way was not sufficient to justify a law.

Hanson concluded, "The Defendant's argument that this Court is precluded from finding a 'fundamental right to same-sex marriage' is not accurate or persuasive."[43] To add weight to his finding, the judge cited *Loving v. Virginia* (1967) in which the U.S. Supreme Court found laws banning interracial marriage to be unconstitutional. "The fact that there was no historical tradition of interracial marriage in Virginia did not preclude the court from holding that the fundamental right to marriage was violated through Virginia's prohibition against interracial marriage."[44]

Almost as remarkably, the judge wrote that the law could not even pass constitutional muster under rational basis, which Kuhle had urged as the standard of review. This was the principle that courts should defer to legislatures and could approve of a law if it was reasonably connected to the governmental interest attempting to be achieved.

Hanson said the defense failed to provide evidence that banning same-sex marriage would have any effect on opposite-sex couples procreating or providing the best environment for raising children: "So far as this Court can tell, Section 595.2(1) operates only to harm same-sex couples and their children."[45]

As the two lawyers paged through the decision, Hanson broached a touchy subject.

"What do we want to do about a stay?" he asked. Without a stay, gay and lesbian couples would have the right to go to any county recorder's office in Iowa and demand they be given a marriage license. Hanson understood his decision was destined for appeal before the Iowa Supreme Court, and he wanted to know what the next move should be.

Kuhle responded that he would file for an immediate stay pending appeal to the Iowa Supreme Court. Johnson said he wasn't exactly sure what the correct procedure would be.

"I need to check with my cocounsel about it," he said. "Obviously, we have to oppose a stay because we are claiming this is an urgent issue." At the same time, something bothered Johnson. It was the thought of couples rushing by the dozens to the Polk County building to get marriage licenses even though Hanson's ruling still could be overturned. They might marry, only to have their official status voided later. In a telephone call to Taylor, he expressed his doubts about fighting a stay. The last thing that he wanted was to have "people run off for the next year and half to get married and have this thing reversed."

The Des Moines attorney later said Taylor had agreed to the stay but wanted to go through the steps of opposing it to eliminate any doubt the plaintiffs wanted to marry. As with some same-sex marriage decisions that have been made since *Varnum*, the possibility that legal marriages might not be recognized became a consideration. For example, when Utah's ban on same-sex marriage was declared unconstitutional in 2014, nearly one thousand couples married there before the U.S. Supreme Court issued a stay pending a final decision by the courts. In court filings, Utah officials said that if their law was upheld by the U.S. Supreme Court, they would refuse to recognize those marriages. The fate of these marriages remains uncertain as this book goes to press.

Hanson's decision to release the ruling late on a Thursday afternoon didn't prevent a media blitz. Front-page headlines about the decision were in most daily newspapers the next day: "Judge: Ban on Gay Marriage Invalid," said the *Des Moines Register*; "Same-Sex Marriage Ban Voided," added the *Gazette* of Cedar Rapids.

But the release of the decision in the late afternoon of August 30 limited newspaper and television stations to focusing on the decisions and the immediate reactions to it. On September 1, newspapers and television gave the story coverage from just about every conceivable angle. The *Des Moines Register* had six stories and an editorial supporting Hanson's decision. One story centered on two men, Iowa State University students, who managed to obtain a waiver of the statutory three-day waiting period from district judge Scott Rosenberg and were quickly married. But they would be the only couple to wed immediately after Hanson's decision. The judge issued a stay pending appeal to the Iowa Supreme Court the day after his decision came out.

Back in Iowa City, Janelle Rettig finally got the telephone call she had been anticipating for nearly three years. She laughed when she heard that Judge Hanson had given the plaintiffs a clear and decisive victory on the way to the Iowa Supreme Court. But Rettig wasn't surprised. As a poker player skilled enough to make the main event of the World Series of Poker, she had watched Hanson closely during the oral arguments.

"The judge looked completely bored when he was listening to the other side," she said after the hearing. "When he was listening to our side, he leaned forward as if to say, 'Tell me more.' With them, he acted like, 'I can't believe you are saying something so stupid.'"

As she had walked out of the courthouse on the day of the hearing with Butler and Taylor, she predicted the outcome. "We won that."

And they had. The only question left: would they win the next one?

Iowa Supreme Court, 2009. Front row (left to right): *Justice Mark Cady, Chief Justice Marsha Ternus, Justice Michael Streit.* Back row (left to right): *Justice Brent Appel, Justice David Wiggins, Justice Daryl Hecht, Justice David Baker. Photograph courtesy of the Iowa Supreme Court.*

Justice Mark Cady. Photograph courtesy of the Iowa Supreme Court.

Marsha Ternus giving her acceptance speech for the Profile in Courage Award. Reproduced by permission of the John F. Kennedy Library Foundation.

Ceremony for the John F. Kennedy Profile in Courage Awards, 2012.
Left to right: Michael Streit, Marsha Ternus, Caroline Kennedy, David Baker.
Reproduced by permission of the John F. Kennedy Library Foundation.

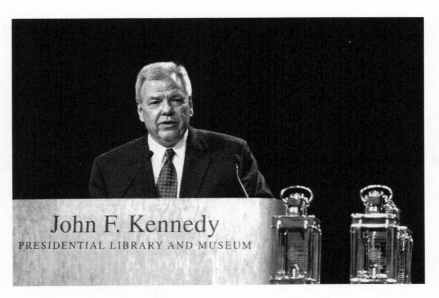

Michael Streit giving his acceptance speech for the Profile in Courage Award.
Reproduced by permission of the John F. Kennedy Library Foundation.

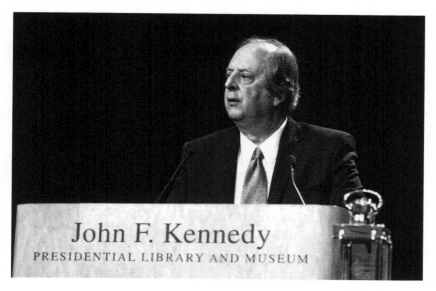

David Baker giving his acceptance speech for the Profile in Courage Award.
Reproduced by permission of the John F. Kennedy Library Foundation.

District court judge Jeffrey Neary. Photograph by
Warren Taylor, reproduced by permission.

District court judge Robert Hanson. Photograph courtesy of Robert Hanson.

*Dennis Johnson.
Photograph courtesy
of Dennis Johnson.*

Camilla Taylor announces the Iowa Supreme Court victory to her clients on April 3, 2009. Photograph from Dan Welk Click! Photography, courtesy of Lambda Legal.

Plaintiffs hearing the news of their victory. Left to right: *David Twombley, Larry Hoch, McKinley BarbouRoske, Dawn BarbouRoske, Jen BarbouRoske, Breeanna BarbouRoske. Photograph from Dan Welk Click! Photography, courtesy of Lambda Legal.*

An emotional moment for four plaintiffs as they receive news of the victory.
Left to right: Patricia Varnum, Katherine Varnum, Jason Morgan, Charles Swaggerty.
Photograph from Dan Welk Click! Photography, courtesy of Lambda Legal.

The BarbouRoske family. Left to right: Dawn, Breeanna, McKinley, Jen.
Photograph courtesy of Lambda Legal.

Connie Mackey, president of the Family Resource Council PAC, speaks to reporters in front of the bus used by the opponents of the retention of three Iowa Supreme Court justices in 2010. Photograph from Jamie Buelt, reproduced by permission.

Congressman Steve King of Iowa campaigning for the ouster of three Iowa Supreme Court justices in 2010. Photograph from Jamie Buelt, reproduced by permission.

Supporters of judicial retention gather at the Iowa Statehouse for a press conference in 2010. Photograph from Jamie Buelt, reproduced by permission.

Opponents of judicial retention provide a contrast to supporters at the Iowa Statehouse in 2010. Photograph from Jamie Buelt, reproduced by permission.

Rick Santorum (center right) *and Bob Vander Plaats* (just behind him)
campaign to oust Justice David Wiggins in Orange City, Iowa, in 2012.
Photograph courtesy of the Iowa State Bar Association.

*Campaign kickoff for the retention of Justice David Wiggins in 2012 at the Iowa
Statehouse. Left to right: Dan Moore, Guy Cook, Christine Branstad.
Photograph courtesy of the Iowa State Bar Association.*

Dan Moore speaking with a television reporter next to the campaign truck in Mason City, Iowa. Photograph courtesy of the Iowa State Bar Association.

||||||||||||||||||||||||||||||||||||||||||||||||||||||||||||||||||||||||||||||||||

CHAPTER EIGHT

All Justices Concur

In fall of 2008, when Chief Justice Marsha Ternus scanned the freshly printed memo listing the seven new Iowa Supreme Court cases to be heard in December, there it was.

Varnum v. Brien—07-1499.

Like the other six court members, Ternus had known an explosive marriage equality case could be inching its way to them since the day it had been filed in district court almost three years before.[1] And for over a year, lawyers for both sides and experts from around the country had been filing friend-of-the-court briefs, exploring the case from every angle. But when 07-1499 showed up at the Judicial Branch Building in November of 2008, the name and number still failed to strike a chord with the chief justice.

"*Varnum v. Brien*," she would say later, "didn't mean a thing to me then."

But Judge Robert Hanson's decision to declare the Iowa DOMA unconstitutional placed the issue directly before the seven members of Iowa's Supreme Court. Like it or not, Ternus and her colleagues now had to decide whether the Iowa Constitution's guarantees of equality and uniform application of the law extended to allowing homosexuals to marry the person of their choice.

For Camilla Taylor and Dennis Johnson, the plaintiffs' lawyers, Hanson's decision meant they would begin the second half of their push to overturn the law with a strongly worded lower court decision on their side of the scoreboard. Now their job was to persuade the court members to go where only a few judges had gone before them.

When Taylor and Johnson surveyed the composition of the court—five of the seven appointed by Democratic governors—Mark Cady was the one who concerned them most, not so much because he was appointed by a Republican and might end up opposing their effort, but mostly because he was so difficult to predict. Johnson felt better after talking to a colleague at his law firm who had clerked for Cady. First and foremost, the colleague said, "Cady is a very conscientious legal scholar." Johnson said he would take his chances any day with a legal scholar who refused to let political ideology enter into his decisions. Taylor hoped he was right.

"Cady is quite an intimidating character," she recalled. "He took some more conservative positions than other members of the court on a number of different things. It wasn't a politically conservative position necessarily, but he was less willing to do what he viewed was extending the court out over past precedent."

Taylor was on the mark. While Cady wasn't against change per se, he was less comfortable with it in great leaps and bounds.[2] Even as a kid growing up in Minnesota and Wisconsin, Mark was the careful, deliberate one. His brother, Roger, was just the opposite. Though Mark was a bright kid, if anyone in the family was brilliant, it was Roger, who turned out to be a physician, researcher, and CEO well-known in the medical field for his groundbreaking work in headache and migraine management.

Roger was almost two years older, and Mark looked up to him—not because he was probably the smartest kid in town, but because Mark was never sure what Roger was going to do next. Big brother had a curiosity that wouldn't quit. Would he blow up the basement chemistry lab or burn down the garage trying some experiment? Or both at the same time? As Mark remembers it, a package from some obscure mail-order outfit seemed to be showing up on the doorstep every other day. While Roger was daring and compulsive, Mark was a portrait of restraint. While Roger scoffed at boundaries, Mark searched for structure.

"Um, Roger, this could be dangerous." Mark must have said that or something similar once a week. "Can we slow down here, Roger, and think this through?"

When Mark Cady grew older, he approached the law the same way. Before *Varnum v. Brien*, he was seen by some as the court's foremost "strict constructionist." Whatever that means. To some it refers to a person who interprets the constitution literally without considering time, place, or evolution of thought. To others, it is simply the opposite of an "activist" jurist. For his part, Cady avoids the term, saying, "If change is supported by what we know, change is good."

One amicus brief after the other pointed to studies confirming the finding that children do better with two parents, whether those parents are two men, two women or one man and one woman. Cady was overwhelmed by the conformity of the research on the subject.

Yet Cady had filed a strongly worded dissent in the RACI II case, which was a major linchpin in the *Varnum* plaintiffs' effort to have the restriction on same-sex marriage overturned. If the court decided to use the rational basis standard, Taylor wondered how Cady, in light of his dissent, would view their position that no rational basis exists for the Defense of Marriage Act. Would he be willing to buck the will of the legislature?

But a closer reading of Cady's dissent shows he wasn't unwilling to buck state lawmakers. Rather, he clearly disapproved of the process used by the majority in arriving at the RACI II decision—applying the equal protection doctrine differently than the court had in a previous decision overturned by the U.S. Supreme Court. Cady thought, in fairness, the court should have used the same analysis method it had used previously and decided the case that way.

Then there was *Callender v. Skiles*, another vital piece of the plaintiffs' argument. In that case about the rights of a natural father, the court essentially said times change and the Iowa Constitution had to recognize that, even if it meant breaking new ground. Like RACI II, the Iowa court's decision on *Callender* ran completely counter to a ruling by the U.S. Supreme Court ten years earlier that decided natural fathers had no due process right to claim paternity. Cady had written the 5–4 majority position and suggested even then a willingness to consider social change in applying the Iowa Constitution's guarantee of equality under the law.

The *Varnum* legal team also had been assessing its chances with the rest of the court. Taylor's reading centered on Ternus. The chief justice's reputation as an insurance defense lawyer and the fact she was a practicing Catholic concerned Johnson but not his Lambda Legal colleague.

"We really did pitch the entire case to Justice Ternus," Taylor later said.

"We didn't think of her as being a particularly liberal person with respect to politics, but we knew that, like Cady, she was incredibly intelligent and that on the RACI decision she was great. And that was necessary as much as anything else."

Ternus had written the RACI II decision for a 5–2 majority of the court. The decision cemented a new standard for analyzing the constitutionality of state laws when using rational basis. Legal scholars might call it "rational basis with teeth" or "bite" to distinguish it from the court's providing deference to the legislative branch's judgment to the point of superficial analysis. The decision signaled two doctrines potentially beneficial to the *Varnum* plaintiffs.

First, the court was now willing to examine the credibility of the means used to achieve a legislative goal, not just whether the legislative goal was rational. For example, if lawmakers claimed that restricting marriage to a man and a woman would promote procreation, the court would ask how banning same-sex couples from marrying encouraged baby making by married opposite-sex couples.

Second, Ternus also established that the court would not be tied to federal precedent when analyzing equal-protection claims brought under the Iowa Constitution. In RACI II, Ternus wrote that while the U.S. Supreme Court had determined the legislature had the authority, under the federal Constitution, to set varying tax rates for racetracks compared to casinos, Iowa's court could come to a different conclusion under the Iowa Constitution. For the *Varnum* plaintiffs, it meant the court might be willing to examine closely whether gays and lesbians might be considered a quasi-suspect or suspect class—something that had never been done on the federal level—forcing the court to impose heightened or strict scrutiny on the law.

Taylor had learned something else:

We were looking for someone who was going to champion the courageous thing to do because that was what the law required. We heard again and again behind the scenes that the only thing that mattered for Justice Ternus was what the law says.

Ternus's commitment to doing "the right thing" regardless of consequence can be traced to a character-forming incident in the first grade.

Her class had been studying Native American music. The students were listening and dancing to songs on a record player. When it was time for recess, they broke off into groups. After recess the teacher asked four girls to come to the front of the class. One was Ternus, who was excited because she thought it was their turn to dance to the music. Her excitement vanished when the teacher said, "These girls did something very mean over recess," and called them out for excluding one of their friends from the group.

Standing at the front of the classroom, knowing she'd done nothing of the kind, Ternus refused to hang her head or feel the least bit guilty. "I'll never forget it," she said years later. "I can still feel myself standing there, saying 'I am not going to look down. She can say what she wants, but I know in my soul I did nothing wrong.'" She wasn't about to let that teacher determine how she viewed herself. From then on, she vowed she would do what is right and let other people make whatever judgments they want. She tried to carry that pledge into adulthood and her professional career.

Ternus, the first person in her family to attend college, had grown up on a farm in east central Iowa. She was one of six children, who arose at dawn every day to do the chores. They fed and milked the cows. They dressed the chickens and canned corn and tomatoes. They were a self-sufficient family, even to the point of making much of their clothing. Ternus still remembers the time her mother let her buy something at a clothing store. She picked out a twenty-dollar dress, which at the time seemed like spending all the money in the world.

The future chief justice didn't take to farming. The exhausting work wasn't a problem, but she much preferred her math and English courses at tiny Washington High School. After graduating, she accepted a tuition scholarship and enrolled in the honors program at the University of Iowa an hour down the road. The "U of I" represented her opportunity to go to college. She majored in home economics with an emphasis in clothing and textiles. Ternus enjoyed almost everything about working in the lab, testing the fabrics.

It was a time of peak campus unrest around the country. The Kent State shootings led to rioting and demonstrations in college towns across the country, including Iowa City. In the spring semester of Ternus's freshman year, the armory adjunct building that housed the writing lab burned down. Students had the option to take their grades and go home or stay for finals. Ternus went home. She had no interest in politics, didn't know the difference between conservative and liberal, and didn't care to know. But the violence frightened her. While other students took to the streets, Ternus stayed in her dorm room and hit the books.

After graduating Phi Beta Kappa, she took a job as a bank teller in Des Moines but found it unchallenging. Working the counter one day, she found herself beside a young woman who was thinking about applying for law school. Taken aback, Ternus thought to herself, "Really? If she can go to law school, so can I." Not long after, Ternus was accepted to Drake University in Des Moines, became editor-in-chief of the *Drake Law Review*, and graduated with high honors. At Drake she enjoyed the tax classes most. Tax work was like a puzzle. She enjoyed the challenge of putting the pieces together — just as she later enjoyed the challenge of working through a court case. Gather the facts and arrange them within the framework of the applicable legal principles. The job isn't done until each piece is accounted for. In Ternus's mind, a disingenuous argument is one that glosses over those missing pieces.

Though Ternus, like Cady, was appointed by Branstad, she says she can't remember a time when she wasn't a registered Independent. She believes Branstad agreed with her on the court's need for the perspective of someone coming from private practice. To his credit, it's also true that Branstad has not been at all hesitant to appoint women.

In sixteen years of civil litigation and insurance law, Ternus sometimes found herself advocating positions she didn't agree with on legal grounds. For most lawyers, that goes with the territory. For Ternus, it was an ethical problem. At one point, she wasn't sure she could bring herself to argue a case on appeal. To Ternus's way of thinking, the legal argument she advocated, while reasonable, would prove problematic over time.

Decades later, when Ternus reached the supreme court, her peers seemed to think her major nemesis would be Louis Lavorato, who became chief justice in 2000 after joining the court in 1986. "I remember people would say that because he was a liberal plaintiff's lawyer and I was a conservative defense lawyer," Ternus said, "we would be clashing all the time." But it didn't happen—in her view, because Lavorato approached the job as she did: "decision-making based on the rule of law."

Ternus also found a structural cause to promote while serving as an associate justice. She saw how the system neglected children, particularly in welfare cases. When Lavorato sent Ternus to a conference on the subject, she immediately recognized the magnitude of the problem. Children were languishing in foster care because child welfare cases had become low priority. She deemed the situation shameful. Why is it more important to try some fender bender, she asked herself, while children wondering where they would go to school in the fall were ignored? Ternus saw thousands of kids sucked into the court system and damaged well into adulthood. Like every other state, she said, Iowa needed to act more quickly on their behalf, and she intended to make it happen.

When Ternus succeeded Lavorato as chief justice in 2006, she decided she would continue to look for wide consensus and not allow the court's discussions to degenerate into ideological street fights. By that time, the membership of the court had been reduced from nine to seven.

"If you're really seeking a synergy in collective decision making," she said years later, "you have to listen to others to find the truth in what they are saying—not figure out how you're going to tear it apart." To emphasize her philosophy, a few weeks after she was elected chief justice, Ternus gathered her colleagues together at a retreat to discuss the future of the court and how to reach consensus. Six of the seven justices at that time would help decide the *Varnum* case. (David Baker, an experienced trial lawyer appointed by Chet Culver, would not arrive until 2008.) In one of their first sessions at the retreat, Ternus told her colleagues she didn't want to head a court driven by politics or ideology. "It was very important for me to make sure we were a public institution with integrity and high principles," Ternus said. "That was our court." Her edict to colleagues was similar to David Bunker's urgings in 1857 to his Constitutional Convention delegates—get "as near the truth as we can."

Of the others, the legal team figured they would get votes from David Wiggins, Brent Appel, Daryl Hecht, and probably David Baker. Johnson had cases with Wiggins when both were in private practice and knew how tough he could be: "The guy never backs down from anybody."

When Johnson was solicitor general, he worked with Appel in the attorney general's office. He liked what he saw there, too. The future justice was smart, thorough, and studious. The latter word comes up most. Nobody researches a case like the studious Appel. It was almost a running gag around the Judicial Branch Building. As part of an initiative to make it easier for citizens outside central Iowa to see the supreme court at work, the justices traveled to Morningside College in Sioux City for oral arguments. As the justices were walking past the school library, someone said, "Keep an eye on Appel. We're going to lose him."

The joke was reality based. To prepare for a case about a citizen's constitutional right to a public education, Appel traveled to Cedar Falls to dig into the research at the University of Northern Iowa library. By all accounts, he dug deep into the *Varnum* case as well.

Brent Appel grew up in Dubuque, went to Stanford for undergraduate and graduate school, and attended Cal Berkeley for his law degree. In private practice in 1999, Appel was a lead lawyer in the state's billion-dollar settlement with the tobacco industry.

Daryl Hecht was a farm kid from Lytton, Iowa, a town of three hundred or so that is at least an hour from any of Iowa's bigger cities, unless you count Fort Dodge and its twenty-five thousand people. When the justice was growing up, Lytton was much bigger—almost four hundred people. He went to Morningside College in Sioux City for undergrad and the University of South Dakota for law school before earning a master's of law degree at the University of Virginia. As a worker's compensation lawyer fighting big business, Hecht earned a reputation as a protector of the little guy and a defender of the rights and liberties of the individual. You wouldn't know it, a lawyer friend said, because he doesn't wear it on his sleeve. "Thoughtful, kind, and deeply progressive at the core" are a few of the other words used to describe Hecht. In 1999, after twenty-two years in private practice, including a term as president of the Iowa Trial Lawyers Association, Hecht joined the court of appeals. He was appointed to the Iowa Supreme Court in 2006.

David Baker was the recent addition to the court. A lifelong Iowan and graduate of Waterloo West High School and the University of Iowa—undergrad and law school—Baker went to work in Cedar Rapids, specializing in tax, estate planning, and corporate law. Marriage equality was far from his radar.[3] Eventually he joined with a colleague to begin his own firm, focusing on personal injury, professional negligence, construction, real estate commercial law, and worker's compensation. As a plaintiff litigator, Baker ultimately found his own legal conclusions conflicting with his client's hopes or desires. In conversations with office colleagues, Baker would sometimes say, "I know what the law says," and the response would be, "Yeah, but how do we get around that?" Baker grew increasingly disinclined to find a way "around that" and increasingly drawn to the writing and researching side of the law. Was he meant to be somewhere else? It was starting to look that way.

In 2004, Tom Vilsack appointed Baker to the district court. Two years later, Vilsack bumped him up to the Iowa Court of Appeals. Vilsack's successor, Chet Culver, quickly sent Baker to the supreme court, just in time to join the *Varnum* decision. His rise was meteoric, as was his fall. When Baker left the court, he was replaced by Bruce Zager, an old kindergarten classmate in Waterloo. The two friends were also Cub Scouts and Boy Scouts together, not to mention swimming teammates in high school. In 2011, one Scout took the other's chair on the Iowa Supreme Court.

Johnson had trouble reading Michael Streit, who had written a few things that seemed sensitive to the rights of gays. Would he be ready to fight this time?

By December 8 — the day Ternus and her court heard oral arguments, took their seats at a conference table in what is called the inner sanctum of the Iowa Judicial Branch Building, and made the decision that would resonate throughout the country — she knew enough about *Varnum v. Brien* to understand with certainty what the court must do. Though the Judicial Branch Building was only a few years old, the inner sanctum spoke to the court's long history. Standing near a window was an antique coat rack with eight double-rounded hooks. Once used for heavy overcoats and top hats, the old wooden relic still holds the court members' black robes between monthly conferences, hearings, and arguments. Like many appeal tribunals, the Iowa Supreme Court pays special attention to tradition. One particular tradition honors the court's history by positioning each member in the seat of the justice who preceded him or (later) her. It's safe to say the court members wearing those top hats never envisioned a case like this one.

Moments earlier in the courtroom nearby, oral arguments had concluded before an overflow crowd that spilled into an area providing closed-circuit TV coverage. For more than two hours, Roger Kuhle, the assistant Polk County attorney representing recorder Timothy J. Brien, had faced off again against Dennis Johnson, the attorney representing the six plaintiff couples. Did the Iowa legislature have a justification to restrict civil marriage licenses to male-female couples only? Or did the law improperly discriminate against a group historically subjected to intolerance?

Kuhle's conclusion: marriage has always been a heterosexual institution necessary to encourage procreation and provide stability to the family unit. As a result, the plaintiffs were prohibited from making a claim of equal protection unless the court was willing to revise the centuries-old definition of marriage. "Marriage is between a man and a woman," the county's lawyer said at one point. "I am not being trite, your honor. But it is an oxymoron to say 'same-sex marriage.'"[4]

Johnson responded by saying his plaintiffs were not asking the court to redefine marriage but rather to recognize this: the right of two homosexuals to marry was no different from that of two heterosexuals. "We are not suggesting a new institution," said the local counsel. "We are suggesting that everybody be able to participate equally in the institution that has existed since the beginning of this state."[5]

He completed the plaintiffs' argument by repeating the story about Jen and Dawn BarbouRoske's search for a preschool. The process was going smoothly until the two moms learned that daughter McKinley would not be permitted to participate in a family-week project like the kids with opposite-sex parents. "They were just about ready to put their money down because they thought they had found a perfect place," Johnson told the court. "But they thought to ask if there was any way their daughter would be treated differently because she had two moms." He then explained the significance. "McKinley was going to be shamed in front of her peers because the government says her family isn't as good as other families."[6]

McKinley and her two moms, sitting off to the side in the front row, had been paying close attention. More than that, McKinley, the ten-year-old *Star Wars* fan, was deliberately staring a hole through Marsha Ternus, trying to reach into the chief justice's unconscious with a Jedi mind trick and influence her decision. "I just really felt confident and comforted by her," the child would say later.

> In my house, girls rule. I just felt I had a connection. I was a little girl fighting for my parents, and I felt she would realize it. At school, the female teachers can always get the crazy little boys to behave. I thought if I got her on my side, I could start moving something with the Force, and she'd tell the rest of them what to do. I was concentrating so hard.

Audio and video devices are prohibited for most Iowa courtroom visitors, but the rules say nothing about shutting down telekinetic powers. For the record, McKinley's moms were almost certain they noticed Ternus returning their child's stare. Alas, that was unlikely. Not wanting to be subconsciously swayed by anything but the facts and the law, Ternus makes a point of keeping her eyes away from the gallery.

While McKinley was attempting to channel the chief justice, her lawyer was sneaking peeks at the clock. Johnson had been talking and taking questions for almost forty minutes, and he still hadn't mentioned the kids and their right to have married parents. Ternus must have noticed Johnson's anxiety because she told him not to worry about the time. "Okay," he thought, "but it has to end sometime, and I have to get this in."

Then it happened. On the last question, Justice Mark Cady provided an opening: "If we believe that the plaintiffs are entitled to the same rights and benefits of marriage but not the title, can we consider some kind of civil union remedy?"[7]

Johnson's response was direct. "If my clients are given civil unions, they will be given the badge of basically second-class citizenship," he said. He talked about how the children of gay people deserve to have two parents like everyone else and should not have to settle for some lesser legal agreement. He used McKinley's experience at the kitchen table and her parents' experience at the preschool as illustrations.

Finally, he pointed to the U.S. Supreme Court's rejection of "separate but equal" in *Brown v. Board of Education*. Quoting from the ruling, John-son pointed out what the court had said. Even if the schools were equal then, the children "would know they were being sent to a separate school because they were deemed to be inferior." They would be hurt in their hearts and minds in a way from which they might never recover.

"These are real harms to people," Johnson told the court, reminiscent of Rufus L. B. Clarke's 1857 prediction that Iowans would one day embrace racial equality. "This lack of respect, dignity, and equality—the state of Iowa should have no part in that. The state should provide full marriage equality under the same name as everyone else."[8]

"There," he said to himself after making his point. "I got it in." Then came a mini panic attack. "Oh, shit. I just ended the argument." Johnson had more to say, but when he looked at the justices, the justices looked back at him. Silence. Three words popped into his head: "This is over." A pause. Then one final thought about the members of the court. "I got them. I got them all."

During his thirty years in the courtroom, Johnson had never experi-enced a moment like that. Though something had happened, he wasn't sure what. Seldom had he been so touched by the emotion of a case. Two memories had stuck in his mind on the morning of oral arguments, and he carried both into the courtroom.

The day they filed the lawsuit, the plaintiffs and their lawyers had held a news conference. Before the plaintiffs met the media, they took part in a session on how to conduct themselves with reporters. While they sat quietly waiting for "class" to begin, someone in this group of strangers broke the silence with a question. "How did you first know?"

Some of the responses elicited knowing smiles. Reva Evans laughed and said she should have known she was gay in high school when she wanted to wear her father's ties. Some were poignant. Jason Morgan said he knew as far back as he could remember. Still others were sad. "Old Fart Number 1," Larry Hoch, trapped in a traditional marriage, spent much of his adulthood in painful denial. Johnson sat in amazement as they told their stories. He had no idea; why would he? He'd never given it much thought. But now he got it. "Imagine going through life hiding your sexual orientation," he thought, "listening to people talk about your immorality in the eyes of God. They live with that all the time."

To Johnson, the notion of people changing their sexual orientation seemed more preposterous than ever. On the morning of oral arguments, he watched each of the plaintiffs, one by one, leave the hotel and board the van to the courthouse. "My only thought," he recounted, "was 'Oh, my God. I have to win this for them.'"

Scanning the court's bench one last time, he mused to himself, "I don't know how any one of you can rule against my clients. I don't see how any of you can."

With oral arguments completed, the court members adjourned to the inner sanctum. Justice Cady began the discussion. A soft-spoken fifty-eight-year-old appointed by the Republican Branstad, Cady would also write the opinion. It would be a four-month project.

Skeptics assumed he drew the assignment because *Varnum* was sure to be explosive. Since he would not face a retention vote until 2016, he was considered least vulnerable. And because he had been appointed by a Republican governor, his voice might carry more weight with conservatives. The theory was news to Cady, who actually earned his place on the hot seat by winning a raffle. Or, some said at the time, by losing it.

In fact, the assignment had been made weeks earlier when Ternus and her administrative assistant, Tamara Barrett, had arranged a double drawing to make it as fair as possible. Slips of paper numbered one through seven were placed in a black cloth bag. The first drawing would determine the order in which the justices pulled the names of seven cases. The order was based on seniority—Ternus, Cady, Michael Streit, David Wiggins, Daryl Hecht, Brent Appel, and David Baker. All cases are important, of course. Isn't that what you're supposed to say? Yet only one had the potential to rip the court and the state in two, changing both forever. And each member of the court knew which case that was.

The room fell silent as Ternus drew first. Cady, next in seniority, reached in and grasped slip number three. On it went, until each justice had pulled a number. Then came the drawing with the names of the cases. Ternus walked around the conference table to each justice, who then drew out a case.

When it was Cady's turn, he reached in, looked down, and—there it was. Ternus remembers hearing him say, *"Varnum v. Brien."* At first, not having paid much attention to the names, he didn't make the connection. As the others scanned their colleague's face for clues, the light came on.

"He got it," Streit said with a laugh.[9]

Ternus, standing over his shoulder, concurred. "Yes," she said, "that's the case."

But where would he go with it?

The answer was obvious: wherever the research led him. After months of reading and note taking and finally absorbing a morning of oral arguments, it was up to Cady to provide a brief analysis and explain to his peers how they should decide *Varnum v. Brien*. The room fell quiet—the mood was somber and serious. Since the double drawing, the justices had barely mentioned the case to one another, much less discussed its merits. How would Iowa's high court respond to the lower court decision? They were about to find out.

Now, starting with Cady, each member of the court disclosed for the first time his or her viewpoint on one of the most contentious issues of the day.

"We should affirm," he said softly, citing the Iowa Constitution's equal protection guarantee, which, in his mind, clearly prohibited limiting civil marriage to a man and a woman. The justice said it was true that any of the three methods of constitutional analysis—rational basis, heightened scrutiny, or strict scrutiny—could be used to uphold Judge Hanson's decision. The county urged the court to use a rational basis analysis for its decision, but Cady thought the county's justifications for maintaining the restriction simply weren't reasonable. If the county couldn't win on rational basis, the law couldn't survive the higher standards of scrutiny.

Those standards required the county to show how the law either fulfills a compelling state interest in the least restrictive way possible or furthers a government interest. Because the case centered on a question related to the group's sexual orientation, Cady considered the plaintiffs to be members of a "quasi-suspect class" and believed heightened scrutiny to be the most appropriate standard of review.

Next, each justice was given the chance to respond. First up was Hecht, who agreed with Cady's assessment. Then came the rest of the dominoes—Streit, Baker, Wiggins, Ternus, Appel. All concurred on the equal protection analysis. Just as Cady had hoped, the plaintiffs' argument would be unanimously upheld as long as he could write an opinion that held everyone together.

This decision, he thought, was too controversial, too volatile for anything less. When it came to *Varnum*, he strongly believed the court should speak in one voice. In writing the decision, he was convinced there was no room for even a concurring opinion—an opinion in agreement with the court's conclusion but not its reasoning.

As one justice after another weighed in, Streit could almost feel a sigh of relief spreading through the room. When it was over, the court members pushed back from the table and silently let the moment sink in. They all knew immediately something unusual had happened—the first unanimous decision by a court declaring unconstitutional a law prohibiting same-sex marriage. Massachusetts's high court had been 4–3 in 2003; so had Connecticut's and California's high courts in 2008. California voters had overturned the decision with Proposition 8, which meant Iowa would be just the third state in the union and the first in America's heartland permitting same-sex couples to marry.

Since the Massachusetts decision, national polls indicated a gradual, but slight increase among those supporting marriage equality. But they still showed only about 40 percent of the nation supporting it. The justices, however, knew the polls didn't matter much. Neither did the backlash they knew loomed ahead. Chief Justice Ternus had made it clear from the beginning of her tenure that what mattered was the law and reaching the right conclusion regardless of political outcome.

On December 8, 2008, the justices knew they had reached a decision destined to pit angry Iowans against one another and the court. Republican attempts to amend Iowa's constitution restricting marriage to a man and a woman had failed in the legislature in 2004 because the Democrats who controlled the Iowa Senate would have nothing to do with it. Elsewhere, however, political opposition to marriage equality was usually a winning issue. Almost all Republicans running for president in 2008 had announced their opposition to same-sex marriage during the Iowa presidential caucus campaigns. So did the eventual president, Democrat

Barack Obama. A *Des Moines Register* Iowa poll taken just weeks before the oral arguments had found only 28 percent of Iowans favoring same-sex marriage and 30 percent backing the establishment of civil unions.

But that couldn't be helped—the law was the law.

"We knew this was right," Michael Streit would say later. "It was so obvious."

But what's obvious at first blush isn't always so obvious upon further review. Cady, as the designated author of *Varnum*, understood that. His assignment would begin the same as always—legal research on top of legal research on top of even more legal research. While the court initially voted in favor of the *Varnum* plaintiffs, Cady knew that could change. Most of the court members had the experience of advocating a particular decision at the initial conference only to reverse it during the researching and writing process. There were even times when the majority-opinion assignment was moved to another justice simply because a turn in the research led the initially assigned justice to a different conclusion.

Cady and his law clerk, Ben Parrott, would spend the rest of December and January reviewing not only the briefs submitted by Polk County and the plaintiffs but also the twenty-six amicus (friend of the court) briefs provided by various advocacy groups and legal scholars. Both Johnson and Kuhle had acknowledged in oral arguments the mountain of legal literature—the district court records and the amicus briefs—the case had dumped in the court's lap. "This court right now has before it the most complete and best record it could ever have to decide this kind of a case," Johnson said. "National advocacy groups follow these cases around. They offer assistance and help if you want it or not."[10]

But Cady, with Parrott's assistance, would also broaden his review beyond what had been filed. Unlike cases involving personal injury, criminal behavior, child custody, or the like, judicial decision making on a constitutional issue isn't based solely on how or when something occurred. Rather, the court considers so-called legislative or constitutional facts, found in social science, physical science, economics, politics, or society in general. No formal rules govern the submission of legislative facts, which the justices themselves and their clerks often find through independent research. This situation meant that Cady and Parrott had to locate legal reviews that discussed how courts should analyze claims of equal protection and due process, then read them in memo form. If possible, they would review every decision related to same-sex marriage.

Work on the *Varnum* case had actually started about six weeks before oral arguments—the day Cady drew the writing assignment. All justices, with the assistance of their clerks, prepare themselves for oral arguments by doing legal research prior to the hearing. After the drawing, Cady had walked to his clerk's office. Parrott, a twenty-seven-year-old Marshall-town, Iowa, native and, like his boss, a Drake Law School graduate, had been working for the court's senior justice for almost a year. "I had read some of Justice Cady's opinions," Parrott said, "particularly his dissenting opinions, and I liked his view on the law, and, of course, I heard what a good boss he was."[11]

As Cady walked into the office, Parrott could tell immediately something serious was up. The clerks all knew the records from the district court case had arrived—a sign the court was about to select the justice responsible for the case. Cady was direct. "We got *Varnum*," he said. "Let's go to work."

Parrott also learned that Chief Justice Ternus had decided to ease their workload. She removed Cady from all other cases until the *Varnum* opinion was completed to every court member's satisfaction. Parrott knew two other things. Though he was only twenty-seven years old, this could turn out to be the biggest challenge he would face in his legal career. And, unfortunately, he couldn't tell anyone what he was doing, not even his wife. As Cady's clerk, Parrott had an attorney-client relationship with his boss. The two would work closely together, but only they and the other six justices would know about their research until decision day.

In law school, ironically, Parrott had received his worst grade in a family law course. Much of that had to do with one poor answer on the final exam. The question asked for an analysis of whether the U.S. Constitution's full faith and credit clause required states to respect another state's decision to permit a same-sex couple to marry. "I just BS'd my way through it," Parrott remembered later. "Same-sex marriage wasn't something I had thought a lot about or spent the bulk of my time studying. And that continued to be true until the day that case arrived on my desk."

The young lawyer's e-mail to Cady had a simple message: "You need to read this." Attached was a *University of California Law Review* article written in 1949 by Professors Joseph Tussman and Jacobus tenBroek, titled "The Equal Protection of the Laws." Parrott discovered the review article as part of his research more than two months after oral argument. The title intrigued him. He and his boss were struggling with an important and complex issue further muddled by the simple phrase, "similarly situated."

Polk County's attorneys as well as several amicus briefs filed by same-sex marriage opponents challenged the plaintiffs' case by denying that gays and lesbians were subjected to discriminatory treatment. How so? Simple, wrote the lawyers for the Catholic fraternal society the Knights of Columbus. "Both men and women may marry someone of the opposite sex, neither may marry someone of the same sex."[12] Translation: equal protection requires only people who are similarly situated to be treated the same, and Iowa's marriage law did, in fact, treat men and women the same. The claim, if upheld, had a serious consequence. Should the plaintiffs be unable to prove that homosexuals wishing to marry were "similarly situated" to heterosexuals wishing to marry, the equal protection guarantee of the Iowa Constitution could not be extended to protect homosexuals wanting to marry. In other words, the court would probably be required to dismiss the lawsuit on grounds that gays and lesbians had no legal standing to challenge the law.

The *Varnum* attorneys asked the court to accept the lower court's decision for a higher level of scrutiny because the law improperly targeted a group of individuals subjected historically to discrimination. As a "suspect class," the six plaintiff couples deserved to have the court examine whether the law was discriminatory under either heightened or strict scrutiny.

For Cady, this presented a vexing problem. How were the couples not permitted to marry in Iowa *similarly situated* to those who were permitted? He knew the answer, but how could he translate the sometimes obtuse jargon of the court into plain English? "I can remember staying up at night," he would say later, "trying and trying to make sure that it was totally understood."

Those difficulties were illuminated when Cady, while serving as an adjunct professor at the Fort Dodge campus of Buena Vista University, gave an exam to his students. After handing out the examination, Cady went to a nearby room where he continued to read and scribble notes on his legal analysis of *Varnum*. "I'm reading, trying to figure out the case," Cady said, "when suddenly the building janitor comes into the room. I look at a clock, and it's midnight. The kids are all long gone, and the janitor is wondering if I am going to be leaving any time soon."

The next morning the chief justice made another discovery. He'd left his notes in the classroom. Returning to campus, he found both the janitor and his notes.

"I didn't look at any of them," the janitor said.

"I didn't think you knew who I was," Cady responded.

Soon after that long evening Cady spent wrestling with concepts, his clerk's "Equal Protection of the Laws" discovery provided him not only with a seminal analysis of the question bedeviling him but also with a structure to analyze whether the legislature's 1998 enactment of DOMA was justified.

The forty-page article had been written after the adjudication of several cases stemming from the federal government's internment of U.S. citizens of Japanese descent during World War II but before the 1954 *Brown v. Board of Education* desegregation case. In it, the authors defined the essential question to be answered when analyzing whether laws that discriminate—say, by singling out people of Japanese or African ancestry—are justified under the Fourteenth Amendment of the U.S. Constitution, which forbids state governments from passing laws not applied equally to all persons. Wrote Tussman and tenBroek: "It is impossible to pass judgment on the reasonableness of a classification without taking into consideration, or identifying, the purpose of the law."[13]

Just what was the Iowa legislature's purpose in amending Chapter 595 to restrict marriage to a man and a woman? Was it simply to keep gays and lesbians from marrying for religious or political purposes? If that were the case, the law would not withstand constitutional scrutiny. Or was there a deeper governmental, nonreligious purpose that could justify it and be proved? The heart of equal protection, Cady thought, is the state's justification for discriminating. So the analysis first must determine if this law discriminates. And if it does, what's the government justification for the discrimination? And how stringently should the court expect the government to justify its actions?

In the justice's mind, the state's two strongest arguments were (1) that homosexuals were not similarly situated to heterosexuals when it came to marriage, and (2) that heterosexual marriage had to be protected to promote the best environment for raising children. Cady concluded that both positions, particularly in light of the Tussman and tenBroek analysis, fell short. Here's why. The proposition that men and women, as a class, were treated equally under the statute amounted to a circular argument. As Tussman and tenBroek wrote,

> "Similarly situated" cannot mean simply "similar in the possession of the classifying trait." All members of any class are similarly situated in this respect and consequently, any classification whatsoever would be reasonable by this test.[14]

Instead, a reasonable classification is one that "includes all persons who are similarly situated with respect to the purpose of the law."[15]

Under that analysis, Cady decided, the only difference between heterosexuals and homosexuals when it comes to the marriage statute was the person they chose to marry—their sexual orientation. All committed couples, both straight and gay, want loving relationships; often want to raise children, if they can; and finally, want a framework of stability and authority to makes decisions about their lives together. They're "similarly situated."

If this is only about sexual orientation, Cady thought, then no substantive legal difference exists between the groups when applied to the civil marriage statute. While most men and women are attracted to the opposite sex, other men and women are attracted to individuals of their own sex. But that difference, Cady concluded, can't be used to undercut their legitimate desire to take advantage of the purposes and benefits of Iowa's civil marriage laws.

With the threshold question answered, the next step was to analyze the county's argument that limiting marriage to heterosexuals accomplished several legitimate government purposes. The county argued five: maintaining traditional marriage, promoting an optimal environment to raise children, promoting procreation, promoting stability in opposite-sex relationships, and conserving state resources by keeping gays and lesbians from receiving the many tax advantages provided to married couples by Iowa law.

Of all the justifications, Cady initially thought the most persuasive might be the county's claim that the statute promoted the best possible environment to raise children. "I always thought the government could justify it best," he recounted, "by saying that it's better for children to grow up in an environment with a mom and a dad because they both offer a perspective that's helpful." But social science research on homosexual families and child rearing brought Cady to the opposite view. He found the briefs citing scientific studies of gay and lesbian families and their children particularly persuasive. According to a group of family law attorneys, medical and child-welfare organizations have uniformly adopted policies recognizing that sexual orientation is not relevant to parental ability. Such organizations urge that children of same-sex parents be provided with the same legal security and protections as other children.

Among the organizations are the American Psychological Association, the American Academy of Pediatrics, the American Psychiatric Association, the American Academy of Child and Adolescent Psychiatry, the American Psychoanalytic Association, the Child Welfare League of America, and the National Association of Social Workers. In a separate brief, the American Psychological Association put it bluntly:

> There is no scientific basis for concluding that gay and lesbian parents are any less fit or capable than heterosexual parents, or that their children are any less psychologically healthy and well-adjusted.[16]

The association's brief said empirical research over the past two decades has failed to provide any meaningful differences in the parenting ability of lesbian and gay parents compared with homosexual parents.

> Scientific research that has directly compared outcomes for children with gay and lesbian parents with outcomes for children with heterosexual parents has been remarkably consistent in showing les-

bian and gay parents are every bit as fit and capable as heterosexual parents, and their children are as psychologically healthy and well-adjusted as children reared by heterosexual parents.[17]

Cady realized that one of the county's pivotal arguments — prohibiting same-sex couples from marriage would result in children being reared in the best possible environment — merited close examination. The test used is called "under-inclusion and over-inclusion." Lawyers call it "the fit." The fit goes this way, according to Tussman and tenBroek: a statute that targets or classifies a group whose rights the government restricts must include everyone who could be subjected to the purpose of the law. For example, if the state argues that allowing same-sex couples to marry would create an atmosphere less optimal, if not harmful, for raising children, then why aren't other people who might be less than great parents included in the marriage ban? Shouldn't the statute prohibit pedophiles or other sex abusers from marrying? Or violent felons convicted of murdering family members? Or men and women known to be child abusers or involved in domestic abuse? Or even parents convicted of drunken driving?

If only homosexuals are to be banned while others who could harm children aren't, the statute is determined to be "under-inclusive" and likely unable to achieve the stated goal of the discriminatory law. At the same time, why would the state want to deny marriage to homosexuals who had no intention of starting a family? If the ban is designed to protect children, those gays and lesbians are being denied marriage by "over-inclusion."

The remaining arguments by the county were even less persuasive under the same test, Cady reasoned. If the statute was meant to promote procreation, why were infertile or sterile couples permitted to marry? If the goal is preserving state resources, why target only an estimated fifty-eight hundred couples in a state of about three million? Why not deny those benefits to African Americans, illegitimate children, or even red-haired individuals?

Cady now felt more than comfortable with his conclusions. His initial impression months earlier when the justices voted to affirm had been correct. Now came the hard part. He and Parrott now faced the task of writing an opinion — a controversial opinion — in a way that could be understood on the streets of Fort Dodge. Ultimately, the opinion's structure, tone, analysis, and writing style were all Cady. But once it was written and rewritten dozens of times, he offered it to the rest of the court to consume and digest. When it came to making changes, some of the justices had bigger appetites than others, but all knew their colleague's draft opinion had hit the target.

Again and again, Michael Streit asked, "Who are we writing this for?" The question stuck with the entire court as the members went word by word, line by line, through the text. Cady, one of the court's clearest writers, had asked himself the same question from the beginning.

"As we did this," Streit wrote later, "we were pulled back — or dragged back — from our instinct to write legal." Streit himself wrote with a flourish. Like a flashy newspaper writer, he was fond of opening his opinions with a line or phrase intended to hook the reader. He wasn't writing for his colleagues or for the approval of law professors.

Streit was the one who kept asking, "Who is the audience?" Though he wanted the opinion to speak to people without law degrees, it wouldn't be easy.

Usually, a justice (with the assistance of a law clerk) will write an opinion, circulate it to the other members, and revise as needed. But this ruling would be different. The court members knew this was an opinion to be written so precisely that no sentence could be misconstrued or taken out of context by critics who were bound to try to spin the opinion into something it wasn't.

Cady and his clerk pounded out seemingly countless versions of the ruling before sharing it with their colleagues and even more versions when the rest of them began to participate. Then everyone met, four times in all, to haggle over the words and phrases appearing on an overhead projector. The conversations were confidential and spirited, but the general view was this: the opinion could not say too much or too little.

Their changes often resulted in the elimination or substitution of a word or phrase in addition to the normal editing. "There were times I drove home just bristling," Cady acknowledged. "I thought the opinion was better ten drafts before the final, but that was the collective process."

Streit had the same concerns. With all the writing-by-committee tinkering, were they sucking the life out of the decision? The scholarly after-the-fact consensus is no. "If anything is remarkable about the form of the opinion itself," wrote Todd E. Pettys of the University of Iowa law school, "it is the great patience and clarity with which the author explained its reasoning." Cady, he said, "seemed to go out of his way to walk through the analysis in a manner that an educated lay reader could easily understand."[18]

While this appeared to be the clear consensus in academia, not every law professor agreed. Robert Nagel, a constitutional law expert at the University of Colorado, told the *New York Times* the ruling was an example of "institutional hubris—this assumption that a judicial opinion can magically transform public attitudes or perhaps make them irrelevant." He added dismissively that the language in the ruling contained "clunky vocabulary" and a "painfully labored analysis."[19]

The decision to use a more informal than legal voice came after Parrott had submitted a first draft. As he read that draft, Cady felt the opinion's voice should have a ring of familiarity and unanimity. As the judge recounted,

> Once I got a grasp of the law and was a hundred percent convinced of the outcome of the opinion, my whole focus was to explain it the best way I could. I wanted to give the people who wanted to read it the same understanding I had achieved in writing it.

As a result, he inserted the word "we" wherever he could in place of "the court." He used the personal pronouns "we" or "our" nearly two hundred times. He did so for a reason, which he later explained,

> It was to convey the understanding that this is all of ours. This is what it is all about. Our process. What we do as a society. It's not the courts. It's our constitution at work. What we are all about.

With Parrott's help, the justice addressed the most likely criticisms and counterarguments. No, the court did not exceed its authority or "legislate from the bench." Cady reviewed the court's powers and duties under the Iowa Constitution. Citing both case law and the debates of the Iowa Constitutional Convention of 1857, he made clear the supreme court's duty as arbiter and protector of the state constitution: "A statute inconsistent with the Iowa Constitution must be declared void, even though it may be supported by strong and deep-seated traditional beliefs and popular opinion."[20]

Then he addressed the likely outrage from mainstream religious communities.

Starting at the district court level, attorneys on both sides had avoided religious arguments. Cady could easily have done the same but decided late in the process to take them on. The decision helped make *Varnum v. Brien* a major turning point.

"It wasn't argued or suggested by anyone," Cady said. "I just realized, once I put the case all together, it was missing the obvious." Parrott was the first to see the revisions. Cady walked into his office one morning and asked him to read a new section. "As I read it," the clerk said, "it was quite clear to me it had to be said. It was genius."

Cady's goal was twofold—to acknowledge the criticism sure to come from the state's religious communities and to assure them they would be protected by the Iowa Constitution's freedom-of-religion guarantee. They would not have to allow same-sex couples to marry in their homes of worship, and clergy could not be required to officiate at such unions. What's more, he noted, a number of denominations not only supported the right of gays and lesbians to marry but also would solemnize their vows. In short, affirming the right of same-sex couples to marry civilly was not a blow against religion. "In the final analysis," Cady wrote,

> we give respect to the views of all Iowans on the issue of same-sex marriage—religious or otherwise—by giving respect to our constitutional principles. These principles require that the state recognize both opposite-sex and same-sex civil marriage. Religious doctrine and views contrary to this principle of law are unaffected, and people can continue to associate with the religion that best reflects their views.[21]

||||||||||||||||||||||||||||||||||||||||||||||||||||||||||||||||||||||||||||||||||||||||

CHAPTER NINE

Decision Day . . . and Beyond

S omething was up. Becky Cady had known that for months but didn't
dare ask her husband about his business.[1] In their almost thirty
years together, she had watched Mark Cady advance from assistant district attorney in 1979 to district court judge to chief judge of the
court of appeals and finally, in 1998, to Iowa Supreme Court justice. Early
in their relationship she had come to understand that Mark's work was
rarely open to discussion. But she also had learned to recognize the signs
when anything big was about to happen. When Mark spent hours in his
home office late into the night, Becky knew she would soon be hearing
about it in the media.

Downtown Des Moines is a ninety-minute drive from the Cady home
in Fort Dodge, an old railroad town almost a hundred miles to the northwest. In the ice and snow of winter, the roads can be difficult to navigate.
By Friday, April 3, 2009, winter still couldn't decide whether to stay or go,
which was typical this time of year in Iowa. But for Mark Cady, this was no
typical day. Though he hadn't mentioned the *Varnum* case to a soul outside
the courthouse, Becky Cady had long suspected her husband was writing
the opinion. He often worked long hours, but not usually for four months
straight. Finally, the night before the ruling's release, he told Becky the
decision would be controversial and he was the author. Without disclos-
ing the result, he told her to prepare for a harsh public response. Becky
awaited the opinion and braced for the backlash.

Cady left home even earlier than usual that morning. Arriving in Des
Moines, he called Becky and their two grown-up children, Kelsi and

Spencer. The decision would be out at approximately 8:30 A.M. "You might want to stay off the computer for a while," he said. "We have a very controversial decision coming out. The response could get nasty."

Emotions were strong when the subject was same-sex marriage, and polls showed that only a small minority of Iowans supported it, with not many more endorsing civil unions. Political science professor David Redlawsk acknowledged that Iowans as a whole weren't ready to embrace gay marriage but were "clearly ready to legally acknowledge same-sex relationships" of some kind.[2] While only 28 percent supported same-sex marriage, 58 percent were ready to accept either civil unions or same-sex marriage. Some kind of legal commitment, yes—but marriage? That was still the hot-button word.

The night before, after making what he thought were the final changes in the *Varnum* text and setting out for home, Cady had caught a glimpse of what was to come. When the justice turned on the radio, Steve Deace, a popular ultraconservative talk-show host, was already bemoaning the decision to come. He knew its release was imminent because, following custom, the court had issued a media advisory Thursday morning: the opinion would be posted on the Iowa Judicial Branch website by 8:30 A.M. Friday.

Let the conjecture begin. Deace and his guests were flatly predicting that the supreme court, with five of the seven members having been selected by Democratic governors, would declare the marriage law unconstitutional. But the talk-show host went further, saying conservatives could take some solace in the fact that the two Republican appointees, Ternus and Cady, would be dissenting. When Cady heard that, he thought, "Well, that's interesting. If he only knew."

Social and religious conservatives were already plotting worst-case strategies, discussing the possibility of the legislature passing a constitutional amendment defining marriage strictly as a relationship between one man and one woman. It would be a tough sell. It had failed in 2004, and the Democrats who still controlled the senate would never allow such a proposal to be debated, much less make it to the ballot.

During the week, there had been conjecture about the timing of the decision. The legislators would be adjourning for the summer in a few days. Would it make sense to wait for them to leave town, thereby avoiding some of the heat? Not to Marsha Ternus. The chief justice was adamant. Politics had nothing to do with this decision or this court, she said. They weren't about to start playing political games now. The opinion goes out when it's ready, and it will be ready for public consumption Friday morning.

As Cady listened to the radio on his Thursday night drive home, Dennis Johnson and his wife, Ann Marie, were in their car heading to Colorado. Checking his voice mail, Johnson found a message from Camilla Taylor giving him a heads-up. Good news, he thought, but he and Ann Marie were almost in Vail; too late to turn back now. Johnson's job was done, anyway. No real need to be there for the postgame.

"Let's go skiing," he said.

But the more he thought about it, the more he realized he had to be there. When Ann Marie agreed, he called Taylor to say he was on his way. The legal architect of the case then slipped him some interesting news. "For your information, the Supreme Court ordered security for themselves and their families. And I don't think they're afraid of *us*."

Johnson's secretary booked him a flight from Denver to Des Moines. He arrived that night and met with the other lawyers Friday morning. When Johnson said he thought it would be unanimous, Lambda's Upton agreed, but Taylor still wasn't ready to celebrate.

The plaintiffs, staying at the nearby Hotel Fort Des Moines, weren't sure what to think. Before the BarbouRoske family left Iowa City for Des Moines on Thursday, they had received a call from Breeanna's school. Their youngest daughter had taken a spill on the playground and had come away with a knot on her head the size of a goose egg. While patching her up, Dawn wondered half in jest how Bre's lump would play on the evening news and in the morning papers. Jen was working late at the hospital, which meant it was up to Dawn to get the girls ready for the two-hour trip west. She also had to prepare them for what might happen and what others might say. People can be cruel, she said. You might hear this or that or something worse. Just don't take it to heart. Some folks are just plain mean.

But most aren't. In all, the Iowa City community was nurturing and supportive. The teachers and administrators watched out for the kids. The BarbouRoskes could feel the compassion and concern. In casual conversation one day at the hospital, a coworker looked at Jen and said, "Before I met you, I was against gay marriage. I thought it was ridiculous. Why would we ever allow something like that? But after working side by side with you for all those hours, I support you one hundred percent because this is just a real-people kind of issue."

With Jen at work, Dawn scurried around the house, trying to get everything organized and packed. Bre, meanwhile, was upstairs plastering monster tattoo stickers all over her face. The good news was that it momentarily took the focus off the bump on her head. While Dawn was busy washing Bre, McKinley, the eleven-year-old coplaintiff, was out of sorts because the tattoos belonged to her. Eventually, they got it resolved, hopped in the car, and headed west for the big announcement the next morning. When Jen met up with them at the hotel after her night shift, she took a quick peek at the younger child's sleeping face. At least one thing was certain about the day ahead. Whatever happens, this well-scrubbed little girl would have the rosiest cheeks in Des Moines.

As the BarbouRoske women were preparing for the trip to Des Moines, Bob Vander Plaats, a well-known Christian conservative, was at home in northwest Iowa watching the youngest of his four sons compete in a basketball game.[3] Vander Plaats hadn't planned on becoming the state's foremost cultural warrior. Growing up as one of eight kids in a middle-class family in Sheldon, Iowa (population just under five thousand), he seemed destined to be a top teacher and successful coach. But before he was thirty, teaching and coaching led to a job as principal of a new high school and later of Sheldon High School. After that, Vander Plaats became executive director and then "president of strategic vision" for a social service agency named Opportunities Unlimited that helps rehabilitate people with physical disabilities and brain injuries. It seemed like a good fit. His third son, Lucas, was born with a severe brain disorder.

Vander Plaats also opened a consulting company, MVP Leadership, and became a self-described "turnaround CEO." The turnaround at Opportunites Unlimited came full circle when fund-raising slipped and, as reported in the *Sioux City Journal*, Vander Plaats either resigned or was forced out as CEO. Though he left the organization, he didn't disappear from view. It didn't take Vander Plaats long to pop up as president and CEO of the new FAMiLY Leader (lowercase *i* to show that God comes first), a Des Moines–area conservative Christian advocacy group. FAMiLY Leader became the parent organization of three other Christian conservative groups: Iowa Family Policy Center, Marriage Matters, and Iowa Family PAC. By April of 2009, Vander Plaats had immersed himself in the battle against marriage equality. On April 2, when he learned the *Varnum* opinion would be released the next morning, Vander Plaats called Chuck Hurley, president of the Iowa Family Policy Center, and asked what he thought.

"I think you need to be down here," Hurley said. Indeed, a man in Vander Plaats's position, with his unwavering belief in the sanctity of traditional marriage, had to be in Des Moines on this historic day. Besides, Vander Plaats was running for governor again. Only a few months before, the former schoolteacher/principal/basketball coach/business consultant from Sioux City had announced the formation of Team Vander Plaats 2010, a committee to kick off his third gubernatorial campaign.

In 2002, Vander Plaats had finished a close third in the Republican primary before Democrat Tom Vilsack defeated Doug Gross in the general election. Four years later, he gave it another try before joining the ticket of Iowa congressman Jim Nussle as lieutenant governor. Nussle suffered a lopsided loss to Democrat Chet Culver. But that wasn't the last Iowa's electorate would hear of Vander Plaats. In 2008, he would help guide conservative Christian Mike Huckabee to an upset victory in the state's presidential caucuses.

Waging a high-profile war against same-sex marriage could only increase Vander Plaats's appeal with the kind of social conservatives gathered outside the Iowa Judicial Branch Building on April 3. Leading the group on this day was Hurley, the state's most visible opponent of same-sex marriage at the time. Hurley had been central to the backlash against district court judge Jeffrey Neary's 2004 dissolution of Kimberly Brown and Jennifer Perez's civil union. As 8 A.M. approached, he told the group that, regardless of the outcome, they should "respond with love, concern, and respect." They formed a semicircle and lowered their heads in prayer.

The Reverend Keith Ratliff, Sr., of the Maple Street Missionary Baptist Church in Des Moines assured God that whatever the supreme court decided to do, the opponents of same-sex marriage would "stand by the word" of a power higher than Iowa's supreme court. Danny Carroll, another vocal foe, who served four terms in the Iowa House before losing his seat in 2006 and becoming a lobbyist for the Iowa Family Policy Center, asked God to free gays and lesbians from "their homosexual lifestyle."

Nearby, another small crowd showed its support for the gay and lesbian plaintiffs. Amid that group was Matt McCoy. Eleven years before, the legislator from Des Moines had voted (against his beliefs) in defense of traditional marriage. Since then, he had successfully battled alcoholism, acknowledged he was gay, and, in 2004, helped block the effort to insert a ban on same-sex unions in the state constitution. As McCoy and his friends waited anxiously for the news, they kept checking the court website with their smart phones. But due to the traffic volume — 1.5 million visitors before 11 A.M. — the overwhelmed website server crashed.

As it turned out, the author of the opinion might have played a small role in the delay. While proofreading the decision in bed the night before, Mark Cady found two minor punctuation changes he wanted to make — one involving a period, the other a semicolon. He decided to deal with it the next morning at work. Unknown to Cady, another law clerk had found the same punctuation errors the night before. Arriving at the Iowa Judicial Branch Building at 7:30 A.M., with the sun shining through the early morning chill, the justice drove past the crowds gathering near the steps on his way to a secured parking area. After taking the elevator to his fourth-floor office, he received permission to go back into the text and make the changes. When Cady was finished tinkering, administrators tried unsuccessfully to post the decision.

At the Hotel Fort Des Moines, the plaintiffs gathered in a private waiting room with orders to stay off their cell phones. According to Taylor's plan, they would hear the news directly from her at a 9:15 news conference. The couples had agreed to let the media record their reactions. Win or lose, it was important to let the public see the impact the decision had on the lives of these people and their families. The media would witness the emotion, interview the plaintiffs, and understand exactly how much this decision meant to them.

An accomplished trial lawyer like Dennis Johnson knew the power of a compelling story. Winning and losing isn't about who can argue the law as much as who best answers the question, "Why should I care?" The world was about to find out.

While the plaintiffs waited to be called into the news conference, their lawyers gathered in Sharon Malheiro's office at the Davis Brown Law firm and tried to pull up the opinion on a computer. Somehow they'd figured out how to bypass the court website and link directly to the text, but it was still slow coming up. As a backup, just in case, a runner was dispatched to the judicial building to retrieve a hard copy.

When the lawyers weren't hitting "refresh" on the computer, they were trying to tally votes. When someone asked Johnson which justices they could count on, he said he wouldn't rule out any of them.

Around 8:40, the opinion popped onto the computer screen. Around the same time, raucous cheering erupted from the entrance of the Judicial Building, where dozens of hard copies were circulating. Standing outside, Vander Plaats wasn't immediately sure who was cheering for whom, but he would soon find out.

"I don't remember ever having a feeling like that before or since," Vander Plaats would say later. "I wasn't angry, and obviously I wasn't happy. My emotions were just kind of void. I don't remember being moved either way, other than knowing this was going to present a huge issue, as a society and a culture, in the gubernatorial campaign."

Others in his group were bitterly disappointed. "It's a perversion," Ratliff said of same-sex marriage, "and it opens the door to more perversions."[4]

In the law offices a mile and a half away, Taylor and Upton quickly scanned the decision. When Taylor saw that Cady had written the majority opinion, she reflexively blurted, "Oh, no!" and asked which justices decided for the plaintiffs. "Who do we have?" she asked. "Who do we have?"

Taylor's assistant scrolled hurriedly to the bottom of the opinion to find the answer: every one. "Affirmed. All justices concur." Johnson was right. Reflexive yelps of approval caromed off the law firm walls.

In that same office in downtown Des Moines, Malheiro, who had done so much to make decision day possible, read the word "affirmed," called her partner, and proposed marriage. After talking about it for twenty years, Malheiro and Sue Ackerman finally were able to do something about it.

The celebration was short and sweet; the job wasn't finished. The lawyers now had to soak in as much of the opinion as possible before joining the plaintiffs and the media. While Taylor and Upton were speed-reading, Johnson sat back and stared out the window. "We won!" he thought to himself. "We won!" Going back over the opinion in his mind, he thought of Cady expressing his concerns about religious freedom, acknowledging the mostly faith-based composition of the opposition, and making sure everyone knew the court wasn't stepping on anyone's religious rights or beliefs. He thought back to Ternus in oral arguments—how she told him not to worry about running out of time and the way she recognized the significance of the moment and the importance of hearing him out.

In the early days of the suit, when Johnson went around talking to editorial boards, newspapers all over the state were less than receptive. But by the time of the oral arguments, most of those same media outlets had come out staunchly in favor of marriage equality.

On a more personal level, Johnson thought about the change he'd seen in his father, a World War II veteran. At first, the elder Johnson hadn't been thrilled about his lawyer son taking the case. He didn't understand. The son didn't understand at first, either. As his thinking shifted, Dennis Johnson understood what his father and other marriage equality skeptics were going through. "He learned," Johnson would say later. "I saw more and more people around me become educated. And I kept thinking if people were anything like I was, it wasn't that they wanted to hurt gay people. They were just unaware of what their lives were like. If they think about it and get to know the people involved, they'll come around quickly."

The momentum was palpable as the plaintiffs were ushered into the media-filled hotel conference room. By that time, they might have been the only adults in the state who *didn't* know how the court had ruled. At first, David Twombley wasn't sure what to think. When he walked into the room, he immediately recognized two dear friends, former student Betty Brim-Hunter and her husband, state representative Bruce Hunter. Initially, noticing the tears in Betty's eyes, Twombley thought the worst.

Then Taylor stepped to the podium with the happy news. "Iowa took its place in the vanguard of the civil rights struggle, and we couldn't be more proud to be part of this."[5]

Thousands of miles from the coastal cultural centers, Iowa had joined Massachusetts and Connecticut to become the third state to allow same-sex marriage. While the couples hugged and kissed, McKinley Barbou-Roske lifted her arms in jubilation. The image of McKinley's reaction appeared in media reports all over the country. She wasn't just a kid anymore. She was a newsmaker telling the *New York Times*, "What I did wasn't just for my family. It was for tons of families."

Earlier, when the plaintiffs were invited to share their thoughts with the media, she stepped right up to the microphone and said, "Hi, I'm McKinley, and I'm really, really happy. I feel that my family has always had this right, and today it is true. No longer shall we be just people who aren't allowed to be married. We are able to get married."[6]

The Varnums had been the first couple to speak. Kate went first. "I'd like to introduce you to my fiancée, Trish Varnum. I never thought I'd be able to say that."

Jason Morgan, who had been with Chuck Swaggerty for twelve years, choked back tears and said, "We've been together in sickness and health, through the death of his mother, through the adoption of our children, through four long years of this legal battle. And if being together through all of that isn't love and commitment or isn't family or isn't marriage, then I don't know what is."[7]

Around the state, same-sex couples were celebrating. In Iowa City, Janelle Rettig and Robin Butler had returned to the scene of their 2004 protest. On that day, couples waited in line at the Johnson County Building for an entire afternoon just for the chance to be refused a marriage license. Now, gathered in a packed conference room anticipating the release of the supreme court's decision, they were kept waiting like everyone else. Losing patience with the court's balky website, Rettig asked state representative Mary Mascher to use her connections in Des Moines to get the decision. Just when it seemed as if nothing was working, Rettig recalled, Mary let out a victory scream.

Rettig joined Butler and Mascher in a tearful group hug. "There was nothing to say," Rettig remembered. "We had come such a long way."

Joining the plaintiffs for the interview session in Des Moines, Johnson called the occasion "a great day for civil rights in Iowa," adding, "We have all of you courageous plaintiffs to thank." Then he offered the final directive: "Go get married. Live happily ever. Live the American dream."[8]

Get married they did. On April 27, the day the law went into effect, the clerk of the Iowa Supreme Court sent the following memo to Timothy J. Brien and all the other county recorders across the state: The appeal is now concluded. Therefore, you are hereby directed to proceed in the manner required by law and consistent with the opinion of the court.[9]

Few same-sex couples were quicker to proceed than Swaggerty and Morgan, who immediately began calling judges in their county, asking to have the three-day waiting period waived. No luck. Then they looked north to Plymouth County, putting in a call, fittingly, to Judge Jeffrey Neary, who six years earlier had inadvertently put the marriage equality legal machinery into motion by signing a divorce decree between two women. Neary said he'd be happy to waive the waiting period, adding "You've waited long enough."

A few minutes after 8 A.M., Swaggerty and Morgan exchanged vows at the Plymouth County Courthouse in Le Mars. Before then, the media had been calling to ask about their plans, assuming they were getting married in downtown Sioux City. The couple had always been self-conscious about public displays of affection and felt uncomfortable about turning this private moment into a sideshow. They said they'd gladly agree to interviews in the days ahead. Somebody told them the media were going to be there anyway with their cameras and microphones. But few knew they were going to Le Mars. That included the minister from Le Mars, who traveled twenty-six miles to Sioux City to take part in a protest.

It turned out to be a good decision. The clerks and other employees in Le Mars were well acquainted with Morgan and Swaggerty. That's where they had completed their first two adoptions. When the office workers asked if they could watch the civil ceremony, the men said, "Why not?" They made sure to send a wedding photo to the *Sioux City Journal*.

Also among the first to apply for a license were Reva Evans and Ingrid Olson. With two-year-old Jamison by their side, they had returned to the Polk County Administration Building, the same place that had sent them home empty-handed in November of 2005.

Musser and Dreaming were wed during a low-key ceremony in their home in Decorah.

When the counties began passing out marriage licenses, the opposition showed up at some of the larger sites with petitions telling the recorders not to worry about heeding the supreme court's decision. In Des Moines, Chuck Hurley, head of the Iowa Family Policy Center, dropped off a pile of petitions at the recorder's office and told reporters the marriage ban was still on the books. Governor Chet Culver, no fan of same-sex marriage in the past, said, sorry, the county recorders do not ignore supreme court rulings. Hurley, the man who once said "homosexual acts are arguably more destructive and potentially more costly to society than smoking,"[10] tried to put a damper on the outcome by reminding everyone that a retention election loomed in 2010.

In typical Hurley fashion, he courteously passed out bottled water to the men and women standing in line — the same men and women he was trying to hold down. He had his reasons. "Our expression is that we love you as a person," Hurley once explained. "It would be the same message as if one of my friends, one of my coworkers was doing something that was contrary to right and good and common sense. I would urge them to reconsider."[11] The people standing in line were not there to reconsider. They were there to exercise their newly won right to marry the person they loved.

That summer at a local park, the BarbouRoskes recreated their commitment ceremony and ring exchange from almost twenty years before. Only this time, their vows carried the weight of the legal system. And this time, McKinley was there to play "Canon in D" on violin while Bre served as flower girl and ring bearer. As for Hoch and Twombley, they were legally wed that September at the First Christian Church in Des Moines. Three weeks after decision day, Trish and Kate Varnum went to the Linn County recorder's office and spent thirty-five dollars for a marriage license. They, too, opted for a September wedding. It was a time of mixed emotions. Trish's younger brother had died in 2008, two days before Kate's father passed away after suffering a brain injury. The anniversary they celebrate is the day of their earlier commitment ceremony. A few years later, the Varnums still say Trish's dad has been great. Kate, a stay-at-home mom after losing her job, says he still treats each of his children's spouses as if he were their own father. Better yet, Trish adds, he loves their adopted son, Alex, as much as any grandparent can love a grandchild.

But not everyone was able to follow Dennis Johnson's "happily ever after" instructions. Reality tells a different story. U.S. Census Bureau data show some 2.4 million divorces in 2012, the vast majority, of course, occurring in heterosexual marriages. Evans and Olson were married in June of 2009 but would ultimately become a Census Bureau casualty. Their divorce became final in February of 2012.

When the marital-equality bliss slowly ebbed over the next several days, a different sort of reality set in. The *Varnum* decision made countless people happy, but it also had the opposite effect; and the justices serving on the Iowa Supreme Court bore the brunt of the unhappiness. Each member of the court was affected. Ternus received death threats and instructed her children to watch for unfamiliar cars pulling into their driveway and not to answer the door.

Cady was confronted at the YMCA near his home. The day after the decision went out, he was lifting weights when a stranger approached. The stranger—bigger, stronger, younger, and in no mood for intellectual discourse—looked at Cady and said, "I'd like to tear your fucking head off. That was the goddamnedest, most fucked-up decision I've ever seen. How could you do that?" Sitting at a weight machine, feeling threatened, the justice rose and braced for a physical confrontation. A former Drake University wrestler, he knew how to defend himself. Still, it had been a while since someone physically tried to take him down, and he had no desire to revisit the experience. Cady told the stranger he understood why people might disagree. But those same people have to understand something, too. It's his job to make these decisions. The stranger spat out a few more expletives, stared at the object of his contempt for a long second or two, and then walked away.

A few days after the ruling, the court received an angry e-mail at the office: "I defended the likes of you—as an American soldier in World War II and Korea. I conclude I served the wrong side—Hitler treated queers the way that they should be treated—in gas chambers. You are bastards."[12] Like the other members of the court, Michael Streit was stunned by the emotion. "We cannot change such raw and intense feeling with nuanced discussion," he said. "But how *do* you change them?" The justice had no answer, but the experience did drive something else home. The gay community and their families face this kind of hostility every day.

The reaction wasn't completely negative. Some of the justices were even more surprised by the outpouring of gratitude and the strength of their emotion. Much of it was touching. The daughter of a college professor and her same-sex partner thought about naming their adopted baby girl Cady. "Even in church," Cady said, "while some people would stare you down, others would hold your hand and say thanks. Sometimes they'd say that's what you had to do, as if they were apologizing."

Ternus, however, eventually stopped going to church. When asked later if she had switched to a different place of worship, she replied, "No, I'm not too impressed with churches right now. I don't attend." Not that she had been shunned or treated badly by members of the congregation. "It was the idea of religious leaders dictating who should and shouldn't be endowed with certain civil rights." In her mind, those who believe in social justice and in strengthening families should be for same-sex marriage, not against.

Bishop Richard Pates of the Catholic Diocese of Des Moines clearly was not in the camp that equated social justice with same-sex marriage. In a statement, Pates said he "wholeheartedly joined" in "strong disagreement" with those who supported the *Varnum* decision and urged Iowans "to rise in support" of a constitutional amendment "to preserve civil marriage as it has been recognized . . . since the beginning of recorded history."[13]

Vander Plaats called for Chet Culver, Iowa's Democratic governor, to keep the ruling from going into effect. The governor, Vander Plaats insisted, could issue an executive order, putting the decision on hold until the legislature had a chance to deal with it. In a news conference four days before Iowa's county recorders began dispensing marriage licenses, Vander Plaats brandished a draft of the executive order, challenged Culver to sign it, and said to do otherwise would be "constitutionally irresponsible." A Culver deputy responded by saying the governor has no such authority, adding, "Somebody who's run for office as often as Mr. Vander Plaats" should have a better grasp of the limits and powers of the office.[14]

Thinking similar thoughts (though not voicing them) were the seven members of the Iowa Supreme Court. The backlash seemed to hit Chief

Justice Ternus hardest. The Great Recession that struck in 2008 had resulted in budget cuts that cost many court reporters and other employees their jobs—which didn't win the chief justice many new friends. Then there was a night of underage drinking that went on at a bonfire on the Ternus family property a half mile from the house that drew a visit from the police. Ternus was criticized for saying she had been asleep in the house and didn't realize her son and several other nineteen-year-old college students had been taking part.

After *Varnum*, state representative Dwayne Alons, a staunch opponent of marriage between same-sex partners, declared that voters would likely remember that incident during the next retention vote. Maybe so. But like the girl standing in front of her first-grade class decades before, Ternus kept plowing ahead, convinced she had no reason to apologize to anyone.

Since Iowa adopted the merit system and stopped electing judges directly in 1962, no supreme court justice had been removed from the bench by a retention vote. But nothing had inflamed the public like same-sex marriage. Few understood that better than Cady. Two months before the decision, he had visited a close friend's father-in-law, who had just weeks to live. The justice and the dying man, "the nicest guy in the world," were alone in the hospice when the man looked up and abruptly changed the subject. Barely speaking above a whisper, he begged Cady not to rule in favor of gay marriage. It meant that much, even on his deathbed.

It meant that much to most conservatives, but they couldn't do much about it after the fact. Many Iowa Republicans called for a constitutional amendment, which sounded good. In the end, however, it would have been a difficult, time-consuming, low-percentage move. The Democrats controlled the senate, and Majority Leader Michael Gronstal was insistent. No way would he allow a vote to take away the civil rights of any individual or group of individuals. Not surprisingly, Congressman Steve King, the contentious, spotlight-hugging Tea Party favorite who had a hammerlock on western Iowa, wanted more than a constitutional amendment. "The legislature," he said, "must also enact marriage license residency requirements so that Iowa does not become the gay marriage mecca due to the supreme court's latest experiment in social engineering."[15]

Maintaining the status quo meant something to certain Democrats, too, including the governor. "We'll do whatever it takes," Culver said, "to protect marriage between a man and a woman."[16] Then slowly he walked it back. The first-term Democrat said his religious beliefs told him marriage is between a man and a woman, yet the Iowa Constitution demands equal protection for all citizens.

Despite all the histrionics, threats, doomsday scenarios, and predictions of retention setbacks, it soon became obvious. On this issue, there would be no turning back—even if it meant the worst for the three justices facing retention elections in 2010.

Streit was one of those three. After the *Varnum* decision's release, a former law clerk e-mailed him a note of congratulations. The justice responded with thanks and a bit of prophecy: "Now we'll see if we keep our jobs."

CHAPTER TEN

||||||||||||||||||||||||||||||||||||||||||||||||||||||||||||||||||||||||||||||||||||||

We the People

In 2009, according to Iowa Department of Health records, 1,783 same-sex couples acquired marriage licenses and exchanged vows after the state removed the same-sex marriage ban. But it wasn't time for complacency. Though marriage equality might have been the will of the Iowa Supreme Court, hundreds of thousands of regular Iowans never would accept it as part of God's plan. The seven justices might have been unanimous, but the people were anything but.

Dennis Johnson saw the division firsthand. The year after he helped win the case for the six plaintiff couples, Johnson took part in RAGBRAI, the *Des Moines Register*'s annual bike ride across Iowa. He had heard about the move to oust the three court members up for retention but figured it was a waste of time. "I thought it was a joke," he said. "I never thought they'd get them." Johnson changed his mind while reading one antiretention road sign after another as he pedaled across the state. Western Iowa, where the most vocal legislative opposition to same-sex marriage lived, was particularly agitated. After the trip, Johnson called Taylor at Lambda to tell her about it. "This is serious," he said.

If Johnson was talking about the black, 4 × 8 feet plywood signs painted to look like ballots that said VOTE NO NOVEMBER 2nd, he was right. The effort to oust the justices in the 2010 midterm election was dead serious. The signs were the handiwork of the Common Sense political action committee, which warned the citizens of Iowa to beware of judicial overreach. "Most Iowans don't pay attention to judicial retention," Johnson said, "but you get that reactionary 35 percent wound up, and they are going to vote."

Bob Vander Plaats had every intention of getting them wound up. He didn't know it on April 3, but the decision would precede an unsettling time in his life. Less than a week after *Varnum*, his World War II–veteran father died of a massive stroke. But just a few days before his death, John Vander Plaats had mentioned *Varnum* to his son. "What the heck happened yesterday? How can they do that? And what can be done about it?"

"I am not exactly sure how it all plays out," the son had responded, "but I *will* find out."

When Vander Plaats went to church the following Sunday, his pastor never mentioned the decision, which disappointed him. "I thought churches were supposed to be biblically sound but culturally relevant," he would say later. "And here's a major cultural issue that shifted the dynamics of God's design for the family. And you're remaining silent?"

At least partly to honor the memory of his father, Vander Plaats began to speak out against the *Varnum* decision. Emphasizing the supreme court's refusal to let the legislature address the issue, he prepared to make a third run for governor.

Chief Justice Marsha Ternus had known the decision would be explosive, but the 2010 retention vote was not her most pressing concern. Her biggest post-*Varnum* challenge was keeping the court system running smoothly in the midst of massive budget cuts, triggered by tumbling tax receipts during the Great Recession. This wasn't just a problem in Iowa. Shrinking budgets and expanding caseloads were common throughout the country. Ternus's options were not good: part-time courts or massive layoffs. Either one, she said, would cripple the system, which was already feeling the effects of unpaid furlough days and closed court offices.

On November 8, 2009, seven months after the *Varnum* decision, Ternus presided over a 7.1 percent spending cut. The governor had announced a similar spending reduction for the executive branch. Belt-tightening was the stark reality.

After much back-and-forth within the court, this much was clear: the options were not good. A consensus was eventually reached, and Ternus unveiled the plan—$11.4 million in reductions, which would lead to 105 layoffs, 10 days of furloughs for all members of the judicial branch, and severe restrictions on courthouse hours throughout the state.

Among those who lost jobs were twenty-three court attendants and thirteen court reporters. The response in the legal community wasn't good. Talk of replacing all court recorders with digital voice recordings did not help morale. Meanwhile, the seven Iowa Supreme Court justices went to work every day in an elegant new five-story marble, limestone, and copper building off by itself on the southern edge of the capitol complex.

All the way from Sioux City, district court judge Jeffrey Neary could sense trouble. Reductions meant heavier workloads for judges and staff and even longer delays in getting to trial for the lawyers. Much of the resentment seemed directed toward Ternus. "They thought I was a shrew," Ternus said in retrospect.

Neary agreed.

The judges out in the state were having a lot of problems with Marsha at the time. I don't disrespect her, and I never did; but there were a lot of hard feelings out there against her. Most of us believed we did the brunt of the work with no recognition of our value.

Add voter fallout from the marriage ruling to the budget cuts, the sputtering economy, plus a growing anti-incumbent mindset, and Ternus was facing severe headwinds. As the 2010 retention election drew near, the chief justice, Streit, and Baker faced another dilemma. Would they fight for their jobs? After talking it over, the answer was no. The three would not respond to political accusations or discuss the *Varnum* decision in any detail with the media. The reason was simple judicial independence.

"My view of the court," Ternus said years later, "is it should not be involved in politics and its decisions should not be based on politics. I simply believed we shouldn't try to influence politics by manipulating how the courts work. That's not our concern."

In June 2010, Vander Plaats also faced a tough decision. He'd just been defeated for the third time in his bid to become the Republican Party candidate for governor. Though he'd received 41 percent of the primary vote, the winner was a familiar name. Terry Branstad, the governor before Tom Vilsack, pulled 50 percent of the vote. He and Vander Plaats met to talk about mending fences and moving the party forward. The meeting, by all accounts, was a bust. Vander Plaats seemed to think the best way to move the party forward was becoming Branstad's running mate. Branstad indicated that was not about to happen, and the *Varnum* fallout was a big reason. Throughout the campaign, Vander Plaats had criticized his opponent for not agreeing, if elected, to stop gays and lesbians from marrying until Iowans were able to vote on a constitutional amendment. Branstad, who holds a law degree from Drake University, scoffed at such a notion. The court, he said, would likely declare any such "executive order" an illegal violation of the separation of powers.

Vander Plaats, the *Iowa Republican* website reported, did something else that did not endear himself to the former governor. He threatened to run as an independent, which would seriously cut into the Branstad vote and return incumbent Chet Culver to office. Craig Robinson, editor and founder of TheIowaRepublican.com and a former party operative, blistered Vander Plaats, saying raising money would be difficult, and it was time to give somebody else a turn.

> Bob Vander Plaats has had his run. For the last ten years, he has been a candidate for governor. Those who think that Vander Plaats getting 40 percent of the vote in his third attempt at the nomination is some sort of great feat need to have their heads examined.[1]

Running as an independent carried substantial risk to Vander Plaats, and he knew it. If his candidacy led to Culver's reelection, he would become anathema to the party. In early August, Vander Plaats called a news conference in front of the Judicial Branch Building to say he would not run as an independent. Instead, he would focus his energies on ousting the three Supreme Court members up for retention.[2] A week later, he summoned reporters back to the same spot for another announcement. Vander Plaats would be launching a "grassroots campaign" called "Iowa for Freedom," whose mission would be unseating the three justices.[3]

One Iowa, the state's most visible LGBT advocacy group, responded to the news with an announcement of its own from executive director Carolyn Jenison:

> Bob Vander Plaats is a failed politician who has nothing better to do than play with the lives of Iowans. He aims to hurt Iowa fami-

lies, divide our communities, and demean our judicial tradition of equality for all. I believe Iowans will reject this campaign this November, just as GOP primary voters rejected Bob Vander Plaats on June 3.[4]

Vander Plaats's new organization wasn't the only one looking to punish the supreme court for the *Varnum* decision. Reports filed with the Iowa Ethics and Campaign Disclosure Board said three additional advocate groups out of the Washington, D.C., area and one out of Tupelo, Mississippi, the American Family Association (AFA), spent approximately a million dollars to send the three justices home. Even the Iowa for Freedom crusade was funded by the Mississippi group, whose "senior issues analyst" said that gays should be "disqualified for public office" because "a man who ignores time-honored standards of sexual behavior simply cannot be trusted with the power of public office."[5] And that was one of Bryan Fischer's less incendiary pronouncements.

As it turned out, Iowa for Freedom was created to spend AFA's money. The new nonprofit had help getting off the ground from a high-profile source. The *Los Angeles Times* and the Associated Press reported that Newt Gingrich, the former U.S. Speaker of the House, had channeled hundreds of thousands of dollars into Iowa for Freedom, whose executive director later said the three justices would still be on the bench without Gingrich's strategic and monetary help.

Citizens United, the conservative lobbying group whose Supreme Court victory helped open the floodgates to corporate money, spent nearly $18,000 on anticourt robo-calls.[6] When a quarter million Iowans picked up their phones, they heard 2008 Iowa Caucus winner Mike Huckabee, calling for the Citizens United Political Victory Fund and decrying "activist judges who put their own self interests ahead of the common good."[7]

The list of "independent spenders" in the 2010 Iowa Supreme Court race, according to Followthemoney.org, includes these organizations:

- For Retention
- Fair Courts for Us: $423,767
- Against Retention
- National Organization for Marriage: $635,628

- AFA Action (political arm of the American Family Association): $171,225
- Campaign for Working Families: $100,000
- Family Research Council Action: $55,997
- Citizens United Political Victory Fund: $17,823
- Iowa Family Policy Center Action: $10,178
    Total $990,851

In 2006, independent political spending in Iowa totaled $152,316. In 2010, it was $4.3 million. Once a nonfactor; now a force. Win or lose, one thing was clear. Vander Plaats had turned one state's judicial retention election into a high-stakes national political referendum on same-sex marriage, and the battle was on.

To get the word out about the "activist judges" who "ruled from the bench," Vander Plaats and an assortment of high-profile allies from the religious Right traveled the state on a four-day, thirteen-hundred-mile, twenty-stop tour in something called the Judge Bus. The vehicle of choice was actually more than just a bus. It was a sleek motor coach that would have been the envy of many rock bands. Posted on the side of the bus were huge head shots of the three Iowa court members with the word "No" stamped on each face. Next to the photos, the catchphrase "Support Iowa Families NOT Activist Judges" was emblazoned in yellow across the top. Inscribed in bright red directly below was "VOTE 'NO Retention' FOR ACTIVIST JUDGES."

One of the heavy hitters aboard was presidential hopeful Rick Santorum, the former senator from Pennsylvania. The idea for the tour, according to a book published by the Vander Plaats–led Iowa-based Family Leader, belonged to Connie Mackey of the Family Research Council political action committee and was "embraced with great enthusiasm" by Family Research Council president Tony Perkins. Perkins, who unsuccessfully had urged the ouster of Neary in 2004 for his decision to allow two lesbians to divorce, approached National Organization for Marriage president Brian Brown, who said he "jumped at the chance" and proceeded to spend more than $635,000 to get the Judge Bus rolling and the judges checking the help-wanted ads.[8] Created in 2007 to put

Proposition 8 (which sought to restore a ban on gay marriage the court had overturned) on the ballot in California, the National Organization for Marriage specialized in attacking same-sex marriage through state legislatures. In sum, the battle in Iowa was clearly only one skirmish in a nationwide holy war to kill same-sex marriage — and to fuel certain politicians' presidential ambitions.

Three weeks before the midterm election, an Iowa-based advocacy group, Fair Courts for Us, materialized to counter the antiretention movement with a "Homegrown for Justice" tour. Included in the group were two respected Republican father figures, former governor Bob Ray and his lieutenant governor, Arthur Neu. Also signing on as cochairs were Christie Vilsack, wife of former Democratic governor Tom Vilsack, and a third moderate Republican, Sioux City lawyer Dan Moore, a past president of the Iowa State Bar Association.

It wasn't party affiliation alone that made the choice of Moore intriguing. He also happened to be the former secretary and treasurer of Vander Plaats's gubernatorial election campaigns. Moore and Vander Plaats had known each other since the early 1990s. They formed a bond after Moore joined the board of human services agency Opportunities Unlimited and Vander Plaats was hired as executive director. Moore found Vander Plaats to be energetic and easygoing.[9] The attorney had always been interested in politics. Years later, he would win a seat on the city council in Sioux City.

In 2000, when Vander Plaats was thinking about running for governor, Moore was offered a cabinet position as legal secretary. Moore played that role, sitting in on cabinet meetings, helping formulate campaign strategy, and watching over financial reports in all three of Vander Plaats's governor races. He found the candidate to be charismatic, organized, and media savvy. Nobody was better at sticking to a script; nobody had a better ear for a good sound bite. In a live interview with the lights on, the video rolling, and the reporters pressing him, Vander Plaats had a way of changing the subject — "I think what your question really is . . ." — to fit the point he wanted to make. This amused and impressed Moore, who kept waiting for someone to say, "Bob, could you answer the original question . . ." but never witnessed it.

The *Varnum* decision severely strained their relationship. To Moore, the best move Iowa ever made for the courts was adopting the merit retention system in the early 1960s. When many of his fellow Republicans went after the justices, he refused to join the hunt. "I could not in good conscience sit this one out and let the courts take the heavy attacks," he said looking back. "I had to stand up."

Moore will probably never take a public position on whether Marsha Ternus's court was right or wrong, but he considered the Cady opinion a gem. After several readings, he found it well organized, well written, and based on sound constitutional principles. Even if he had been unimpressed with the logic, Moore still would have had trouble finding fault. "As a lawyer," he said later, "I'm licensed by the Iowa Supreme Court. Every fiber in my body supports our judiciary and judicial system."

It was almost as if Moore's family itself was under attack. He clearly remembered Ternus in law school at Drake University—her active participation in class, her articles as editor-in-chief of the law review. "She wrote the law review," he says with a smile. "I read it. I like to joke about how I held her up in our class. I was at the bottom. She was at the top. Marsha was one of the smart ones. You remember the smart ones. It was very hard for me to watch those attacks on her."

After the 7–0 vote, when Vander Plaats urged Governor Culver to issue an executive order stopping same-sex marriages until the legislature could act, he anticipated Moore's dismay and left him out of the discussion. Their relationship continued to slide. Wherever Iowa for Freedom went on the Judge Bus tour, Moore and a group from Fair Courts for Us would show up nearby. Even without a team tour bus at their disposal, they would make their case. Moore would tell the crowd about his unique perspective as a lifelong Republican and longtime Vander Plaats lieutenant. But this, he would add, is where the two part ways. In his talking points, Moore would mention his former friend by name and launch into a series of questions for "Bob" or "Mr. Vander Plaats."

Citing a September 2010 poll released by the *Des Moines Register* showing a plurality of Iowans likely to vote to retain the three justices, Moore asked three questions:

- Do you believe your focus on the courts is out of touch with the real issues facing Iowans?
- Do you support impeachment proceedings for the remaining jus-

tices even though polls find the majority of Iowans are against them and they will have no effect on the law regarding same-sex marriage in Iowa?

- Will you and the American Family Association finally come clean about the donors who gave nearly a million dollars to inject politic into Iowa's courts?
- Do you support legislation that violates the Iowa Constitution and our system of checks and balances?
- Do you support legislation that prevents the Iowa Supreme Court from reviewing laws?

The questions were being asked. But was anybody listening?

The road show began on a cool, gray, late October Monday morning at the Iowa statehouse. The proretention group kicked it off with short presentations from Neu, Iowa Department of Public Safety commissioner Eugene Meyer, and former Iowa attorney general Bonnie Campbell, who concluded her remarks by saying, "I don't believe that out-of-state special interest groups riding around Iowa in a bus with Montana plates, presuming they know what is best for Iowans, have considered at all the full impact of their actions. On the other hand, why do they have to? They won't be here after November 3, but the rest of us will."[10]

Serving as a backdrop were supporters holding green signs that said "TURN THE BALLOT OVER" on one side and "VOTE YES YES YES" on the other.

Around the same time, the antiretention crowd gathered for its kickoff rally. Among the participants were Iowa representative Steve King, an architect of Iowa's Defense of Marriage Act in 1998, and house colleague Louis Gohmert of Texas, Republican National Committee member Kim Lehman, and National Organization for Marriage president Brian Brown. Said King, "You send a message to these judges on November second, and I will tell you, it will echo all across this land in all fifty states."[11] While he spoke, a group of retention dissenters held red signs that said "NO activist judges."

The tour ended the following Thursday at the Judicial Branch Building in Des Moines—just five days before midterm elections and the retention vote. Except for a reported "Yes to Iowa judges" crowd of 150 plus at the

Linn County Courthouse in Cedar Rapids, daily attendance for both sides was sparse—usually between three and four dozen for either side. Nevertheless, Brian Brown called the bus tour a "great success." He turned out to be right.

Fair Courts reported spending more than $417,267 on direct mail, radio, online advertising, and their own little traveling show, but time and fire power conspired against them. In his prime, former governor Ray had been the voice of assurance, able to step into any important role in a pinch. But this wasn't the governor at the top of his game. His radio spot began with football sounds in the background, then the tweet of a whistle and Ray offering a lukewarm endorsement. "We'll never agree with every call, but you shouldn't fire the good referees over just one call. The same is true for the Iowa Supreme Court."[12] To many, it almost sounded like an apology: even the best make mistakes, so don't be too hard on us.

In a Fair Courts for Us news release on October 13, 2012, Neu gave it a shot. "Iowa's judicial system is one of the best in the nation. To change it simply because some are unhappy about one decision would be foolish."[13] Though he might have been correct, the message didn't take, and time was running out.

The election-night outlook was not good. It was an off year, and Janelle Rettig's former party, the GOP, had done a good job nurturing strong anti-government sentiment in Iowa and beyond. The "activist judges, legislating from the bench" theme song had taken a foothold. By this time, too, the long struggle for marriage equality seemed to be taking a toll even on those who would most benefit. "The message," Rettig said in retrospect, "came from the justices themselves and their handlers that a campaign wasn't welcomed. People had been fighting this fight for decades and now they feel like they are human beings and want to live their lives and be with their children. Is that abandonment or is it that 'I'm tired and need to do something else with my life'?"

Ternus, Streit, and Baker made few public appearances and refused to campaign or raise money to defend themselves. Litigants, they agreed, should never have to wonder whose lawyer gave how much money to a judge's reelection campaign. Three weeks before the election, however,

Ternus broke her silence during an appearance at Iowa State University in Ames. And she didn't hold back. "These critics," she said, "are blinded by their own ideology. They simply refuse to accept that an impartial, legally sound, and fair reading of the law can lead to an unpopular decision."[14]

She also criticized the Iowa for Freedom antiretention campaign as well as Bob Vander Plaats for telling the court to send the matter to the state legislature. Ternus also had harsh words for the American Family Association, the Mississippi-based group that wants the court to be "servants" to "ideology rather than servants of the law."[15]

The reviews were good, but to no avail. On election night, the final tally wasn't close. For the first time in the state's history, voters had removed three members of the Iowa Supreme Court. The triple ouster was the result of a "perfect storm." Republicans won back the Iowa House, as well as returning Terry Branstad to the governor's chair after defeating incumbent Chet Culver. And yet the victory wasn't total.

Every ten years, Iowans are asked to vote for or against a constitutional convention. In 2010, they rejected the proposal. What's more, Democrats maintained a slim majority in the Iowa Senate, where Michael Gronstal made it clear he would reject all attempts to push a constitutional amendment onto the senate floor. That now meant the earliest a vote could be held on a constitutional amendment would be 2016.

In 1962, when Iowans changed to a merit retention system for judges, they did so to let voters have a say in the selection process while holding politics to a minimum. In 2010, that objective was severely tested. The election night numbers were basically the same for Ternus, Streit, and Baker. Each failed to receive 50 percent of the votes and would be leaving office December 31. We the People had spoken.

Two months later, Interim Chief Justice Mark Cady walked down the center aisle of the Iowa House of Representatives to make the annual State of the Judiciary speech. The annual speech seldom drew much attention. On this occasion the event attracted a standing-room-only crowd in the chamber and gallery of the Iowa House. It was the first time a member of the court would speak formally to lawmakers post-*Varnum*. Cady, who would soon be elected chief justice by his peers, made no attempt to dodge the issue.

He told lawmakers he understood the controversy but refused to back down. The decision, Cady said, was the product of a court that had

> worked hard to author a written decision to fully explain our reasoning to all Iowans, and we understand how Iowans could reach differing opinions about this decision. . . . This discourse is not new for Iowa, although I doubt it has ever been so strong. . . . Our court . . . has many times in the past decided cases involving civil rights that were once controversial, yet over time those cases have become a celebrated part of the proud and rich Iowa history of equality for all.

The line drew a standing ovation from the public gallery on both sides of the house and about half the chamber. Republican legislators remained seated and silent.

Cady then spoke directly to the critics—to those who believed the legislature should have been given time to act before marriage licenses were issued to same-sex couples. Those critics, he said, didn't understand the role of the judiciary.

"Courts serve the law, . . . not the demands of special interest groups," he said. "By serving that law, courts protect the civil, political, economic, and social rights of all citizens."[16] When Cady ended his speech, the public gallery again stood and applauded. Walking up the center aisle toward the exit, he turned, smiled, and waved to the gallery on the north side of the chamber, exiting to even greater applause.

Some Republicans in the legislature found Cady's remarks condescending. Senator Kent Sorenson, a Republican from Indianola, said the chief justice "came in here with a pompous, arrogant attitude and tried to give the legislature a history lesson. . . . You come in here and you make a speech like that—well, you saw the reaction. I don't think it was received very well when he started going down that road."[17] Sorenson was one of several Republican legislators who criticized Cady for addressing the *Varnum* decision and for his comments on the separation of powers.

Senator Merlin Bartz, a Republican from Grafton, said Cady "just poured a five-gallon can of gasoline on the fire"—a line that was echoed by other Republican lawmakers.[18] Bartz said Cady also acted in a political manner when he waved to supporters in the public balconies after his speech and when he mentioned the marriage ruling: "I think he frankly should have been silent on the decision. Sometimes you have to leave the elephant standing in the room and just not discuss it."[19]

Two years later, a prominent foundation in Boston came to the opposite conclusion. The foundation thought the three justices who were ousted deserved to be recognized and called their action a profile in courage.

CHAPTER ELEVEN

|||||||||||||||||||||||||||||||||||||||||||||||||||||||||||||||||||||||||||||||||||||||

Buyer's Remorse

C hief Justice Mark Cady ignored the buzzing noise in his pocket
and kept talking. The phone would have to wait. Addressing the
crowd at the 2012 John F. Kennedy Profile in Courage Awards
breakfast, he surveyed the room. The chairs and tables were filled with
Boston dignitaries and well-wishers. Seated next to him was Caroline
Kennedy, the fifty-four-year-old daughter of the late president. She and
the rest of the attendees listened intently as Cady explained why three of
his former colleagues on Iowa's high court so richly deserved the honor
they were about to receive.

If only the folks back home were so accepting. While some 450,000
Iowans had voted to retain them in 2009, more than 530,000 chose to
send them home.

The *Varnum* decision and the way Cady framed the issue had earned
high marks in law schools around the country and in much of the legal
community. Kennedy, president of the JFK Library Foundation and author
of nine books on constitutional law, read a few lines from Cady's opinion
at the ceremony:

> In the final analysis, we give respect to the views of all Iowans on the
> issue of same-sex marriage—religious or otherwise—by giving re-
> spect to our constitutional principles. These principles require that
> the state recognize both opposite-sex and same-sex civil marriage.[1]

Unlike previous rulings, this decision came from middle America. The
significance was clear to many of the elites outside the heartland: gays

and lesbians deserve equal rights no matter where they live. Not just in the heavily populated urban centers on the two coasts, but everywhere between. Yes, *Varnum v. Brien* made Iowa only the third state, along with Massachusetts and Connecticut, to lift a ban on same-sex marriage. But many Iowans disagreed strongly with the legal reasoning and had exacted a heavy retribution.

Obviously, the law professors and the lawyers did not have the final word, and Cady's noisy cell phone was a stark reminder of the power of ordinary voters. After talking at length with Kennedy at the awards breakfast, after praising his colleagues for their grace under fire, Cady strolled across the hall for the awards ceremony and stopped to check his messages.

That buzzing sound was a call from his wife, Becky, texting from Iowa: "BVP says this award is an insult to a half million voters and constitutionally astute Iowans!" Cady saw the initials and sighed. Bob Vander Plaats, the head of the FAMiLY Leader, was going off again. An hour before the awards ceremony, no less.[2]

"Can you believe it?" the chief justice asked a friend. "Can you believe this guy? Wasn't it enough, spending all that time, raising all that money to remove three honorable people from the bench? Couldn't he at least have the decency to let them enjoy the moment?"[3] While the deposed justices were waiting to be honored, Vander Plaats was trashing them in the Iowa media thirteen hundred miles away. Vander Plaats told reporters,

> I see this as a deliberate slap in the face of the people of Iowa. It should never be a profile in courage when you go outside the bounds of the constitution that you swear an oath to. And I really believe the people of Iowa deserve the "Bold and Courageous Award" for holding activist judges in check when they go outside their constitutional authority. This is how elitists work.[4]

Cady showed his wife's text to David Wiggins, who was next up on the retention chopping block. Wiggins shook his head. When he returned to Des Moines, he would waste no time making it known he wasn't about to sit back and be bullied. Wiggins would fight for his job.

Cady wasn't up for retention until 2016, but Vander Plaats's reaction to the Profile in Courage Award was not what he wanted to hear on this sunny spring day along Boston Harbor—this day of affirmation. When the ceremony began in the library auditorium, the chairman of the Kennedy Library Foundation peered out at the crowd of four hundred and smiled. "Is there anyone left in Iowa today?" he said. The answer: some three million residents, including several hundred thousand who had serious doubts about same-sex marriage.

Touring the presidential library the day before, Cady and Streit were taken by the words of the president's younger brother. The words came from a 1966 address in South Africa less than two years before Robert Kennedy's run for president ended tragically.

> Each time a man stands up for an ideal, or acts to improve the lot of others, or strikes out against injustice, he sends forth a tiny ripple of hope, and . . . those ripples build a current which can sweep down the mightiest walls of oppression and resistance.[5]

Streit, in his acceptance speech, said that was his dream for *Varnum*: a tiny ripple becoming a strong current, washing away the hate.

In Boston, Baker, Ternus, Streit, and their colleagues who remained on the bench were caught between two worlds—the nurturing, supportive crowd in Boston and the angry defenders of traditional marriage ready to finish the job back home. But for those few days in Boston, all was good. Before the *Varnum* decision, these former justices and their supreme court peers were rarely, if ever, called "black-robed masters." That was Michele Bachmann's oft-repeated description for "activist judges" who "legislate from the bench." To the Kennedy foundation, however, the justices were public servants who "made courageous decisions of conscience without regard for personal or professional consequences."[6]

The library staff chatted excitedly about a recent Frank Bruni column in the *New York Times* focusing on the second woman to be appointed to the Iowa Supreme Court and the first to become chief justice.

Caroline Kennedy, president of the library foundation, praised the honored guests.

> They don't think they did anything special. They were just doing their job. But for public officials, just doing their job often demands a special kind of courage. Standing up for human rights requires

courage. Serving the interest of all citizens, not just the majority, requires courage.

What pleased the justices even more than the honor was the recognition that much more than three jobs was at stake—an insistence that judges interpret the law rather than obey the popular will. Kennedy continued,

> This award is usually given to elected officials in the legislative branch of government. But in honoring these three principled jurists, we seek to remind all Americans of the importance of an independent judiciary and its role in safeguarding our most fundamental rights.[7]

None of the three was expecting to hear this from Kennedy. They were shocked to hear from her at all. Baker had received a call from a woman who said the library was planning its fiftieth anniversary celebration and was looking into the issue of judicial independence. The caller asked Baker would it be all right if one of the library researchers called for an interview. If so, would Monday at 10:30 work? When the phone rang on Monday, the voice on the other end of the phone said, "Hello, this is Caroline Kennedy."

"The real Caroline Kennedy?" Baker replied.

The real one laughed into the phone.

For the schoolkids on a field trip to the library, the awards ceremony was more than just an opportunity to skip class. Sam Ganem, an eighth-grader at Brown Middle School in nearby Newton, was one of four members representing the school's fledgling gay-straight alliance. Sam had two mothers and believed decisions like *Varnum* were long overdue. "What none of us gets is why this is an issue," he said. "People should be allowed to be happy with each other, and marriage can make people happy."[8]

During the ceremony at least a third of the auditorium's four hundred seats were filled with supportive Iowans, who watched as Ternus, Baker, and Streit each received a sterling silver lantern symbolizing a beacon of hope.

While Sonya Streit sat on stage with the spouses of the other two justices, the Streits' ten-year-old son, Ashton, was perched near three current members of the Iowa Supreme Court, a former Iowa House Speaker, and the recently retired chief federal judge for the Southern District of

Iowa. He listened intently as his father stood at the podium and talked about the *Varnum* decision and how it had generated the most vicious hate mail any of the justices had seen.

When Michael Streit listened to the arguments against marriage equality, he couldn't help thinking about Asian-born Sonya and their son. Many were the exact arguments raised against interracial marriage.

- Certain truths are eternal, based on natural law, taught by God, church, and the Bible.
- The family is the cornerstone of society, held in place by traditional marriage.
- The children will be harmed by anything other than the traditional family.

Whenever he heard them, he had the same thought: "Those arguments were shot down thirty, forty years ago, yet you still want to resurrect them?"

Soon after the decision had come out, Streit had taken part in a swearing-in ceremony for three new lawyers. Before they began, the justice met some of their family members and gave them a tour of the Iowa Judicial Branch Building. Streit enjoyed taking visitors around the new place. Stately and intimidating from the outside, the Judicial Branch Building on the inside looks much like any other new office complex. After the ceremony, an elderly black woman approached Streit and thanked him for his role in the *Varnum* case, calling it one of the most important civil rights decisions the Iowa Supreme Court had ever made. Opponents of marital equality had said it was an insult to African Americans to compare same-sex marriage with interracial marriage. The ban on interracial marriage was completely different, they argued. Yet the woman in Streit's office had no trouble linking the two. Taken aback, Streit asked the woman why she thought the *Varnum* decision was so important. She began to cry and introduced him to her husband, who was white.

Walking through Streit's office, she had noticed a family photo. She recalled how she and her husband had to leave their southern home state to marry. "Where we were from," she said, "you couldn't have married one another. If you had lived in our time, you would not have had that beautiful boy." When Streit tells that story, he has trouble getting past the "beautiful boy" part without pausing to collect himself.

In a strange coincidence, he and Vander Plaats, the person who played such a big role in shoving him out the door, grew up in the same small community. Streit can't remember ever having crossed paths with Vander Plaats in the northwest Iowa town of Sheldon. That's not surprising considering the age gap: Streit is thirteen years older. They also attended different high schools. Streit went to Sheldon High; Vander Plaats attended Western Christian fifteen miles away in nearby Hull. Though Sheldon is far from microscopic by Iowa standards, the chance of two men from the same community in the rural Midwest butting heads over a court case of national consequence is slim. Maybe it's evidence, or maybe not, that small towns in conservative strongholds can indeed produce diversity of thought.

After graduating from the University of Iowa in 1972, Streit enrolled at the University of San Diego law school, where he wrote for the law review. After law school, Streit entered private practice in Chariton, Iowa, before becoming an assistant county attorney and then county attorney. In his climb to the top rung of Iowa's judicial system, Streit was the model for bipartisan nominations. Republican Terry Branstad appointed him to the district court in 1983 and to the court of appeals in 1996. In 2001, Democrat Tom Vilsack put him on the supreme court. After spending twenty-eight years on the bench and writing hundreds of opinions, he was gone.

When it was Baker's turn to speak in Boston, he said it would have been a mistake for the three to fight for their jobs. The rules allowed them to form campaign committees, but they had decided against it. "Had we chosen to form campaigns," Baker told the crowd, "we would have tacitly admitted that we were what we claimed not to be — politicians." He mentioned the million-dollar current flowing into Iowa from outside its borders. The 2009 retention vote wasn't just about removing three members of the court, Baker said. It was an attempt to "intimidate judges, not only in Iowa, but nationally. That is why outside money was there. The outside groups were in Iowa to take the blindfold off [Lady Justice] and have every judge looking over their shoulder, thinking that if you vote contrary to us, we're coming after you."[9]

Like the others preparing for the case, Baker had read through a pile of documents. He even took them to his daughter's swimming meets. Once you take religion out of the mix, he kept thinking, there's nothing here. The ability of the churches to define marriage any way they saw fit was still intact. So what's the problem? Baker had little trouble dismissing the counterargument: if the government sanctions marriage of same-sex couples, it must then allow the same kind of contract between multiple parties—in other words, polygamy. At that point, he reasoned, the state could advance justifiable reasons for not allowing polygamy. Finding empirical evidence pointing to the potential for harm among multiple spouses would not be difficult.

Last up was Ternus, who steered away from the emotion of the moment, stuck with the law, and echoed what she'd told the *New York Times*: she just wanted to be fair. Then she cited the words of United States Supreme Court Justice Anthony Kennedy: "Judicial independence does not give judges the freedom to rule as they wish; it gives them the freedom to rule as they must." Judges, she continued, cannot base their decisions on popular opinion or even on their own personal beliefs. "When judges begin to do that, we cease to be a government based on law."[10]

When the ceremony was over, when the applause faded and the photographers packed up their cameras, the celebration continued at a reception in the library atrium. Family and friends of the recipients mingled and munched tea sandwiches and pizza. Bright sunlight poured through huge windows that offered a spectacular view of the harbor washing up against the library grounds. On that perfect spring day in New England, Sonya Streit still had one question. "Do you think there's any buyer's remorse back home?"[11]

Not much. Not yet. Not among the people whose votes had cost her husband his job. On the first Tuesday in November, with David Wiggins's future in the balance, they would begin to find out.

The Sunday before the November retention vote, the *Des Moines Register*'s Iowa Poll put the odds of Wiggins surviving at a bit less than fifty-fifty. Few who knew the justice well doubted his smarts or his devotion to the rule of law, but his career offered some potential pitfalls. Being seen in some circles as Governor Tom Vilsack's liberal buddy didn't always work in his favor. And at times, Wiggins could be blunt. Before the retention vote, when asked about the likelihood of following Ternus, Streit, and Baker off the bench in the next retention vote, he had said, "Quite frankly, all three are probably making twice as much as they were here professionally, and I'm not going to worry about it. I gave up a position where I was making three times what I'm making here."[12] Brash? Yes, but does it really matter? Nobody on that court was more gregarious and personable than Michael Streit, and it didn't help him keep his job.

Like Ternus and the others, Wiggins had a compelling story to tell. How does a bright Jewish kid from Skokie, Illinois, in the near-north suburbs of Chicago, end up on the Iowa Supreme Court? His father had a wholesale egg and butter business, and Wiggins would travel to Iowa with him to deal with suppliers.

He wasn't one of those lawyers who'd always had his heart set on becoming a supreme court justice. When asked before the retention vote what attracted him to the job, he said, "Nothing." In twenty-seven years in private practice, Wiggins barely gave it a thought until the governor asked him to throw his name in, convincing him it was an opportunity to make a difference. And he did.

The Wiggins story isn't warm and fuzzy, but there is much to admire about his professional climb. Like many college students of his era, Wiggins could have been mistaken for a member of the counterculture. He wasn't exactly a full-blooded hippie when he enrolled at what is known now as the University of Illinois at Chicago (he planned on becoming an actuary, for heaven sakes), but he spent ample time exploring the city. Why go away to college when everything you need is a bus or subway ride away? The actuary plans didn't last long. As a freshman in the business school in 1969, he took a required philosophy course, which included a heavy dose of current events and rock 'n' roll. Philosophy quickly became his major.

By graduation, Wiggins still hadn't figured out what to do with his philosophy degree. He thought about medical school, but that meant four more years of college. When someone told him to take the Law School Admission Test, he didn't know what it was, and the application deadline had passed. But he paid the penalty fee and did well enough to be admitted to Tulane, DePaul, and Drake Universities. He chose Drake because it gave him the best financial deal. When Wiggins heard he would be required to take something called "torts," he had to look it up. He thought they were talking about pastries.

An enterprising young man, Wiggins and a friend decided to place a table in the lobby of the law school and sell used textbooks. Students would set a price. The two entrepreneurs would make the sale and take 10 percent. Not long after, according to Wiggins lore, the university bookstore started selling used textbooks.

After seeing a notice on the bulletin board inviting students to join *Drake Law Review*, Wiggins signed on and became an editor. He landed a job clerking for a Des Moines firm that included Louis Lavarato, who would later become chief justice of the Iowa Supreme Court. Wiggins was such a quick study that in his final year at Drake, the bosses at Williams, Hart, Lavorato and Kirtley gave him a key role in a trial.

After finishing first in his spring graduating class, Wiggins was ready to take a job in Chicago with the Democratic Party political machine. That's when Lavorato talked him into staying. Wiggins tried thirteen civil jury cases in his first six months on the job and lost them all. Lavorato finally confessed, telling Wiggins he was assigned the cases because they were losers, and the firm just wanted to be done with them. Undeterred, Wiggins went on to make more money than he could ever earn in all the years he'll spend on Iowa's highest court. He hit his first big verdict in 1980. The state was warehousing children and young adults at a facility for the developmentally and mentally disabled, emphasizing drugs over therapy. The firm's thirty-three-year-old client suffered from a neurological muscle disorder caused by the tranquilizers he was given over the years. The final payment on the judgment exceeded $860,000—a huge award for a medical negligence case at the time.

A young Tom Vilsack was practicing law in Mount Pleasant, Iowa, when he and Wiggins became friends. If Vilsack had any lofty political ambitions at the time, Wiggins says he wasn't aware of them. Every so often, the two would meet in Pella with their spouses. Wiggins's wife, Marsha, is also from Chicago. They planned on staying in Des Moines only a few years before heading home. But Williams, Hart, Lavorato, and Kirtley kept giving this up-and-comer more responsibility, more big cases, and the kind of financial opportunity that might have taken years to earn in a big Chicago firm. In less than two years on the job, he became a partner.

When Vilsack was elected president of the Iowa Trial Lawyers Association in 1985, Wiggins followed him a year later. When Vilsack was elected mayor of Mount Pleasant after Edward King was murdered during a council meeting, he and Wiggins remained friends. When Vilsack was elected to the Iowa Senate, the bond grew stronger. Shortly after Vilsack became governor, Wiggins's neighbor noticed in the paper that the Indianapolis 500 was on the governor's bucket list. "Would Tom like to go?"

The three piled into an suv with Vilsack's son, Jess, and drove to Indianapolis and back. On the road, Vilsack and Wiggins found time to talk about the latest supreme court vacancy. It took some convincing, but Wiggins finally agreed to apply for the job. "The governor told me not a lot of people get a chance to make a difference in public service," Wiggins recounted during the retention battle. "It was like a once in a lifetime opportunity. I had a great law career and made a substantial amount of money, so I thought it was time to give something back."

Wiggins had few illusions about his appointment. He knew his friendship with Vilsack helped him land the job. He also knew he wouldn't have been asked if he hadn't been right for the position. "Tom has a lot of friends," Wiggins said later, "but he didn't ask *them* to do it."

While future supreme court colleagues Brent Appel and Daryl Hecht were temporarily left behind in the process that year, Wiggins zipped through in what might have been record time. The nomination, however, came with a cost. "I gave up my personal beliefs in 2003," he said. "My religion teaches against same-sex marriage. I voted against my personal and religious beliefs because the law requires it." It was a price he was willing to pay and a telling admission. In one sentence, Wiggins had explained what the job is all about.

Though he no longer represented victims of personal injury and malpractice, in a way he remained a "lawyer for the little guy." During each retention skirmish, he did little to help dispel his image as a passionate social liberal. Though he is no longer a regular at the synagogue, Wiggins attended Hebrew school as a child and says he still tries to live by the traditional tenets he learned, while not allowing his personal and religious beliefs to influence his interpretation of the law.

After his three colleagues had been removed, Wiggins mentioned something else particularly noteworthy about the *Varnum* decision. "It's like any other decision we make. We didn't find a right in this case. We found a suspect class. California found that same-sex marriage was a fundamental right. We didn't."

Either way, *Varnum* is a case that generates emotion. Doesn't it?

"No, it doesn't. It is a case of constitutional law. There is no emotion to it," Wiggins said.

We found that people who are in committed same-sex relationships were similarly situated to opposite-sex couples in committed relationships. If marriage was a fundamental right, you have to use "strict scrutiny." I don't know if marriage is a fundamental right. The right to reproduce is a fundamental right.

During the buildup to the retention vote, a high-profile Republican privately accused Wiggins of masterminding the *Varnum* decision, persuading Ternus and Cady to go along. Wiggins called the accusation "the most absurd thing I ever heard." Ternus and Cady, he said, might be the least easily manipulated people he knows. What's more, nobody on that court pressured anyone to take one side or the other. "Ternus is more strong-willed than I ever was," Wiggins said.

When she didn't agree, you couldn't change her mind on it. You couldn't talk her into things she didn't agree with. She wouldn't even hold her nose and vote for something if she disagreed with it. Some people will hold their nose and vote in a particular way, but she never would do that. . . . Mark is the same way. He probably has written more dissents over the years than anyone [else] on the bench.

I wish I had that much power to tell seven other people smarter than me what to do. Let me tell you about the process. Nobody talks about a case before oral argument. Nobody talks about it.

Facing his retention vote, Wiggins promised he wouldn't be bullied. If Vander Plaats or someone else on the other side spoke out against him, Wiggins promised he would answer. He saw how refusing comment seemed to work against his colleagues. "They stood there and did the rope-a-dope," Wiggins said, alluding to a passive, though effective, Muhammad

Ali boxing tactic designed to sap an opponent's energy. "I'm not going to do that. If they say something, I'll respond." Wiggins responded by writing an op-ed piece for the *Des Moines Register*.

Several lawyers formed a committee to raise money for his campaign. While judges are permitted to form campaign committees, the judicial code forbids them from becoming actively involved in the fund-raising. He wasn't comfortable with the idea of campaign fund-raising, and the antiretention crowd kept hammering away.

In 2011, when Wiggins was the chair of the supreme court's judicial nominating committee, one of the candidates was law professor Angela Onwuachi-Willig, who was not licensed to practice law in Iowa. In Wiggins's first question to the candidate, he noted that holding a license is mandatory for judges under the state constitution.

> Our charge is to send people who meet the qualifications, either by age or by license, to the governor. We have to send nine people, but if we send you without a license we're really sending eight people. So tell me in your best way, how we can get around the Iowa Constitution and do that?[13]

To some who saw the video, there was nothing menacing about the rhetorical question. It seemed like a polite way of saying, "There's clearly no way of getting around that, so what now? Are you going to get a license?"

It was a misleading sound bite that became proof to *Varnum*-decision detractors that Wiggins wouldn't think twice about stomping on the constitution and should be tossed overboard. With the next retention vote less than six months away, would Wiggins be the one in need of a life raft? At this point, it was anyone's guess. Whatever the voters had planned for Wiggins, he wouldn't be doing the rope-a-dope.

||||||||||||||||||||||||||||||||||||||||||||||||||||||||||||||||||||||||||||||||||

CHAPTER TWELVE

Enough Is Enough

W hen the vice president of the Iowa State Bar Association opened his e-mail early in the summer of 2011, he noticed a message from the president.[1] It was Robert Waterman asking Guy Cook for a favor. The brother of Iowa Supreme Court Justice Thomas Waterman wanted to know whether Cook would chair the Iowans for Fair and Impartial Courts committee. Cook knew the task wasn't as painless as it sounded. He understood what was at stake — preventing a fourth Iowa Supreme Court justice from losing a retention battle. Of all the bar president's many duties, none was more important than saving David Wiggins.

Sitting in his downtown Des Moines office, Cook opened Waterman's e-mail, closed it, opened it again to make sure he hadn't missed anything, filed it away one last time, and leaned back in his chair. Cook had pretty much done it all in his three decades of law practice: tricky civil cases that brought million-dollar verdicts, white-collar criminal fraud of all stripes, medical malpractice, products liability, breach of contract, false arrest.

Chairing the Fair and Impartial Courts committee wouldn't be just a difficult assignment. It would also require a healthy time commitment. For most of the year, Cook looked forward to his annual deep-sea fishing excursion on the Pacific Ocean. He also enjoyed hanging out on the Des Moines River in his boat, the aptly named "Not Guilty." The water would have to wait if Cook decided to focus his energy on convincing the public that Bob Vander Plaats had it wrong.

From the bar association's perspective, the retention vote looked like a food fight waiting to happen. With eight thousand plus members, many holding strong views one way or the other on same-sex marriage and the direction of the bar association, the organization might provoke an intramural skirmish.

The legal community took a hit after the last retention vote for sitting back and letting the other side control the tempo. Dennis Johnson, the local lawyer who had represented the plaintiffs in the *Varnum* case, said the bar association should have been embarrassed for being so timid. In his mind, the way the legal community left Ternus, Streit, and Baker hanging out to dry was "a travesty." Cook wouldn't go that far. Nobody had known what to expect in 2010, which involved a big dose of seat-of-the-pants decision making. With the 2012 elections moving into view, the state's lawyers could see the problem and the solution more clearly.

It wasn't a matter of changing minds or defending the decision supporting same-sex marriage. It was a matter of effectively yet simply explaining the supreme court's role in upholding the constitution. Vowing not to repeat the mistake of "taking a law book to a knife fight," Cook accepted the assignment.

First, at the advice of consultants, the proretention people had some repair work to do. They had to get the legal "family" back together. Some of the lawyers, mostly in the rural areas, had turned on the courts. Instead of blaming the legislature for judicial budget cuts and the resulting furloughs and layoffs, they had taken it out on Ternus, Streit, and Baker. Some of the *judges* had even announced their intention to vote no.

Trying to reverse the momentum, Cook and others met regularly with the association's numerous governing boards across the state. They reiterated the importance of getting behind the court and getting out in the community—at service club meetings, coffee shops, wherever—to explain why one decision shouldn't determine a judge's qualifications. After studying everything that went wrong in 2010 and everything that didn't, Cook decided the problem wasn't so much getting caught flat-footed without a game plan, as many suggested. What really had put them in a deep hole was getting such a late start after failing to anticipate the effort needed.

Beginning in August of 2011, the new committee met almost every month leading up to the November 2012 election. Cook laid out a plan for the sequel—a plan much like the one put together by Judge Jeff Neary when he was facing ouster in 2004. If Vander Plaats or anyone else set out to attack the judiciary before the 2012 vote, the bar association would waste no time responding. If Vander Plaats told a gathering that the *Varnum* justices went "outside of the constitution" and "amended the constitution from the bench," Cook quickly went online or on radio and fired back.

The justices did not go outside the constitution, he explained. "Iowa's constitution proclaims that all citizens are to be treated equally. The justices simply applied the equal protection clause of the constitution."

Nor did they amend the constitution from the bench. "They applied the constitution. The constitution remains the same.

"Removing more justices will not change the law; only Iowa's legislature can do that by amending the state's constitution.

"Removing more justices will only serve to weaken our courts and deny individual freedoms and liberty.

"Bob Vander Plaats's efforts to politicize justice in Iowa is good for no one, including those who disagree with the court ruling."

In the past, the bar association had been more likely to dodge controversy, leaving the brush fires to the trial lawyers and other smaller advocacy groups within the larger association. This time, however, the smaller groups would coordinate their activities: same direction, same message, same page. When Vander Plaats said the bar was split on marriage equality, it would be the legal community's professional duty as officers of the court to explain why this claim was patently untrue. Even the lawyers who opposed same-sex marriage would at least agree on the importance of protecting a judiciary under siege.

Two years earlier, a bar association poll had found that more than 80 percent of the membership approved of Streit's and Baker's performance and more than 70 percent were positive about Ternus. Either the public didn't know or didn't care. Iowans for Fair and Impartial Courts would try to change that.

When the opponents of marriage equality complained about not having had a say in the *Varnum* case, Cook wanted a quick, firm rebuttal:

Correct. That's how the system works. The United States is not a pure democracy. It is a republic with three branches of government.

You had no say in the marriage decision? Correct again. When was the last time you were able to vote on a murder conviction or weigh in on a child support decision?

To those who believed the law should have been sent back to the legislature with orders to fix it, the answer was, "Not an option. This is not like the U.S. Supreme Court, which decides whether to take a case or not." In the Iowa district court, the lawsuit had been filed and assigned. Judge Robert Hanson didn't ask for it. When it showed up on his desk, he did the research and made the call. When Polk County appealed, the case went to the Iowa Supreme Court. As a "case of first impression," *Varnum v. Brien* presented a legal question without precedent, and the state's high court was duty bound to accept it. As Cook said,

> The justices didn't just wake up one day and say, "You know what? Let's legalize gay marriage, then next week let's take away their guns." That's the mythology some people buy into about judges. They were not activists.

To voters with strong beliefs about the sanctity of traditional marriage, Cook's argument was a tough sell. There's nothing illegal or immoral about voting no for a judge, even if the reason has nothing to do with the constitutionality of a law. Voters are not required to come to the polls with an explanation for their decisions, which meant the procourt forces had some heavy lifting ahead.

Cook started by building a roster for the Yes committee that, same as two years ago, included Republicans and Democrats alike. One of the Republicans was Christine Branstad, the lawyer and niece of Iowa governor Terry Branstad. When she asked to be included, Cook said welcome aboard. Another was a veteran of the last retention campaign, Dan Moore, who wanted a second chance at protecting the judiciary.

In a guest column for the *Des Moines Register* between retention elections, Moore had a few things to say about Bob Vander Plaats, his former close friend. Vander Plaats was so obsessed with the gay-marriage issue . . . he would rather see the Iowa judicial system destroyed, instead of pursuing a change in the law within the channels provided.

The Iowa judicial branch has a long history of exceptional service, distinguished and acclaimed decisions—and now it is being raked through the mud, disparaged, criticized, and harangued daily.

That wasn't all. The "senseless attacks" on the Iowa Supreme Court are led by groups that

want to turn back the clock fifty years and politicize Iowa's judicial branch.

Their motives center on one decision that they don't like, and their tactics are misleading with the intent to scare Iowa voters."[2]

Because the judicial branch had next to no media machinery or public relations juice pushing them forward, Cook decided that role belonged to the lawyers. Teaming with acting bar association president Cynthia Moser, Cook set out to neutralize what same-sex marriage proponents called the "scare tactics, misinformation, and lies of the other side."

As Cook plotted strategy, he thought of the old line, often attributed to Mark Twain, that described what they were up against: "A lie travels half-way around the world while the truth is still putting on its shoes." To give the truth a fighting chance, the proretention team had to be more coordinated, more proactive than before. The bar had some forty governors (the very definition of an unwieldy group), who were encouraged to serve as spokespersons in their communities. Each was given the same set of materials with the same talking points.

Then there was the "Yes" panel truck. Unlike 2010, the proretention group would have an answer to the enemy's rock-star motor coach and tour. The bar association had been monitoring the antiretention faction's financial disclosure statements to see whether the faction was planning another tour. The answer was yes. Following Dan Moore's suggestion, Cook and company decided to hit the same eighteen stops and add two more—the politically receptive college towns of Iowa City and Ames. Wherever the sleek "No Wiggins" motor coach went, the humble "Yes Judges" so-called mobile display vehicle would be right behind.

The owner was bar president Waterman, who carted his dogs around in it. Cook suggested they borrow it to shadow Vander Plaats. "We don't have to sleep in the damn thing," he said. "We can stay in hotels." It wasn't the ultimate in either luxury or technology. According to at least one witness, it resembled an ice cream truck, but why not? Cook spruced it up by designing the red, white, and blue bumper sticker that said, "Yes Freedom, Yes Liberty, Yes Iowa Judges." The message was bannered across the sides.

In Cook's mind, Vander Plaats had appropriated words like "liberty" and "freedom," and it was time to take them back. To make sure the voters knew a retention vote was coming, the bar association trumpeted the news in red, white, and blue at the top of its website:

Turn the ballot over and vote
    YES
  For our Iowa judges
Why? Because a yes vote
1) helps keep politics and out-of-state money out of our courts.
2) keeps our Iowa judges and justices accountable to the constitution, not to political pressure or popular opinion.
3) helps ensure fair hearing regardless of financial status, gender, ethnic background, or political affiliation.

It was less "about agreeing with the *Varnum* decision" and more about making sure the standing judge in question is "competent, ethical, and works hard to resolve the day-to-day legal issues of Iowans."[3] The lawyers developed relationships with the advocacy groups and encouraged all to work as a team. They answered accusations and misinformation quickly and aggressively.

Every year the bar association sponsors a booth at the Iowa State Fair. In the summer of 2012, the theme was "Fair and Impartial." They made brochures for each judge on the ballot—Wiggins, as well as newcomers Edward Mansfield, Thomas Waterman, and Bruce Zager—and answered questions.

Cook thought it important to bring the sitting justices down from their lofty perch and turn them into real people. The public, he believed, should know more about them and their stories and the vetting processes they had survived on the way to the supreme court. Each of the seven on the court had been nominated, reviewed, and pitted against three other finalists. They were among the state's best and brightest, appointed by members of both parties.

From Cook's perspective, the complete picture largely remained a secret during the 2010 election season. To insiders like him, Ternus was nothing like the caricature her critics portrayed. Though she fared the worst of the three in the first retention vote, she wasn't arrogant or aloof so much as guarded, intense, and painstakingly meticulous.

Ternus's life story—4H all-star, home economics major, editor-in-chief of the *Drake Law Review*—was a combination of Iowa smarts and integrity. In his mind, she was the brainy farm girl who said, "I can do better than this," went to law school, and overcame her home state's then puzzling reluctance to elect or even appoint women to some of its highest positions. If anyone should have been able to appreciate Ternus, it was regular, everyday Iowans. She, as well as Streit and Baker, had some distinct selling points in 2010 that went largely unsold.

But Ternus, Streit, and Baker were the election past. Wiggins was Cook's concern now, and it looked as if another nasty battle loomed. As the retention election approached, Wiggins received 63 percent on the 2012 biannual Judicial Performance Review—the second-lowest rating since the retention process had gone into effect fifty years before. Cook knew Vander Plaats would pound on what appeared to be Wiggins's low class ranking. He also knew the reasons had nothing to do with Wiggins's legal acumen or skill on the bench. The man isn't a backslapper or a chronic people pleaser. He doesn't always do the best job of hiding the fact that he's probably smarter than you and could be making a lot more money in private practice. Take him or leave him; he doesn't care which.

At 9 A.M. Monday, September 24, six weeks from the general election, Vander Plaats was ready to leave him behind. Standing outside the state capitol, the head of FAMiLY Leader got the tour rolling by acknowledging the half million Iowans who voted no to Ternus, Streit, and Baker in 2010. It was now time, he added, to send their colleague away with them. If they'll "redefine the institution of marriage," Vander Plaats said, hauling out one of his favorite refrains, "then they won't blink an eye when they take away your private property, when they take away your guns, . . . when they take away your freedom of religion or freedom of speech."[4]

Rick Santorum, the presidential hopeful from Pennsylvania, who had finished thirty-four votes ahead of eventual nominee Mitt Romney to win the Iowa caucuses earlier that year, was along for a repeat tour. "Even if you don't agree with my position on the issue of marriage," he said, "understand the danger of allowing judges to determine what the law of the land is, running roughshod over the constitution and the laws of the state. It is a danger to people on both sides of the aisle."[5]

Nine months earlier, Vander Plaats had endorsed Santorum for president. Two days after that, an ABC News report quoted an anonymous source who said Santorum had paid Vander Plaats a million dollars for the endorsement. Santorum kept the story alive by saying Vander Plaats "needed money to promote the endorsement."

Vander Plaats explained the situation to the *Des Moines Register*. "You can't say, 'We endorse you; now see you later.' That's not going to do a lot in the long run."[6]

But that storm somehow passed, and Santorum and Vander Plaats were together again. Standing near the statehouse on day one, Vander Plaats didn't wait long to mention Wiggins's 63 percent favorability rating among the Iowa lawyers:

What they said in that scoring instrument is Judge Wiggins is arrogant. He's confrontational. He's not all that bright and, above all, he's lazy. . . . Now, ladies and gentlemen, take that *Varnum* decision out of there. He does not deserve to be on the bench, and we need to vote Wiggins out on November 6.[7]

While Santorum was scheduled for appearances in Des Moines, Pella, Ottumwa, Burlington, and Muscatine on the first day, Louisiana governor Bobby Jindal, another leading Republican, was booked for Mason City, Marshalltown, Fort Dodge, and Carroll two days later. Not one for understatement, Jindal called November 6 possibly "the most important election in our lifetimes." Then he added,

From the top of the ticket on down, our freedoms and values are at stake. It's critical we do everything we can to encourage conservatives to go to the polls and vote to uphold our values, freedoms, and constitutional rights.[8]

For four days, Vander Plaats did just that. And wherever he and the tour bus went, the ice cream truck followed in their wake. When "No Wiggins" rolled away from the statehouse, "Yes Iowa Judges" returned the fire. But not before Vander Plaats accused them of being copycats. "We know the bar association is going to do the chicken thing, and they're going to follow us around because they don't have what it takes to develop their own tour."[9]

Chicken thing? The other side enjoyed that description as much as anyone. Which group, they laughed, won't be setting foot in either Ames or Iowa City? Besides, the proretention forces failed to "do the chicken thing" the first time and ended up paying the price. This time they would do whatever they could to change a losing game. To send the message that these were more than a series of political "rallies," the "Yes" group preferred to call them "seminars" or "educational forums."

An important objective the second time around was staying on the attack. Two years before, the state board association played more defense than offense. The second time around, they spent fifty thousand dollars to implement their plan. They cranked up a little-used printing press. They were quick about updating their website with the latest news on why Wiggins deserved the voters' approval. The lawyers also got help. Iowa's Democratic Party, which had been largely silent during the 2010 retention election, and gay and lesbian activists—organized and unorganized—joined the fray.

"For Democrats, it became a litmus test," Janelle Rettig remembered. "The party finally got the message that if we weren't going to defend this, there was no reason for us to be Democrats."

Together, the various groups spoke clearly about what was at stake.

Ironically enough, Roger Kuhle also gave the court a boost. The assistant Polk County attorney, who twice argued for county recorder Timothy Brien against the *Varnum* plaintiffs, called the opinion "well reasoned and carefully written only after methodically addressing the issues required by the framework that exists in every constitutional challenge."[10]

When Cook took his turn at the microphone on that first day, he mentioned the United States Chamber of Commerce, which has the Iowa court system consistently near the top of its national rankings. He also had a few things to say about the 63 percent bar association approval rating. If Wiggins were a politician, Cook said, that 63 percent would be considered a landslide. "And if you look at it comparatively to politicians, which he's not, Congress is at twelve. President Obama is somewhere around forty-six, forty-seven percent. Governor Branstad is somewhere in the low fifties."

Next up was Christine Branstad, who was not shy about poking holes in the opposition's arguments. She had no difficulty chiding outsiders like Jindal and Santorum. If they wanted to discuss low judicial ratings, she instructed, they should check the United States Chamber of Commerce numbers for their own states. Iowa, consistently top ten. Pennsylvania, fortieth. Louisiana, forty-ninth. Perhaps the problem wasn't Iowa. The "No Wiggins" bus? The one that says "Your vote, your voice, your values"? It's from South Carolina, Branstad said. And the money comes from outside the state, too.

> Bob Vander Plaats said he was going to get rid of the justices in a grassroots campaign. What he did was bring in millions from Tupelo, Mississippi, and PAC money into the judiciary . . . and that was wrong. We don't want a judicial system where judges are campaigning and where clients are giving judges money.[11]

When it was Dan Moore's turn to speak, a man with a "No Wiggins" sign continued to chime in, yelling, "Sodomy is against the law!" Moore couldn't understand what the man was saying, but he kept talking, only louder. Moore, too, had learned from the last experience. This time, he avoided any mention of Vander Plaats. Instead he pecked away at his former friend's arguments, one by one. "The truth of the matter is, the unanimous Iowa Supreme Court," he prefaced each point,

- Applied the constitution to protect the freedoms and liberties of the citizens
- Followed its sworn oath
- Did what the separation of powers called for and applied the constitution unanimously[12]

When Cook wrapped it up by taking questions, it was on to the next stop—and the next and the next. At the end of the week, Bob Vander Plaats and Cynthia Moser made a joint appearance on Iowa Public Television and continued the debate on Wiggins's report card.

Vander Plaats was fond of calling the justice's 63 percent approval rating the equivalent of a D-minus. The former schoolteacher he often summons from within decided it doesn't get much worse than that.

Moser countered by saying the retention vote wasn't a "classroom exercise" and 63 percent is much higher than the 51 it takes to win retention. A politician would be "delighted" with that kind of majority—a not-so-veiled shot at Vander Plaats and his win-loss record as a candidate for governor.

Wiggins, Moser added, scored in the high satisfactory range in each category. She had more: the judicial retention survey meant nothing to Vander Plaats when Ternus, Streit, and Baker scored in the well-above-passing seventies and eighties. If it didn't matter then, why did it matter now?[13]

Christopher Rants had been out of office for more than two years. He had ended his legislative career and his political aspirations to become governor on February 18, 2010, when he faced reality. Neither he nor anyone else in the Republican Party could beat former governor Terry Branstad in the party primary that year. Rants had hoped to get the nomination based on his near twenty years of legislative experience, combined with the fact that no other Republican notables were running for the job to oppose incumbent Democrat Chet Culver. But that ended when the party leaders successfully begged Branstad, who had served from 1983 through 1998, to come out of political retirement and some of the party's wealthiest supporters infused the former governor's campaign with more money than the rest of the field could raise. Now, two years later, Rants traveled the country as a political consultant but maintained his home in Sioux City. He also wrote an occasional column for the *Sioux City Journal* about various political issues.

On September 30, 2012, Rants unexpectedly used his column to recount his meeting in late 2003 with Chuck Hurley, the conservative lobbyist who had insisted that the Republican leaders push for passage of a constitutional amendment restricting marriage to a man and a woman. That attempt had failed in the Iowa Senate, removing a major obstacle to the filing of the *Varnum* lawsuit. In the column, Rants recounted for the first time publicly how Hurley had asked for the meeting and expressed concern that the Iowa law restricting marriage to a man and a woman had to be enshrined in the Iowa Constitution.

But then Rants struck what would be viewed as a stunning blow to the effort to oust Wiggins.

> The FAMiLY Leader, out on their bus tour, would have us believe that our supreme court hijacked the constitution, usurping the roles of chief executive and legislature. Justice Wiggins must go or the republic will fail.
>
> That is not true. That is why I will vote YES to retain Justice Wiggins.

Rants went on to explain that during the 2003 meeting he and Hurley had even discussed the likelihood that the Iowa Supreme Court would overturn the law if it ever reached them. That's why, he said. Iowa voters needed to understand that the members of the Iowa Supreme Court who decided *Varnum* had just been doing their job.

> I share this story because those who want to toss Justice Wiggins are the same ones who came to me knowing the law wouldn't stand up to constitutional scrutiny. Why else put it in the constitution? Every lawyer I talked to in advance of the ruling who read the briefs submitted to the court told me the law was going to be tossed. In short, the court did what we expected.

Rants then said that those who opposed the decision held as much responsibility for allowing the decision to stand as the court itself.

> The blame lies with us. We didn't put it in the Constitution despite ample opportunity. By "we" I mean all of us. There have been three elections since our first attempt, and Iowans apparently have chosen to not elect a legislature to do that.

Rants concluded with a shot at the leaders of the effort to oust Wiggins.

> The last thing we want in Iowa is a court that is engaged in political campaigns, raising money from PACs, and worried about their poll numbers. We especially do not want them responding to threats from bullies.[14]

Within a week, Rants's column had been reprinted in various newspapers across the state and, as one would expect, drew criticsm from those pushing for Wiggins's ouster. Hurley, in a response printed the following week in the *Sioux City Journal*, urged voters to reject Wiggins's retention, contending his behavior threatens all of our freedoms.

> When Judge Wiggins and his fellow activist judges concluded that they should recognize a brand new "right, heretofore unimagined" by creating (legislating) a new category of marriage, they stepped out of their constititutional bounds. If we allow them to "legislate from the bench" without the voters holding them accountable, no right is safe.

Of Rants's column, Hurley pointed out that the former legislator had wrongly identified most of the court members as Branstad appointees but acknowledged "that groups like ours have been concerned for nearly a decade that Wiggins & Co. would try to legislate from the bench."

"Finally, Rants calls people like us who resist power-grabbing judges 'bullies,'" Hurley wrote, invoking Thomas Jefferson's criticism of the potential dangers of the judiciary becoming an oligarchical institution. "I'll humbly join his company. But I prefer the term 'patriot.'"[15]

The transformation of Jeff Angelo, the former Republican state senator, was one of the signs that things were changing. He could have been a poster boy for the shifting attitudes on marriage equality. In 1998, he and fellow conservative Steve King had voted against the state's Defense of Marriage Act because it didn't go far enough. To Angelo's way of thinking in those days, same-sex couples wanting to marry weren't asking for equal rights. They were asking for "special rights," which meant the sacred institution of marriage was under attack, and it was up to the defenders of traditional marriage to help rescue it. Same-sex couples just didn't understand. They already had the same rights as heterosexuals. They could marry a member of the opposite sex if they wanted. It was simply their choice to go the other way. Besides, kids need a mom and a dad. That was the secular reasoning.

But like many evangelical conservatives, Angelo was mostly against same-sex marriage on religious grounds. If you believed in the separation of church and state, though, it was more difficult to make the argument. So Angelo stayed away from the line of reasoning that truly convinced him: marriage was strictly between a man and a woman because that's how God wanted it. The Iowa Constitution reflected the will of God. That's just the way it was.

When Angelo helped chase Jonathan Wilson off the Des Moines school board in 1995 after twelve years of service, it wasn't because the man was doing a bad job. It was because he was gay. Years later, Angelo acknowledged the truth.

"Was it religious in nature? Completely." But over time, it became increasingly more difficult for the conservative legislator to make that claim. Being gay wasn't like exceeding the speed limit on the highway. It wasn't something you could stop.

As late as 2004—a year before Robert Hanson's decision on behalf of the *Varnum* plaintiffs in Polk County—Angelo was a lead sponsor on the constitutional amendment to protect marriage. It was win-win politics.

When Angelo read Hanson's decision on *Varnum*, he shrugged and said, "Activist judge." Unlike some politicians, however, Angelo never felt the need to surround himself with people who only agreed with him. Then, as now, he had gay friends. When he'd launch into his love-the-sinner-hate-the-sin monologue, his closer friends would call him out. No, they really weren't okay with that. It made them feel like second-class citizens.

One legislator in particular, Sandy Vopalka, the founder and president of Equality Iowa, had become one of Angelo's statehouse breakfast buddies. Before he left office, she sat down with him and explained the difficulties gay people encounter every day. "Look," she told him, "when I walk into a hospital, I can't get information about my significant other because I'm not related to her."[16]

Angelo began to think about a farmer from his district who died of AIDS, leaving his partner behind. Their relationship was no secret, and nobody seemed to care. He was the stereotypical farmer: tractor, seed corn cap. Angelo vowed to do whatever he could to push for more AIDS funding. He started talking to other gay and lesbian people, asking them questions. He decided not run for reelection and left office at the end of 2008.

After the *Varnum* decision a few months later, a gay couple who owned one of the best restaurants in Ames, asked Angelo's wife, Tara van Brederode, to be the witness when they applied for their marriage license. "They weren't sure how long they had before a temporary stay was issued," Angelo said. "They ran up to the courthouse with Tara in tow. It was a moment when I said, Okay, how do I really feel about this?"

Angelo's view on same-sex marriage began to change, but he didn't say much about it publicly. His slow transformation stunned his liberal wife. Before getting married, they had promised neither would ever try to convert the other on a political issue or ideological belief. Tara never sat down with him and said, "Let me give you ten points why you should be in favor of same-sex marriage."

Angelo's metamorphosis continued. Over time, he met more people and got to know them. Angelo was at a park in Ames about a month before the 2010 retention vote when he ran into a gay friend handing out leaflets saying Iowa needed to keep all three on the ballot. Later Angelo said,

Here we are in a retention fight. We're having this long conversation, and he says, "You know what, Jeff? Being a gay man in Iowa is really great." That jolted me. I said how can you say that in the middle of all this? He said, "Jeff, what's going on politically is not reflected in the community. We're a live-and-let-live state. Everybody knows I'm gay. I've never been hassled for it. I've always felt comfortable here. I understand the politics just don't reflect that right now."

Those words had an impact. As he thought about it, one thing became clear to him: the public's attitude on homosexuality had changed, but the politicians' hadn't. "I gave that a lot of thought. The whole political debate is divorced from what goes on in the communities," Angelo said.

The tipping point came when a Republican lobbyist friend for One Iowa, the LGBT organization, asked Angelo if he would testify against the constitutional amendment banning gay marriage at an Iowa House hearing in 2011. He said he'd be willing to testify that this is not how the constitution should be used but didn't want to go further.

"No, Jeff," the woman said, "I need someone who'll stand up and say, 'I'm a Republican and I think gay marriage is okay.'" Angelo took a day to think about it, called his friend, and said he was in. As Angelo said years later,

Folks like Bob Vander Plaats have done a very good job saying there isn't any real disagreement in the Republican Party on this. Well, there is. Somebody has to organize the Republicans who think differently. As my wife is fond of telling me — and she's exactly right — who's moving to other side of this issue? Every time you see movement, it's movement toward marriage equality. You know it's the right thing to do. You know history is going to be on your side.

I'm a hardened activist Republican. Somebody needs to say it: "Dudes, we're wrong on this issue." Then a few more people have to say it and a few more . . . and a few more.

On the night of the 2012 judicial retention vote, Angelo got his wish. A few more and a few more added up to 680,284 "yes" votes for David Wiggins to 567,024 "no" votes — or some 110,000 more than he needed to keep his job. The rules don't allow the justice to go back in time to 2010 and transfer some of the overflow to Ternus, Streit, and Baker, but they would have come in handy. Iowa's secretary of state laid out the numbers. Wiggins received 54.6 percent of the "yes" votes. Compare that with the 54 percent "no" Marsha Ternus collected two years before. And the 54.4 percent "no" for Streit and the 54.2 percent "no" for Baker.

Only nine of Iowa's ninety-nine counties voted yes in 2010. Two years later, the number was thirty-four. The difference was turnout: 2010 — 1.13 million voters; 2012 — 1.589 million.

Wiggins gave all the credit to the presidential election and Obama's coattails. Rightly so, but that's turnout and timing for you. And don't forget money. According to statistics compiled by the Brennan Center for Justice at the New York University School of Law, the difference in Retention Battle Two reflected a number of factors besides the quick and unrelenting response of Justice Not Politics. In 2012, antiretention groups spent more than a half million dollars less than they had two years before. Still, they outspent the opposition by more than a hundred thousand dollars.

The court members did a better job connecting with the electorate. They left their chambers more often, speaking to various groups, holding oral arguments, talking to students. They began live-streaming oral arguments.

Yet Wiggins wasn't the only winner that night. Senate Majority Leader Michael Gronstal, who had stood with his Democratic colleagues and refused to allow a vote on a constitutional amendment to reverse *Varnum* since 2009, won reelection to another four-year term with 55 percent of the vote. Democrats also maintained control of the Iowa Senate, thus delaying any possibility of a vote on a constitutional amendment until 2018.

But something else was happening, though it would be days before the final results were in. The push nationally for marriage equality had gained momentum. Voters in three states — Maryland, Maine, and Washington — upheld state laws permitting same-sex couples to marry. What's more, Minnesota voters rejected a proposed constitutional amendment restricting marriage to a man and a woman. Six months later, Minnesota governor Mark Dayton signed legislation making it legal for same-sex couples to marry. Minnesota — as in 1868 when it had joined Iowa to become the second state in the union to approve black male suffrage — became the second state in the Midwest to permit the marriage of same-sex couples.

On election night, somewhere around the time Republican pundits Karl Rove and Dick Morris finally stopped insisting vehemently on Fox News that Romney would win going away, it was time for Vander Plaats to pop out of seclusion and talk about what had just happened. Much of the crowd in the beautiful big home in Grimes that served as election night headquarters for the "no" campaign had dispersed. Vander Plaats and his retention crew were going over the postmortem in another part of the house.

Earlier in the evening, a party room off the swimming pool had been filled with laughter and good vibes. People huddled in small groups, eating snacks, sipping soft drinks, laughing, chatting, and watching the big flatscreen TV above the fireplace. Every so often Vander Plaats or Chuck Hurley or one of the younger Family Leaders wandered through on the way to or from a meeting room. Reporters set up their cameras and laptops in anticipation of what was to come.

When Vander Plaats materialized after the results were in, he wasn't quite as upbeat and cheerful as usual. He echoed the turnout chorus, saying Obama probably had fifty vote-generating offices around the state. He passed on recycling his dueling-bus-tour comments about Wiggins being "arrogant," "confrontational," "not all that bright," and "lazy." He didn't say much about Wiggins at all. Except this: "So the Wiggins thing. The educator in me says we still won. Whether he gets unseated or not, we still won."[17]

For the old coach in Vander Plaats, whose victories and defeats were always decided by the unimpeachable numbers on a scoreboard, it was an interesting perspective.

CHAPTER THIRTEEN

Iowa

After the Iowa Supreme Court handed down its unanimous decision in *Varnum v. Brien*, shock waves had rippled through the country—not only that day, but long after.

Carlos Moreno, a retired member of the California Supreme Court, remembers exactly where he was April 3, 2009, when he heard about the decision.[1] "I was driving from Hartford to New Haven for a legal conference, and it came over the radio." Moreno's interest was strong. He and the rest of California's high court had just heard oral arguments over the constitutionality of Proposition 8, an initiative by California voters requiring a return to one-man, one-woman marriages.

"When I heard the Iowa Supreme Court had voted unanimously to allow same-sex marriage, I was quite surprised," Moreno said. "I knew it was significant because it was from the heartland, and it was unanimous." So significant, in fact, that Moreno quoted liberally from the decision in a concurring and dissenting opinion after the court upheld Proposition 8 less than two months after *Varnum*. Moreno's opinion even opened with a direct quote from *Varnum*: "the 'absolute equality of all' persons before the law [is] 'the very foundation principle of our government' (*Varnum v. Brien* (Iowa 2009) 763 N.W.2d 862, 877)."[2]

This initial decision upholding Proposition 8 was only the start of four litigious years in the debate over same-sex marriage in California. In 2013, the U.S. Supreme Court let stand a decision by U.S. District Court judge Vaughn Walker declaring Proposition 8 unconstitutional.

Jim Nelson also remembers the first time he read the *Varnum* decision.

As an equal-rights advocate for the gays, lesbians, bisexuals, and transgendered of Montana, the associate justice of the Montana Supreme Court believed the Iowa decision could sway his colleagues.[3] "What is remarkable about the ruling is its courage and clarity," he said. "It was unanimous, had common sense, and was classic equal-protection analysis. It impressed me greatly." Nelson had hoped *Varnum* would persuade his colleagues on the Montana bench to open the door to same-sex civil unions despite a constitutional amendment against same-sex marriage. He was wrong. In his words, the Montana court had succeeded only in "punting its responsibilities." In his 2012 dissent after the court's 4–3 decision, Nelson cited *Varnum* extensively.[4]

But *Varnum*'s impact wasn't just immediate. In April 2014, Judge Carlos Lucero of the Tenth Circuit Court of Appeals in Denver asked an attorney defending Utah's constitutional ban on same-sex marriage about two of the plaintiffs in the case. They were Dr. Karen Archer, a sixty-eight-year-old retired physician, and Kate Call, Archer's sixty-year-old spouse. Archer and Call had married in Iowa "out of the necessity of providing whatever security they could for their relationship."[5]

Because Utah's law prohibited recognition of the couple's marriage, Lucero asked how their circumstances were different from the case involving a slave named Dred Scott. "There are plaintiffs here who validly married in Iowa, but they came to Utah and they can never, forever be married. The door has been locked, the key thrown away, and it has been destroyed by whoever found it." He then asked Gene Schaerr, an attorney representing Utah, how Archer and Call's claim to be recognized as a married couple was any different from Scott's claim to be recognized as a free man after he had spent years living in states where human bondage was illegal. It was only when Scott returned to Missouri, a slave state, that he could no longer claim his freedom. "It seems to me, this is an identical situation," Lucero said.[6] In 2013 his argument was bolstered by the U.S. Supreme Court, which ruled unconstitutional a federal law denying federal benefits to legally married same-sex couples in any state.

A month later, two army veterans—Marla Cattermole, fifty-eight, and Julia Lobur, fifty-four—had their 2009 Iowa marriage finally recognized in Pennsylvania. The state's governor, Thomas Corbett, threw in the towel on that case in May 2014 when a federal court judge ruled unconstitutional the state law limiting marriage to a man and a woman. The two women, who had married in Lobur's home town of Carroll, Iowa, but were residents of Pennsylvania, had been in a committed relationship for twenty-seven years after meeting during basic training.

In his decision, Corbett, a former Pennsylvania attorney general, drew a distinction between his personal beliefs and his view of the law, much like *Varnum*. "As a Roman Catholic, the traditional teaching of my faith has not wavered," Corbett said. "I continue to maintain the belief that marriage is between one man and one woman." But he added,

> My duties as governor require that I follow the laws as interpreted by the courts and make a judgment as to the likelihood of a successful appeal. . . .
>
> It is my hope that as the important issue of same-sex relationships continues to be addressed in our society, that [*sic*] all involved be treated with respect.[7]

A month after Corbett's decision, Judge Lucero of the Tenth Circuit would write the majority opinion in declaring Utah's constitutional amendment limiting marriage to a man and a woman unconstitutional. He also would find marriage of gays and lesbians to be a fundamental right. In his opinion, Lucero wrote,

> We hold that the Fourteenth Amendment protects the fundamental right to marry, establish a family, raise children, and enjoy the full protection of a state's marital laws. A state may not deny the issuance of a marriage license to two persons, or refuse to recognize their marriage, based solely upon the sex of the persons in the marriage union.[8]

The momentum behind broad social acceptance of the argument the Iowa Supreme Court justices made in the *Varnum* decision continues to grow.

- Since 2009, thirty-five states and the District of Columbia have either approved same-sex marriage legislatively or have been forced to allow it through court order. Iowa was the first state in the Midwest to approve same-sex marriage and was joined by Minnesota and Illinois, but not until 2013.

- The vast majority of court decisions related to same-sex marriage bans throughout the country cite *Varnum*. More than four hundred law review articles now refer to the decision.
- Since the *Varnum* decision, polls show Iowans have gradually come to accept same-sex marriage with a shrug more than anything else. An Iowa poll conducted by the *Des Moines Register* and published in March 2014 found that 36 percent of the population didn't care about same-sex marriage one way or the other. The poll revealed that 34 percent of the population remained disappointed by the *Varnum* decision, but 28 percent were proud. A separate poll in 2012 also found that 56 percent of Iowans opposed amending the state's constitution to ban same-sex marriage.
- Cries for impeachment or ouster have waned. Calls for the heads of the remaining *Varnum* justices are intended more for political posturing and fund-raising and aren't taken seriously. Though Justices Cady, Hecht, and Appel face retention elections in 2016 and a likely challenge from conservative groups, they appear much more secure than were Ternus, Baker, Streit, or Wiggins.
- As a political issue, the fervor about marriage equality has waned to the degree that some Republicans prefer to let the matter drop. For example, Republicans in Iowa's First and Second Districts urged their platform writers to reject any plank calling for a constitutional ban on same-sex marriage for the 2014 election. The issue Republicans had regarded as a political winner in 2004, they now are more apt to avoid. Further proof: the once-hot marriage equality issue was seldom mentioned by candidates of either party during the 2014 campaign. Despite reelecting Republican Terry Branstad governor and lifting Republican state senator Joni Ernst to the U.S. Senate, voters kept Democrats in control of the Iowa Senate by a slim 26–24 margin. Both Branstad and Ernst have advocated a constitutional amendment restricting marriage to a man and a woman. But Iowa voters, including those from the

district that reelected its state senator Matt McCoy, made certain a marriage amendment vote would be held no earlier than 2020.

- Finally, a decision by the U.S. Supreme Court on whether same-sex marriage is a right under the Fourteenth Amendment appeared likely, despite the apparent reluctance of the court to take up the issue. On October 6, 2014, the court declined to grant certiorari to any of the five appeals overturning same-sex marriage bans in Utah, Wisconsin, Indiana, Oklahoma, and Virginia. Within weeks, bans fell in eight other states as well: Arizona, Alaska, Colorado, Idaho, West Virginia, Wyoming, Nevada, and North Carolina. For the first time a majority of states permitted gay and lesbian partners to marry. But a month later, on a 2–1 vote, the Sixth Circuit Court of Appeals ruled four states— Michigan, Ohio, Tennessee, and Kentucky—could continue to restrict marriage to a man and a woman. That ruling conflicted with decisions in the Fourth, Seventh, Ninth, and Tenth Circuits that found such restrictions unconstitutional. As a result, the U.S. Supreme Court was expected to take up the issue either in 2015 or 2016 to resolve the conflict.

In 1997, Richard Posner, the prolific legal commentator, economist, and member of the Seventh Circuit Court of Appeals, wrote a review of William N. Eskridge's book, *The Case for Same-Sex Marriage*. In it, Posner voiced opposition to the U.S. Supreme Court taking on the constitutional issue as proposed by Eskridge.

A decision by the Supreme Court holding that the Constitution entitles people to marry others of the same sex would be far more radical than any of the decisions cited by Eskridge. Its moorings in text, precedent, public policy, and public opinion would be too tenuous to rally even minimum public support. It would be an unprecedented example of judicial immodesty. That well-worn epithet "usurpative" would finally fit.[9]

Posner feared a court ruling permitting homosexuals to marry—"a radical social policy . . . that exists in no other country of the world"—would prompt a backlash severely damaging to the judiciary's credibility.[10] Simply put, Posner said, the public's opposition at that time was too strong and too widespread for a prudent judiciary to confront. Much of the public believed removing the restrictions amounted to societal approval of the homosexual lifestyle.

But Posner, who acknowledged, despite some misgivings, that allowing same-sex marriage had merit, recommended a remedy—one quite prophetic considering what would take place over the following two decades. In his book review, he wrote,

> Let a state legislature or activist (but elected, and hence democratically responsive) state court adopt homosexual marriage as a policy in one state, and let the rest of the country learn from the results of its experiment.[11]

Posner even provided a template of what a court decision upholding a right to marriage for same-sex couples must include.

> If it is truly a new right, as a right to same-sex marriage would be, text and precedent are not going to dictate the judges' conclusion. They will have to go beyond the technical legal materials of decision and consider moral, political, empirical, prudential, and institutional issues, including the public acceptability of a decision recognizing the new right.[12]

Did the *Varnum* decision meet that standard?

Clearly, Iowans who voted three justices of the Iowa Supreme Court off the bench in 2010 didn't think so. But two years later—when 73 percent of Iowans voted, as opposed to 53 percent two years earlier—the judgment was quite different: David Wiggins was retained.

Interestingly, Wiggins, in an interview for this book before his retention election, took issue with the claim that he and his colleagues had found that gays and lesbians have a fundamental right to marry a person of the same sex or even that they had changed the definition of marriage. "We said that people who are in committed same-sex relationships were similarly situated to opposite-sex couples in committed relationships," he said. "We never found a fundamental right."

By that wording, Wiggins also provided the court a means to avoid the next inevitable firestorm. Posner and other conservative commentators suggest that recognizing a fundamental right to marry opens the door for polygamy.

Ironically, Posner would reverse his 1997 view when he wrote the decision on bans in Wisconsin and Indiana for the Seventh Circuit Court of Appeals. Posner, whose ruling was released just nine days after oral arguments, echoed Cady's analysis regarding the justifications for limiting marriage to a man and a woman.

> The challenged laws discriminate against a minority defined by an immutable characteristic, and the only rationale that the states put forth with any conviction—that same-sex couples and their children don't *need* marriage because same-sex couples can't *produce* children, intended or unintended—is so full of holes that it cannot be taken seriously.[13]

Was *Varnum* the tipping point in the national debate over same-sex marriage? That's debatable. Was it more important than the 2003 Massachusetts decision? Or the U.S. District Court's reversal of California's constitutional ban in 2010? More important than the 2013 U.S. Supreme Court decision invalidating the federal DOMA for New Yorker Edith Windsor?

Each decision played a part in what has become one of the quickest turnarounds in the country's judicial history. But *Varnum*'s significance runs deeper than that. It's also about a group of little-known, everyday Iowans, who fought for their rights against great odds and persuaded powerful people to do the right thing.

For his part, Mark Cady doesn't dwell on the significance of the decision. When the opinion's lead writer runs into critics, he smiles and thanks them for sharing their views. From the beginning, he understood not everyone would approve. To grateful supporters, Cady's response seldom varies—"Just doing my job"—which doesn't mean he takes their kind words for granted. On four occasions since the *Varnum* decision, he has officiated marriages of same-sex couples and was deeply moved each time.

"When I see same-sex couples share in everything that goes with marriage—after they were denied—it gets to me," he said, adding he wished all could see the value of the judicial process and how it can make life better for more people.

Cady became chief justice after the 2010 ouster of his three colleagues. In response to the losing retention vote, he developed a strategy to make sure Iowans had greater access to the court and its members. Several times each year the seven justices travel to a different city where oral arguments on actual cases are held in front of large audiences. Oral arguments in Des Moines are streamed live on the Internet. Cady and the other justices also go out into the various communities and talk about the state's judiciary and how it operates.

"The public will respond in a positive way to the courts when they can see them as they are instead of how those with an agenda want the courts to be seen," he said. The chief justice also has taken time to think about the *Varnum* decision and what ultimately prompted him to lead the court into historic civil rights territory. He acknowledged that he once believed the state could justify a ban on same-sex marriage simply by saying "it's better for children to grow up in an environment with a mom and a dad because they both offer a perspective that's helpful. But," Cady added,

what I realized and what was confirmed by the evidence is I felt that way only because I grew up with a mom and dad, and I valued having a mom and dad. When you dig down hard enough, you find out it doesn't make a whit of difference to children whether they have two moms or two dads or a mom and a dad or one mom and a dad in prison for life.

Cady said that realization no longer allowed him to continue to think as he had in the past. "You get behind the arc when you refuse to look at the reality that the world is starting to show something different."

He admits that even the Iowa court has fallen victim to such thinking. As an example, he cites a 1911 Iowa Supreme Court decision in which the court upheld a state law forbidding female pharmacists from dispensing drugs containing alcohol or alcoholic products like whiskey. When a female pharmacist from Mason City objected to the law on the grounds of equal protection, the court ruled against her, saying there was a legislative justification for it. As Cady sees it, "They basically said we all know there are just some things that men do better than women." Similarly, early same-sex marriage cases were written to maintain the status quo and echoed the attitude of the Iowa Supreme Court back in 1911.

Judges were saying it's better to have both a mom and dad in the family. But those were judges who just couldn't break away from past thinking. And that is what the whole evolution of equal protection is about. It's breaking away from the way we used to think when the old way of thinking is no longer valid.

Cady also has praise for the work of Roger Kuhle and Michael O'Meara, who represented Polk County in the case. The chief justice said that any suggestion from critics that the defense team's legal effort was halfhearted or incomplete is wrong. "Roger and Mike are good lawyers. They did the job they were called to do and did it in a professional way. I respected their approach to this case very much."

For Dennis Johnson, the local cocounsel, his work on the case illuminated how badly gay and lesbian Iowans had been treated for years and how they dealt with it. He said,

Now I realize how unbelievably ignorant I was of the whole situation of being gay in America. And that is what I learned. The insensitivity shocks me yet. It wasn't malicious. It was just pure ignorance as a straight person.

Johnson and his wife had gay and lesbian friends, but they had never talked to them about "how hard it was to be gay."

I never had that conversation with anybody. I should have thought about it. No one ever talked to me — none of the couples — about how disadvantaged they were by not being able to be married.

Camilla Taylor, the lead lawyer from Lambda and now the group's marriage director, said she knew from the beginning Iowa's court system was to be respected, but the impact of the *Varnum* decision nationally is difficult to exaggerate. She acknowledged that three other states — Massachusetts, Connecticut, and California — had moved before Iowa to allow same-sex couples to marry, but she described the Iowa decision as "a game-changer."

"It was transformative," she said, "because for the first time it was a unanimous decision from a state high court and it was a decision from the middle of the country." Taylor said that Iowa will now be seen by same-sex marriage advocates as the place that made it possible for them to gain the right to marry. Until the *Varnum* decision, even advocates had considered the issue mostly as something regional or, at minimum, something potentially viable only on the liberal coasts. As she views it,

> the courage of the court here created courage many, many other places and precipitated wins that we might not have been able to get otherwise. What has happened in legislatures in the weeks, months, and years since the *Varnum* decision has illustrated that.

But Christopher Rants, the former speaker of the Iowa House, might have the best assessment of the true impact of the *Varnum* decision. After all the years of fighting the decision, Rants believes *Varnum* simply started the country down a road that now seems inevitable. He says,

> The *Will and Grace* generation has decided this issue. They have mobilized and done a masterful job at working this issue. So often in politics we try to change people's minds before we change their hearts. They went and changed hearts.
>
> The battle has been lost on this issue . . . or won depending on your perspective. But it's been decided.

It certainly has been decided for McKinley BarbouRoske and her sister, Bre, who have had married parents for more than five years now. And, given the direction of court decisions, it appears likely to be decided for everyone, whether it is done in one fell swoop by the U.S. Supreme Court in the next year or two or on a state-by-state basis.

As Chief Justice Cady has remarked in public appearances since the decision, "It is the way civil rights evolves in America and the way we move toward that 'more perfect Union' just as our Founders hoped.

"In that way, we all win; it just will not be seen by all at the same time."

Appendix: Figures of Importance

PLAINTIFF COUPLES

Jen and Dawn BarbouRoske: The couple lives in Iowa City and has two children, McKinley and Breeanna.

Larry Hoch and David Twombley: The couple, both former schoolteachers, lives in the Des Moines area in retirement.

Bill Musser and Otter Dreaming: The two musicians (among countless other pursuits) had played at many weddings. Eight years after meeting in 2001, they finally were married at their home in Decorah.

Ingrid Olson and Reva Evans: The Council Bluffs couple and their son, Jamison, lived for a while in the former home of Evans's grandmother, who'd spent sixty years there. Married in June 2009, Evans and Olson divorced two and a half years later.

Chuck and Jason Swaggerty-Morgan: The couple lives in Sioux City, where they care for their five adopted children: Ta'John and Reed, biological brothers adopted on the same day; Rain and Micah, biological sister and brother; and Torrey.

Katherine and Patricia Varnum: The couple lives in the Cedar Rapids area and has adopted a son, Alex.

CHILDREN OF PLAINTIFF COUPLES NAMED AS
MINOR CHILDREN PLAINTIFFS IN *VARNUM* LAWSUIT

Breeanna BarbouRoske: Adopted child of Dawn and Jen BarbouRoske. Born in 2002, she was three weeks old when placed with the BarbouRoskes as a foster child. Jointly adopted in 2003.

McKinley BarbouRoske: Biological daughter of Jen BarbouRoske, who was forced to temporarily terminate her parental rights to allow partner Dawn BarbouRoske to finalize a second-parent adoption agreement. Described by Lambda Legal attorney Camilla Taylor as "the heart and soul" of the *Varnum* case.

Jamison Olson: Son of Reva Evans and Ingrid Olson. Conceived through donor insemination and born to Evans in 2006.

Brent Appel: Iowa Supreme Court justice for *Varnum v. Brien* up for retention in 2016.

David Baker: Iowa Supreme Court justice voted out (with Ternus) in 2010 retention vote.

Mark S. Cady: Chief justice of the Iowa Supreme Court as of 2010 after the 2009 retention vote. Cady is up for retention in 2016. Principal author of *Varnum v. Brien*.

Robert Hanson: District court judge who initially ruled that Iowa's law restricting marriage to a man and a woman was unconstitutional under the due process and equal protection guarantees of the Iowa Constitution.

Daryl Hecht: Iowa Supreme Court justice for *Varnum v. Brien*, up for retention in 2016.

Edward Mansfield: Appointed to the Iowa Supreme Court by Iowa governor Terry Branstad to replace one of the justices voted out in 2009.

Margaret Marshall: Chief justice of the Supreme Judicial Court of Massachusetts from 1999 to 2010. She wrote the decision in *Goodridge v. Department of Public Health*, which made Massachusetts the first state to legalize marriage between same-sex couples.

Jeff Neary: District court judge who set the *Varnum* decision into motion by dissolving the marriage of a lesbian couple at a time when same-sex marriage was not legal in Iowa.

Michael Streit: Iowa Supreme Court justice for *Varnum v. Brien*; voted out (with Ternus and Baker) in 2010 retention vote.

Marsha Ternus: Chief justice for *Varnum v. Brien*; voted out in the 2010 retention vote.

Thomas Waterman: Appointed to the Iowa Supreme Court by Iowa governor Terry Branstad to replace one of the justices voted out in 2009.

David Wiggins: Iowa Supreme Court justice for *Varnum v. Brien*, who survived 2012 retention vote to serve another eight-year term.

Bruce Zager: Appointed to the Iowa Supreme Court by Iowa governor Terry Branstad to replace one of the justices voted out in 2009.

Jeff Angelo: Former Iowa state legislator who began his career as a strident opponent of allowing same-sex couples to marry. He later changed his position to become an outspoken advocate of marriage equality.

Christine Branstad: Lawyer and niece of Republican governor Terry Brandstad.

She was an active participant on a 2012 tour of Iowa towns in an effort to retain David Wiggins.

Timothy J. Brien: Polk County recorder. The Brien in *Varnum v. Brien*.

Guy Cook: Iowa State Bar Association president after Cynthia Moser. As president-elect, Cook led the Iowa State Bar Association effort (including a much-publicized bus tour) for David Wiggins in the 2012 judicial retention vote.

Richard Eychaner: A Des Moines businessman who ran for the Republican Party nomination for congress twice in the 1980s. Eychaner's foundation also sponsors the Matthew Shepard Scholarship Award for outstanding gay, lesbian, and transgender high school students.

Chuck Hurley: Social conservative activist and lobbyist for FAMiLY Leader. Hurley is a former Iowa state legislator.

Dennis Johnson: Des Moines lawyer and cocounsel to plaintiffs in the *Varnum* lawsuit. Johnson handled the oral arguments before district court judge Robert Hanson and the Iowa Supreme Court.

Roger Kuhle: Des Moines lawyer serving in the civil division of the Polk County attorney's office. Kuhle was the lead attorney in defending the Iowa marriage restriction law before Judge Hanson and the Iowa Supreme Court.

Sharon Malheiro: Des Moines lawyer specializing in representing gays, lesbians, and transgenders and a gay advocacy activist.

Cynthia Moser: Iowa State Bar Association president between Robert Waterman and Guy Cook.

Ben Parrott: Law clerk to Justice Mark Cady at the time of the *Varnum* decision. He later became an assistant Iowa attorney general.

Janelle Rettig: Gay and lesbian rights activist who is a former staff member for Iowa congressman Jim Leach. She married Robin Butler in 2003 in Toronto. Rettig also has been elected to the Johnson County board of supervisors.

Dennis Ringgenberg: Sioux City lawyer who handled the divorce petition of *Kimberly Jean Brown v. Jennifer Sue Perez* before Judge Neary.

Camilla Taylor: Marriage project director for Lambda Legal and cocounsel for the plaintiffs in *Varnum v. Brien*.

Bob Vander Plaats: Social conservative activist and president of FAMiLY Leader. Vander Plaats led the successful effort against the retention of justices Ternus, Streit, and Baker.

Jonathan Wilson: Des Moines school board member removed by voters after a whisper campaign focusing on his homosexuality.

Terry Branstad: Republican Iowa governor who appointed two of the *Varnum* justices. Branstad was reelected to the governorship in 2010.

Michael Gronstal: Longtime Democrat, Iowa state legislator from Council Bluffs. Since 2007, Gronstal has refused to allow a senate vote on a constitutional amendment restricting marriage to a man and a woman. He was reelected in 2012.

Steve King: Former Iowa state legislator and now a U.S. congressman from Iowa's Fourth District.

Mary Lundby: Legislator from Marion who would become the Iowa Senate Republican leader prior to her death in 2009 from cervical cancer.

Matt McCoy: A member of the Iowa Senate in 1998 who voted to restrict marriage to a man and a woman. Six years later, McCoy acknowledged he was gay and actively fought an attempt to place the restriction in the Iowa Constitution.

Christopher Rants: Former Republican Speaker of the Iowa House from Sioux City who served nearly twenty years in the legislature.

Tom Vilsack: A member of the Iowa Senate in 1998 who also would vote to restrict marriage to a man and a woman. Later that year, he became the first Democrat to hold the governor's office in almost thirty years. Vilsack was appointed U.S. secretary of agriculture by President Barack Obama and served in both terms of the Obama administration.

HISTORICAL FIGURES

David Bunker: Republican delegate to the Iowa Constitutional Convention of 1857 from Washington County and an Iowa state lawmaker. Bunker was instrumental in getting the convention to adopt new language to Article I, Section 1, of the Iowa Constitution so it would begin "All men are, by nature, free and equal."

Rufus L. B. Clarke: Republican delegate to the Iowa Constitutional Convention of 1857 who advocated for black suffrage as well as for removing all racial references from the constitution.

Amos Harris: Democratic delegate to the Iowa Constitutional Convention of 1857 from Appanoose County and an Iowa state lawmaker. He opposed allowing freed slaves and those of mixed race to settle in Iowa.

Ralph: Missouri slave who crossed into the Iowa territory with the permission of his owner. On Independence Day 1839, Ralph became a free man as a result of the first decision by the Iowa Territorial Supreme Court.

Notes

CHAPTER 1

1. Authors' interviews with Jen and Dawn BarbouRoske, September 8, 2012, and October 25, 2013. All recollections and quotations by the BarbouRoskes—Jen, Dawn, and daughter McKinley—in this and subsequent chapters are from the authors' interview unless otherwise noted.

2. Goodridge v. Department of Public Health, 440 Mass. 309, 312 (2003).

3. Varnum v. Brien, 763 N.W. 2d, 862 (Iowa 2009).

4. "Is America Warming to Same-Sex Marriage?," Kenji Yoshino interview by Michel Martin, *Tell Me More*, National Public Radio podcast audio, April 10, 2009.

5. Kenji Yoshino, "Invoking Iowa's History of Civil Rights," *New York Times*, April 3, 2009.

6. Patricia A. Cain, "Contextualizing Varnum v. Brien," 13 *Journal of Gender, Race & Justice* 27 (2009): 47–49.

7. Oral Arguments, Hollingsworth v. Perry, 12-144 (March 26, 2013), 21.

CHAPTER 2

1. Authors' interview with Matt McCoy, May 15, 2014. All McCoy recollections and quotations in this and subsequent chapters are from the authors' interview unless otherwise noted.

2. Andrew Koppelman, *Same Sex, Different States* (New Haven, CT: Yale University Press, 2006), 117.

3. Ralph U. Whitten, "Full Faith and Credit for Dummies," *Creighton Law Review* 38, no. 465 (2005): 479.

4. Keyes and Buchanan quotations are from "Campaign to Protect Marriage Rally," C-SPAN video, February 10, 1996, http://www.c-span.org/video/?69857-1/campaign-protect-marriage-rally.

5. Authors' interview with Dan Johnston, May 22, 2012. All Johnston recollections and quotations are from the authors' interview unless otherwise noted.

6. *Des Moines (IA) Register*, February 1, 1978.

7. Authors' interview with Janelle Rettig and Robin Butler, October 25, 2013. All recollections and quotations of Rettig and Butler in this and subsequent chapters are from the authors' interview unless otherwise noted.

8. Authors' interview with Jeff Angelo, July 6, 2012. All Angelo recollections and quotations in this and subsequent chapters are from the authors' interview unless otherwise noted.

9. Authors' telephone interview with Secretary of Agriculture Tom Vilsack, August 29, 2014. All Vilsack recollections and quotations in this and subsequent chapters are from the authors' interview unless otherwise noted.

CHAPTER 3

1. *The Debates of the Constitutional Convention of the State of Iowa, Assembled at Iowa City* (Davenport: Luse, Lane & Co., 1857), 1:103–104.

2. William Salter, *The Life of James W. Grimes: Governor of Iowa, 1854–1858; A Senator of the United States, 1859–1869* (New York: Appleton, 1876), 59.

3. In the Matter of Ralph (A Colored Man) on Habeas Corpus, in *Reports of Cases Argued and Determined in the Supreme Court of Iowa, 1839* (Davenport: Griggs, Watson & Day, 1870), 1:1.

4. Ibid., 1:8.

5. Ibid., 1:9–10.

6. Robert Dykstra, *Bright Radical Star: Black Freedom and White Supremacy on the Hawkeye Frontier* (Cambridge, MA: Harvard University Press, 1993), 111–112.

7. Ibid., 113.

8. Ibid., 160.

9. *Debates of the Constitutional Convention*, 1:133–134.

10. Ibid., 1:133.

11. Ibid., 2:1068.

12. Ibid., 1:103.

13. Ibid., 2:733.

14. Ibid.

15. Ibid., 2:733–734.

16. Ibid., 1:200–201.

17. Ibid., 2:668–669.

18. Ibid., 2:833.

19. Ibid., 2:834.

20. Ibid., 2:836.

21. Ibid., 2:837.

22. Dykstra, *Bright Radical Star*, 208.

23. Ibid., 209.

24. Ibid., 210.

25. J. Morgan Kousser, *Dead End: The Development of Nineteenth-Century Litigation on Racial Discrimination in Schools; An Inaugural Lecture Delivered before the University of Oxford on 28 February 1985* (Oxford, UK: Oxford University Press, 1986), 16.

26. Clark v. Board of Education, in *Reports of Cases in Law and Equity, Deter-*

mined in the Supreme Court of the State of Iowa, vol. 24 (Chicago: Flood, 1892), 3:274.

27. *Chicago Legal News*, February 5, 1870, quoted in *Women Lawyers' Journal* 16–19 (1928): 32, http://books.google.com/books?id=AopJAQAAIAAJ.

28. Clark v. Board, in *Reports of Cases in Law*, 3:276.

29. Coger v. the North West. Union Packet Co., in *Reports of Cases in Law*, vol. 37, 16:149.

30. Ibid., 16:154–155.

31. Ibid., 16:153.

32. Plessy v. Ferguson, 163 U.S. 537, 551 (1896).

CHAPTER 4

1. Authors' interview with Jeffrey Neary, August 2, 2012. All Neary recollections and quotations in this and subsequent chapters are from the authors' interview unless otherwise noted.

2. Authors' interview with Nick Hytrek, April 3, 2014. All Hytrek recollections and quotations are from the authors' interview unless otherwise noted.

3. Associated Press, "Judge Changes Ruling on Lesbian Couple," *Boston Globe*, December 31, 2003.

4. Nick Hytrek, "Divorce Granted to Lesbian Couple Doesn't Mean Iowa Accepts Union," *Sioux City (IA) Journal*, December 6, 2003.

5. Authors' interview with Sharon Malheiro, April 24, 2012. All Malheiro recollections and quotations in this and subsequent chapters are from the authors' interview unless otherwise noted.

CHAPTER 5

1. Authors' interview with Christopher Rants, April 23, 2014. All Rants recollections and quotations are from the authors' interview unless otherwise noted.

2. Goodridge v. Department of Public Health, 440 Mass. 309, 337 (2003).

3. George W. Bush, "State of the Union Address to the 108th Congress, Second Session," January 20, 2004.

4. Authors' interview with Camilla Taylor and Ken Upton, Lambda Legal lawyers, September 14, 2012. Recollections and quotations of Taylor and Upton in this and subsequent chapters are from the authors' interview unless otherwise noted.

5. Racing Association of Central Iowa v. Fitzgerald, 675 N.W. 2d, 1 (2004).

6. Kim Painter, "No Marriage License to Gays, Despite My Beliefs," *Des Moines Register*, March 14, 2004.

7. Authors' interview with state representative Daniel Lundby, October 19, 2014.

8. Authors' interview with Maggie Tinsman, May 22, 2014. Tinsman recollections and quotations are from the authors' interview unless otherwise noted.

9. Jonathan Roos, "Iowa Senate Panel Acts on Gay Marriage," *Des Moines Register*, February 26, 2004.

10. Gronstal and Kibbie quoted by.Matt McCoy in interview with authors, May 15, 2014.

11. Jonathan Roos, "Senate Rejects Marriage Proposal," *Des Moines Register*, March 24, 2004.

12. Ibid.

13. Ibid.

CHAPTER 6

1. Authors' interview with Larry Hoch and David Twombley, September 10, 2012. All recollections and quotations of Hoch and Twombley in this and subsequent chapters are from the authors' interview unless otherwise noted.

2. William Clinton, "President's Statement on DOMA," September 20, 1996.

3. Authors' interview with Chuck and Jason Swaggerty-Morgan, September 6, 2013. All recollections and quotations of both Swaggerty-Morgans — Chuck and Jason — in this and subsequent chapters are from the authors' interview unless otherwise noted.

4. Lynn Zerschling, "City Council Weighs Impact of Decision," *Sioux City Journal*, February 28, 2004.

5. Passages related to Reva Evans and Ingrid Olson were reviewed and corrected by Olson.

6. Authors' interview with Kate Varnum and Patricia Hyde Varnum, September 30, 2013. All recollections and quotations of the Varnums — Kate and Trish — in this and subsequent chapters are from the authors' interview unless otherwise noted.

7. "Waltzing on Out: Decorah Couple Deals with Challenges of Being Gay in a Small Town," *Decorah (IA) Newspapers*, June 19, 2002.

8. Lissa Greiner, "Panelists Discuss Marriage Equality at Forum," *Decorah Newspapers*, January 26, 2010.

9. Petition, Varnum v. Brien, CV5965, Iowa District Court for Polk County, December 13, 2005.

CHAPTER 7

1. Authors' interview with Robert Hanson, August 21, 2014. All Hanson recollections and quotations in this and subsequent chapters are from the authors' interview unless otherwise noted.

2. Jeff Eckhoff, "Six Couples File Gay Marriage Lawsuit," *Des Moines Register*, December 14, 2005.

3. E-mail provided to authors by Jeffrey Neary on July 11, 2012.

4. Jesse Claeys, "Speakers Back Traditional Marriage at Sioux City Rally," *Sioux City Journal*, October 3, 2004.

5. Ibid.

6. Associated Press, "Judge Granting Lesbian Divorce Invites Dr. Dobson to Discussion," *Waterloo–Cedar Falls (IA) Courier*, September 30, 2004.

7. People for Judicial Quality, Independence, and Integrity, Press release, October 12, 2004.

8. Alons v. Iowa District Court, Iowa Supreme Court, 03-1982 (2005) 17, 22.

9. Jeffrey Neary e-mail.

10. Authors' interview with Dennis Johnson, October 18, 2013. All Johnson recollections and quotations in this and subsequent chapters are from the authors' interview unless otherwise noted.

11. Williams v. Brewer, 375 F. Supp. 170 (S.D. Iowa 1974).

12. Jeff Eckhoff, "Carr Given Two Life Terms in Teen's Slaying," *Des Moines Register*, November 4, 2004.

13. Camilla Taylor, Lambda Legal memorandum, September 29, 2005.

14. Authors' interview with Roger Kuhle and Michael O'Meara, June 7, 2012. All recollections and quotations of Kuhle and O'Meara in this and subsequent chapters are from the authors' interview unless otherwise noted.

15. Linda Greenhouse, "Wedding Bells," *New York Times*, March 20, 2013.

16. Ibid.

17. Ibid.

18. Hernandez v. Robles, 855 N.E. 2d, 1, 7 (N.Y. 2006).

19. Transcript of legal arguments, Varnum v. Brien, cv5965, 12 (May 4, 2007).

20. Ibid., 12–13.

21. Ibid., 14.

22. Ibid., 19.

23. Ibid., 17.

24. Ibid., 18.

25. Ibid., 27.

26. Ibid., 28.

27. Ibid., 29.

28. Ibid., 32.

29. Ibid., 33.

30. Ibid., 52.

31. Ibid., 54.

32. Ibid., 54–55.

33. Ibid., 55.

34. Ibid., 82.

35. Ruling on Plaintiffs' and Defendant's Motions for Summary Judgment, Varnum v. Brien, cv5965, 22 (August 30, 2007).

36. Ibid., 23.

37. Ibid., 28.

38. Ibid., 29.

39. *Constitution for the State of Iowa* (Iowa City: Abraham Palmer, 1846), 5.

40. *Debates of the Constitutional Convention*, 1:14.

41. Legal arguments, Varnum v. Brien, cv5965, 37 (May 4, 2007).

42. Ruling on Summary Judgment, Varnum v. Brien, cv5965, 44 (August 30, 2007).

43. Ibid.

44. Ibid., 45.

45. Ibid., 56.

CHAPTER 8

1. Authors' interview with Marsha Ternus, September 14, 2012. All Ternus recollections and quotations in this and subsequent chapters are from the authors' interview unless otherwise noted.

2. Authors' interview with Mark Cady, April 15, 2014. All Cady recollections and quotations in this and subsequent chapters are from the authors' interview unless otherwise noted.

3. Authors' interview with David Baker, April 23, 2012. All Baker recollections and quotations in this and subsequent chapters are from the authors' interview unless otherwise noted.

4. Oral arguments before the Iowa Supreme Court, Varnum v. Brien, December 9, 2008, Courtroom View Network video, http://cvn.com/proceedings/varnum-v -brien-oral-argument-2008-12-09.

5. Ibid.

6. Ibid.

7. Ibid.

8. Ibid.

9. Authors' interview with Michael Streit, August 8, 2012. All Streit recollections and quotations in this and subsequent chapters are from the authors' interview unless otherwise noted.

10. Oral arguments, Varnum v. Brien, CVN video.

11. Authors' interview with Ben Parrott, April 24, 2013. All Parrott recollections and quotations in this and subsequent chapters are from the authors' interview unless otherwise noted.

12. Amicus brief, Knights of Columbus, Varnum v. Brien, 07-1499, December 2007, 11.

13. Joseph Tussman and Jacobus tenBroek, "The Equal Protection of the Laws," *California Law Review* 37, no. 3 (September 1949): 347.

14. Ibid., 345.

15. Ibid., 346.

16. Amicus brief in support of plaintiffs, American Psychological Association, Varnum v. Brien, 07-1499, May 2008, 16.

17. Ibid., 17.

18. Todd Pettys, "Letter from Iowa: Same-Sex Marriage and the Ouster of Three Justices," *Kansas Law Review* 59, no. 4 (2011): 718.

19. Robert Nagel, "A Painfully Labored Analysis," *New York Times*, April 3, 2009.

20. Varnum v. Brien, 763 N.W. 2d, 862, 875 (Iowa 2009).

21. Ibid. at 906.

CHAPTER 9

1. Authors' interview with Mark Cady, April 15, 2014. All Cady recollections and quotations in this and subsequent chapters are from the authors' interview unless otherwise noted.

2. University of Iowa, Press release, November 25, 2008.

3. Authors' interview with Bob Vander Plaats, December 18, 2012. All recollections and quotations of Vander Plaats in this and subsequent chapters are from the authors' interview unless otherwise noted.

4. Associated Press, "Iowa Supreme Court Rules Same-Sex Marriage Ban Violates Gay, Lesbian Rights," *Iowa State Daily*, April 3, 2009.

5. "Iowa Marriage No Longer Limited to One Man, One Woman," *Des Moines Register*, April 3, 2009, http://www.amnation.com/vfr/archives/012897.html.

6. "Iowa Court Backs Gay Marriage," CNN *Politics*, April 3, 2009, http://www.cnn.com/2009/POLITICS/04/03/iowa.same.sex/index.html?iref=allsearch.

7. Ibid.

8. Amy Lorentzen, Associated Press, "Iowa Supreme Court Legalizes Gay Marriage," April 3, 2009.

9. Procedendo, Clerk of Court, Iowa Supreme Court, Varnum v. Brien, 7-1499, April 27, 2009.

10. Jason Clayworth, "Gay Marriage More Destructive Than Smoking, Hurley Says," *Des Moines Register*, March 12, 2010.

11. "No Problems Reported with Same-Sex Couples Seeking Marriage Licenses, ACLU Says," *(Cedar Rapids) Gazette*, April 27, 2009.

12. Quoted by Justice Michael Streit in his speech at the 2012 John F. Kennedy Profile in Courage Award ceremony, Boston, Massachusetts, May 7, 2012.

13. Jeff Eckhoff and Grant Schulte, "Iowa Gays Have a Right to Marry, Justices Rule," *Des Moines Register*, April 4, 2009.

14. Charlotte Eby, "Vander Plaats: Culver Irresponsible for Not Stopping Gay Marriage," *Sioux City Journal*, April 23, 2009.

15. "King Statement on Same-Sex Marriage in Iowa," Press release, April 27, 2009, http://steveking.house.gov/media-center/press-releases/king-statement-on-same-sex-marriage-in-iowa.

16. Jennifer Jacobs and Jason Clayworth, "Culver Says He'll Review the Ruling," *Des Moines Register*, April 3, 2009.

1. Craig Robinson, "Vander Plaats Mulls Independent Bid after Being Rejected for Lt. Governor," *Iowa Republican*, June 17, 2010, http://theiowarepublican.com/2010/vander-plaats-mulls-independent-bid-after-being-rejected-for-lt-governor.

2. Jason Clayworth, "Vander Plaats Won't Seek an Independent Run, but Will Try to Unseat Supreme Court," *Des Moines Register*, August 6, 2010.

3. O. Kay Henderson, "Vander Plaats Names New Group 'Iowa for Freedom,'" *Radio Iowa*, August 11, 2010, http://www.radioiowa.com/2010/08/11/vander-plaats-names-new-group-iowa-for-freedom.

4. Ibid.

5. Kyle Mantyla, "Fischer: Gays Are Inherently Disqualified from Serving in Public Office," *Right Wing Watch*, August 18, 2014, http://www.rightwingwatch.org/content/fischer-gays-are-inherently-disqualified-serving-public-office.

6. Independent Expenditure by an Organization, Citizens United Political Victory Fund, October 29, 2010, Iowa Ethics and Campaign Disclosure Board, https://webapp.iecdb.iowa.gov/PublicView/IndepExpend/2010/Citizens%20United%20Political%20Victory%20Fund_OIE_2010_10_29_13.24.45.pdf.

7. Alexis Levinson, "Huckabee Makes Himself Heard in Iowa," *Daily Caller*, October 29, 2010.

8. Barb Heki and Vicki Crawford, *We Overrule: How Iowa Turned Judicial Tyranny into a Triumph for Freedom* (Urbandale, IA: FAMiLY Leader, 2012), 58.

9. Authors' interview with Dan Moore, September 16, 2013. All Moore recollections and quotations in this and subsequent chapters are from the authors' interview unless otherwise noted.

10. "Fair Courts for Us Press Conference, Des Moines, October 25, 2010," Homegrown Justice Tour Facebook page, October 26, 2010, video, https://www.facebook.com/pages/Homegrown-Justice-Tour/134613026591007.

11. Tyler Kingkade, "Battle over Judge Retention in Iowa," *Huffington Post*, November 2, 2010.

12. Fair Courts for Us Committee, Proretention radio commercial, October 15, 2010.

13. Ibid.

14. Grant Schulte, "Ternus: Anti-retention Campaigns 'Blinded by Their Own Ideology,'" *Des Moines Register*, October 12, 2010.

15. State of the Judiciary 2011, Joint Session of the Iowa General Assembly at the State Capitol in Des Moines, January 4, 2011, http://www.iptv.org/iowapress/story.cfm/1900/video/soj_20110112_state_judiciary.

16. Ibid.

17. Grant Schulte, "Cady Says Judges Serve Law, Not Political Interests, *Des Moines Register*, January 13, 2011.

18. Ibid.

19. Ibid.

CHAPTER 11

1. Prepared remarks of Caroline Kennedy, John F. Kennedy Profile in Courage Awards Ceremony, Kennedy Presidential Library, Boston, May 7, 2012.

2. Jeff Eckhoff, "Ousted Judges Honored by Kennedy Presidential Library for Their Profiles in Courage," *Des Moines Register*, May 7, 2012.

3. Cady's remarks to authors at the John F. Kennedy Profile in Courage Awards Ceremony, Kennedy Presidential Library, Boston, May 7, 2012.

4. Bob Vander Plaats, Press release, FAMiLY Leader, May 7, 2012.

5. Robert Kennedy, "Ripple of Hope" speech, University of Cape Town, Cape Town, South Africa, June 6, 1966.

6. Program notes, John F. Kennedy Profile in Courage Awards Ceremony, Kennedy Presidential Library, Boston, May 7, 2012.

7. Prepared remarks of Caroline Kennedy, John F. Kennedy Profile in Courage Awards Ceremony, Kennedy Presidential Library, Boston, May 7, 2012.

8. Authors' interview with Sam Ganem, John F. Kennedy Profile in Courage Awards Ceremony, Kennedy Presidential Library, Boston, May 7, 2012.

9. Prepared remarks of David Baker, John F. Kennedy Profile in Courage Awards Ceremony, Kennedy Presidential Library, Boston, May 7, 2012.

10. Prepared remarks of Marsha Ternus, John F. Kennedy Profile in Courage Awards Ceremony, Kennedy Presidential Library, Boston, May 7, 2012.

11. Sonya Streit, comment made to author Witosky in Boston, May 7, 2012.

12. Authors' interview with David Wiggins, June 7, 2012. All Wiggins recollections and quotations in this and subsequent chapters are from the authors' interview unless otherwise noted.

13. Gary Marx, "Part 2: How We Can Get Around the Iowa Constitution," *National Review Online*, February 22, 2011, http://www.nationalreview.com/bench-memos /260388/part-2-how-we-can-get-around-iowa-constitution-gary-marx.

CHAPTER 12

1. Authors' interview with Guy Cook, January 11, 2012. All Cook recollections and quotations are from the authors' interview unless otherwise noted.

2. Dan Moore, "Obsessed with Gay Marriage, Vander Plaats Has Gone Too Far," *Des Moines Register*, January 2, 2011.

3. Melanie in IA, "Turn the Ballot Over and Vote YES to Retain Judges," *Daily Kos*, November 2, 2012, http://www.dailykos.com/story/2012/11/02/1154193/-GOTV -Iowa-Same-Day-Registration-Vote-to-Retain-Judges.

4. Jeff Eckhoff, "'No Wiggins' Tour Rolls Out Its Message," *Des Moines Register*, September 25, 2012.

5. Shane Vander Hart, "Rick Santorum Helps Kick Off Wiggins Tour," *Caffeinated Thoughts*, September 24, 2002, http://caffeinatedthoughts.com/2012/09/rick-san torum-helps-kick-off-no-wiggins-tour-in-iowa.

6. Jennifer Jacobs, "2012 Iowa Caucuses: Iowa Evangelicals Skeptical They Can Unite behind One Candidate for Caucuses," *Des Moines Register*, December 20, 2011.

7. Kevin Hall, "Vander Plaats, Santorum Launch 'No Wiggins' Bus Tour," *Iowa Republican*, September 25, 2012, http://theiowarepublican.com/2012/vander-plaats -santorum-launch-no-wiggins-bus-tour.

8. William Petroski, "Jindal, Santorum to Join Statewide Bus Tour Opposing Iowa Justice Wiggins, *Des Moines Register*, September 18, 2012.

9. Mike Wiser, "Dueling Bus Tours Take on Iowa Justice Vote," *Sioux City Journal*, September 24, 2012.

10. Roger Kuhle, "Anti-Wiggins Crusade Is about Motivating Conservative Voters," *Des Moines Register*, October 31, 2012.

11. Trish Mehaffey, "Dueling Bus Tours in the Judicial Retention Battle Stop in Cedar Rapids," *(Cedar Rapids) Gazette*, September 25, 2012.

12. Bill Shea, "Retention of Iowa Supreme Court Justice Wiggins Is Shadowed by Politics," *Messenger News*, September 27, 2012, http://www.messengernews.net /page/content.detail/id/551358/Retention-of-Iowa-Supreme-Court-Justice-Wiggins -is-shadowed-by-politics.html?nav=5010.

13. "First 'No Wiggins' TV Ad and Other Iowa Judicial Retention News," *Bleeding Heartland*, October 9, 2012, http://www.bleedingheartland.com/diary/5767/first-no -wiggins-tv-ad-and-other-iowa-judicial-retention-news.

14. Christopher Rants, "THE REGULARS: Outrage over Court's Gay Marriage Decision Rings Hollow," *Sioux City Journal*, September 30, 2012.

15. Chuck Hurley, "OTHER VOICES: Retention Election Is about More Than Gay Marriage," *Sioux City Journal*, October 7, 2012.

16. Quoted by Jeff Angelo in his interview with the authors, July 6, 2012.

17. Press conference after the announcement of the retention vote results, November 6, 2012.

CHAPTER 13

1. Authors' interview with former California Supreme Court Justice Carlos Moreno, May 16, 2013. All Moreno recollections and quotations are from the authors' interview unless otherwise noted.

2. "Concurring and Dissenting Opinion by Moreno, J.," Strauss v. Horton, 207 P.3d 48 (2009).

3. Authors' interview with former Montana Supreme Court justice James Nelson, May 6, 2013. Nelson recollections and quotations are from the authors' interview, unless otherwise noted.

4. Donaldson and Guggenheim et al. v. State of Montana, 11-0451.

5. Kitchen v. Herbert, "Utah Same-Sex Marriage Ban Oral Argument," C-SPAN video, April 10, 2014, http://www.c-span.org/video/?318832-1/utah-samesex -marriage-ban-oral-argument.

6. Ibid.

7. Amy Worden and Angel Couloumbis, "Corbett Won't Appeal Decision Striking Pa. Same-Sex Marriage Ban," *(Philadelphia) Inquirer*, May 23, 2014, http://articles .philly.com/2014-05-23/news/50033080_1_gay-marriage-corbett-pennsylvania -family-institute.

8. Kitchen v. Herbert, Tenth Circuit Court of Appeals, 13-4178 (June 25, 2014), 3.

9. Richard A. Posner, "Should There Be Homosexual Marriage? If So, Who Should Decide? Reviewing William N. Eskridge, Jr., *The Case for Same-Sex Marriage: From Sexual Liberty to Civilized Commitment* (1996)," *Michigan Law Review* 95, no. 6 (1997): 1585.

10. Ibid., 1584.

11. Ibid., 1585–1586.

12. Ibid., 1585.

13. Baskin v. Bogan 14-2386 to 14-2388 and Wolf v. Walker, 14-2526 (September 4, 2014), 7.

Index

Iowa and the Midwest Experience